Making Connections

An Interactive Approach to Academic Reading

Kenneth J. Pakenham

University of Akron

St. Martin's Press • New York

To Pamela, Bethany, Michael, and Kate

GOID 4776

Editor: Naomi Silverman
Manager, publishing services: Emily Berleth
Project management: Denise Quirk
Graphics: Laurie Mobley
Cover art and design: Hothouse Design, Inc.

Library of Congress Catalog Card Number: 92-62784

Copyright © 1994 by St. Martin's Press, Inc.

Manufactured in the United States of America.

8 7 6 5 4
f e d c b a

For information, write:
St. Martin's Press, Inc.
175 Fifth Avenue
New York, NY 10010

ISBN: 0-312-06515-9

PREFACE

AUDIENCE

The goal of *Making Connections* is to equip students of English as a second language (ESL) with language skills and reading strategies necessary for the efficient processing of general academic texts. It is designed for use with students whose entry-level proficiency is in the range covered by reasonably balanced TOEFL[1] scores of 430–460 (Section 3 scores in the range 40–46). (Depending on the character of their student body, different ESL programs will have different labels for classes in this proficiency range—intermediate, high intermediate, or low advanced.) In the process of development, the book has been extensively field tested with students in this proficiency range at the English Language Institute, University of Akron. Students who typically complete the level of the program in which *Making Connections* is used are qualified either to begin full-time undergraduate study or to continue their English studies in more advanced classes where the mean TOEFL score on entry is 510.

    Making Connections is intended for use in intensive and nonintensive ESL reading classes. It could also be used, with appropriate complementary writing materials, in a combined academic reading-writing class.

APPROACH

In its content and organization, *Making Connections* reflects a number of beliefs about reading and reading instruction, most based on research in native-speaker and ESL reading, others based on personal observations accumulated over twenty years of teaching EFL/ESL. The most important of these are as follows:

[1]TOEFL is a registered trademark of Educational Testing Service, Princeton, NJ.

iii

1. Successful reading is the result of a balanced interaction between top-down and bottom-up processing skills. The necessary balance requires linguistic preparedness (for the bottom-up processing) and conceptual preparedness (for top-down processing).

2. Reading is also goal-oriented and strategic, that is, it requires readers to use a range of strategies to accomplish whatever goals they have identified as appropriate.

3. Students' ability to activate relevant reading strategies is enhanced when they are made consciously aware of potentially valuable strategies and given frequent, explicit, and meaningful opportunities to use such strategies.

4. While they are reading, good readers are actively engaged in searching for connections in meaning between adjacent sentences (local coherence) and for the main ideas and topics of longer passages of text (global coherence).

5. Effective use of reading strategies will be increased if reading instruction seeks to intervene *during* the reading process, not merely during the prereading and postreading stages.

6. Notwithstanding the need for process-oriented intervention during reading, students judge themselves and know that they will be judged on the product of their reading. Product-oriented activities, in the form of comprehension checks, remain an important means of student self-assessment.

7. Good readers have the ability to deal effectively with unknown vocabulary. The ability to do so is dependent partly on readers' knowledge of the topic discussed in the given reading and partly on their having sufficient lexical knowledge to gain easy access to the vocabulary that provides the context for the unknown vocabulary.

8. ESL readers at the entry proficiency level for *Making Connections* need to consciously develop their vocabulary and to practice effective strategies for doing so. Reading and reading classes provide an appropriate context for such vocabulary development.

9. The more frequently students see an unfamiliar lexical item in a meaningful context, the more likely students are to retain that item.

Following these beliefs, *Making Connections* seeks to develop in ESL readers relevant linguistic skills (knowledge of vocabulary, text structure, and text organization) and to foster their use of effective, process-oriented reading strategies. To these ends, the book employs a re-current organizational sequence by which the target vocabulary, features of text structure and organization, and reading strategies can be (1) introduced in context, (2) explained and practiced intensively, and (3) reintroduced and practiced during the reading process.

OVERVIEW AND ORGANIZATION OF THE BOOK

Making Connections consists of five units and a Vocabulary Study section. Each unit has a general theme that links the six readings within it. Two unit themes were chosen for the international nature and relevance of the information and ideas presented in them—world health-care issues (Unit 1) and global environmental issues (Unit 4). Two unit themes were chosen with an eye to providing ESL students with interesting insights into elements of North American culture—cultural diversity (Unit 2) and family life (Unit 5). The fifth theme, language (Unit 3) was chosen as an entry-point to academic textbook reading because it is a theme of common interest to ESL students with a wide range of future majors.

Within each unit, five shorter background readings (*Reading Passages*) precede the main article (*Main Reading*). The shorter readings provide background knowledge in the general topic area and offer students the chance (1) to meet target vocabulary and other textual elements (for example, sentence structures and methods of rhetorical organization), and (2) to practice various reading strategies in context before they tackle the much longer main article. Prereading activities (*Getting a First Idea*) are provided for each main reading. Intervention in the reading process is provided for all readings in the form of *Comprehension Building Tasks*, activities that appear in the margins of the reading passages and encourage students to activate relevant processing strategies while they are reading. Ideas for other intervention activities for the background reading passages appear in the *Instructor's Manual* that accompanies the text. Postreading activities for all readings include a global coherence check (*Main Idea Check*) and a more detailed comprehension check (*A Closer Look*), topics for reader discussion and input (*What Do You Think?*), and a listing of additional (unexplained) vocabulary that readers are responsible for (*Vocabulary in Context*).

Twelve to fifteen target vocabulary items, chosen for their potential usefulness in general academic English, are introduced in each background reading passage. These items also appear with definitions and examples in the *Vocabulary Study* section at the end of the book. Here they are cross-referenced with the appropriate reading passage and listed in order of their appearance in the passage.

Additional vocabulary building activities (*Vocabulary Practice*) appear after the first two and final three background readings in each unit. These offer students the opportunity to consolidate their learning of the target vocabulary items in the unit and to integrate the items into their existing knowledge, as well as to practice reading for local coherence. After their initial introduction, target lexical items are reintroduced in the later readings of the unit and of following units.

Each unit also contains one or two sections (*Text Study*) that introduce students to important features of the structure and organization of general academic English texts. The text study sections offer practice in the recognition of the given textual features and in strategies that use the acquired textual knowledge for more effective reading. The text features introduced in a given text study section are present in the background reading passages and main reading passage that follow. They also recur in the readings of subsequent units.

GENERAL GUIDELINES FOR USE

Because of the general organizational principles of *Making Connections*, Units 1 to 5 should be read in the sequence in which they appear. For the same reason, within each unit, the background readings are best handled in order of appearance and before students tackle the more challenging main reading. Decisions on when to have students work through the relevant pages of the Vocabulary Study will depend on your own preferences and your awareness of your students' needs and learning styles. Each text study section has been written presupposing only familiarity with linguistic or topical material from the preceding pages of the book. This will permit you to introduce a text study section *before* reading the background reading passage that follows it. Alternatively, you may choose to deal with it *after* the appropriate reading passage, that is, after the features that are the focus of the text study have been introduced in a more general reading context.

The *Instructor's Manual* that accompanies *Making Connections* contains more specific suggestions for the use of the materials in the book, as well as quizzes, supplementary materials, and keys to the exercises. Given this, I will limit further suggestions on how to exploit the material in the book to one based on an insight that I confess I have come to belatedly.

I used to believe that my mastery of a given text (that is, a good comprehension of its content and an awareness of what structures and organization it exploited) was the necessary and sufficient basis for teaching students how to read. While I still believe such mastery is necessary in order to teach effectively, it is clearly not sufficient. Among other things, we need to be aware of the strategies we have employed (with more or less success) in *the process of making sense of the text*.

With apologies for belaboring the obvious to colleagues whose approach to reading instruction already includes consideration of their own processing strategies for the text, I therefore suggest the following: When you are preparing a passage for a class, observe yourself reading the passage for the first and second time. Keep notes on what you are doing and thinking as you come to grips with the text. Use the insights from such self-observation to formulate other processing strategies, and use these strategies to complement or supplement the process-oriented intervention activities included in this book (*Comprehension Building Tasks*).

Finally, an invitation: There is little, perhaps nothing, in the field of ESL reading theory and practice that is not being incorporated into his or her instruction by some instructor somewhere. I know, therefore, that you will take the content and activities of this book and move in original and pedagogically exciting directions that I have not imagined. When you do, and if you have the time for professional exchange, I would greatly enjoy hearing from you.

ACKNOWLEDGMENTS

My completion of this book would not have been possible without the help and support of a large number of people. My thanks go to the editorial and production staff at St. Martin's Press, especially Naomi Silverman, and to the following reviewers: Richard Abend, Monterey Peninsula College; Maureen Burke, University of Iowa; Mark Clarke, University of Colorado, Denver; Jewel Dhuru, Marquette University; Margaret Lindstrom, Colorado State College; Colleen McGovern, University of Colorado, Boulder; Jennifer McKenzie, University of Missouri; Marianne Phinney, University of Texas, El Paso. Thanks also to Laurie Mobley for her artwork, to my colleagues at the English Language Institute, University of Akron, and to the many students whose experiences with the developing text helped determine its final form. Most importantly, I give thanks to my family, whose love and forbearance kept me going.

CONTENTS

UNIT TWO

The Challenge of Diversity

Section 1

Section 2

Section 3

Section 4

UNIT THREE

Aspects of Language

Section 1

UNIT FOUR

Looking after Planet Earth

Section 1

Vocabulary Index

Unit One

World Health in the 1990s

Text Study 1.
Identifying Continuing Ideas

You can already understand sentences like these:

1. I went to see a movie last night. I really enjoyed *it*.

2. Two old friends came to see me on Friday. *They* were in town for a business meeting.

In these examples, the second sentence is connected to the first sentence by the words (pronouns) *it* and *they*. Both *it* and *they* continue ideas that first appeared in the earlier sentences.

In sentence 1, *it* = the film that I went to see last night

In sentence 2, *they* = the two old friends who visited me on Friday

Now we are going to examine other ways in which writers continue talking about an idea from an earlier sentence.

EXAMPLES AND EXPLANATIONS

Look at the examples below. Each example contains two connected sentences. The second sentence of each example repeats an idea from the first sentence. The words that repeat the idea are in *italics*. What idea is being continued or repeated in each example?

1. On Tuesday and Wednesday, it snowed heavily for twenty-four hours. *This* forced the university to close for the rest of the week.

this = the heavy snow that fell for twenty-four hours.

3

Writers often use the word *this* in order to repeat an idea from the sentence before. If you read *this* in a sentence, normally you can look for its meaning in the sentence before. Sometimes, however, the word *this* is not clear enough alone. Therefore, writers often add a noun after it.

2. A number of countries have introduced birth-control programs. The populations of *these countries* is increasing too rapidly.

these countries = the countries that have introduced birth-control programs

Here the writer just uses *these* + the *same noun* that was used in the earlier sentence.

3. The government has decided to build a new factory on the west side of town. *The decision* has angered a lot of residents, who fear that the factory will destroy the beauty of their neighborhood.

the decision = the government's decision to build a factory on the west side of town

Here the writer uses *the* + *noun*. The noun *decision* comes from the same word family as the important verb *decide* of the earlier sentence.

4. According to new statistics from the government, unemployment has fallen in the last six months. *These figures* suggest that the economy is improving.

these figures = the government statistics that show that unemployment has fallen in the last six months

Here the writer uses *these* + *noun*. The noun *figures* is a **synonym** of the noun *statistics* in the earlier sentence. Writers often connect sentences with synonyms, so you need to build your vocabulary in order to understand this type of connection. It is not enough to know only one single word for one idea.

5. On April 15, 1912, the *Titanic*, the largest passenger ship in the world at that time, sank in the North Atlantic. A total of 1,522 passengers and crew lost their lives. *The disaster* shocked the world.

the disaster = the sinking of the *Titanic* and the deaths of 1,522 people

Here the writer again uses *the* + *noun*. This time the noun is a **general word** that describes something in the earlier sentence. You know the meaning of *disaster*, so the connection between the sentences is clear. Here are some other general words that English writers use to make connections in their texts:

For Things That Happen	For Things That We Do	For Things That We Think
incident	action	
event	move	idea
occurrence	reaction	view
situation	behavior	attitude
circumstances	practice	
development	achievement	
tendency	tendency	tendency

READING STRATEGIES

When you read, pay attention to how ideas continue from one sentence into the next sentence. Make sure that you look for and understand connections like the connections you have just studied. In order to understand them, you must

1. Look for　*this*
　　　　　　this or *these* + *noun*
　　　　　　the + *noun*

2. Look for the same idea in an earlier sentence.

3. Use your knowledge of vocabulary and word families.

EXERCISES

Understanding Connections 1

In each of the following, an idea in the first sentence appears again in the second sentence. You should:

1. Underline the continuing idea in the second sentence.

2. Answer the comprehension question.

Example
　　Today a lot of people are criticizing the public schools in the United States. Much of <u>this criticism</u> is coming from dissatisfied parents of public school students.

　　What are dissatisfied parents criticizing today?
　　You answer: *the public schools in the United States.*

1. The government has developed a plan to reduce unemployment in our part of the country. The plan is being welcomed by most people in this part of the country.

   What is being welcomed by the people who live here?

2. The traffic was stopped on the interstate this morning because of an accident. This made me thirty minutes late for my classes.

   What caused me to be late for my classes this morning?

3. The cost of living here is quite high, and wages for many people are rather low. This means that both husband and wife often must work outside the home in order to afford a decent standard of living.

   What forces both husband and wife to find jobs outside the home?

4. A lot of people are realizing that exercise is important for preventing heart disease. This realization is one of the reasons for the great increase in the number of Americans who are becoming members of health clubs.

   What is one of the reasons why many Americans are joining health clubs?

5. The people of ancient Greece and Egypt knew a great deal about the movements of the Earth and about the positions of stars in the night sky. Today some scientists believe that with this knowledge, sailors from ancient Greece or Egypt were able to sail across the Atlantic and reach America over three thousand years ago.

   What perhaps made it possible for the ancient Greeks or Egyptians to reach America long ago?

6. In high school, students who have no interest in school often disturb the classes. This means that students who really want to learn are often prevented from doing so.

   What may stop good students from being able to learn in high school?

Recognizing Synonyms

Write the number of each word or phrase in Column 1 beside its synonym in Column 2. (For any words you are not sure about, use your dictionary or ask your instructor.)

Column 1	Column 2
1. to say that something will happen	_4_ assistance
2. not being happy or pleased	_9_ progress
3. to ask strongly for something	_8_ attempt
4. help or support	_10_ increase
5. law	_1_ predict
6. can or could	_3_ demand
7. to find	_2_ dissatisfaction
8. to try	_6_ be possible
9. improvement	_5_ legislation
10. to rise	_7_ discover

Understanding Connections 2

In the following, the writer uses *synonyms* or *general words* to repeat an idea from the first sentence in the second sentence. You should:

1. Underline the continuing idea in the second sentence.

2. Answer the comprehension question.

1. The condition of the patient has improved greatly in the last twenty-four hours. If this progress continues, the patient will soon be able to leave the hospital.

   What needs to continue if the patient is to go home soon?

2. The workers are asking for a 20 percent wage increase, longer vacations, and better medical insurance. But it is not expected that the company will agree to all of these demands.

   What are the workers demanding?

3. Tom's father stayed calm and did not get angry with Tom when Tom had an accident and wrecked the family car. This reaction surprised Tom, who was expecting an explosion!

   What surprised Tom?

4. In the southern states of the United States, black children were not allowed to go to the same schools as white children; they were sent to all-black schools. This practice continued until the 1960s and ended when the federal government passed laws against separate schools for blacks and whites.

   What was stopped by federal laws in the 1960s?

5. A number of developing countries have tried to introduce birth-control programs for their people. However, many of these attempts have failed because the family planning experts did not know enough about the lives and traditions of the people.

   What have not been successful?

6. In 1960, scientists found the remains of an old European town in Canada. This discovery proved that Europeans reached North America in the eleventh century.

   What shows us clearly that Europeans came to America nine hundred years ago?

7. Some people in the United States believe that the federal government should have more control over the public schools. But there are others who are completely against this idea.

   What idea does the second group of people disagree with?

8. A large number of people are not happy with the government's recent actions—it has introduced new taxes, reduced money for education, and arrested some opponents. The dissatisfaction has even reached people who, a year ago, supported the government without question.

   Why are some supporters of the government now dissatisfied?

9. In Europe, soccer fans often cause trouble on their way to and from professional soccer games; they fight with fans of other teams, attack people in the streets, and damage cars and businesses. Americans are hoping that this kind of behavior doesn't spread to fans of U.S. professional sports.

   What do Americans not want to see in the United States?

10. The year 1968 was very bad for politics in the United States. In that year, both Martin Luther King, Jr., the leader of the civil rights movement, and Bobby Kennedy, who was running for president, were murdered. These events shocked the country.

    What shocked the United States in 1968?

Background Reading and Vocabulary Development

READING PASSAGE 1.1

Read this passage as many times as you need to. However, during your first reading, you should:

1. Stop reading at the end of each sentence that contains boldface words, and complete the Comprehension Building Task in the left margin. Then continue with your reading.

2. Try to identify the most important idea the writer wants to communicate to you in this passage.

Heart Disease and Changing Attitudes

In the recent past, medical researchers have shown that heart disease is associated with certain factors in our day-to-day lives: with stress, with smoking, with poor nutrition, and with a lack of exercise. Doctors and other health experts have begun to emphasize the fact that we can often reduce the risk of heart disease by paying more attention to **these factors.**

More and more people are realizing that there is a connection between heart disease and the way they live. As a result of **this new awareness,** attitudes toward health are changing: in the past, people tended to think that it was sufficient for good health to have a good doctor who could be relied on to know exactly what to do when they became ill. Now they are realizing that merely receiving the best treatment for illness or injury is not enough. They are learning that they must take more responsibility for their own

What is the meaning of these factors? *Check in previous sentences.*

What is the meaning of this new awareness? *Check in previous sentences.*

1

2

5

10

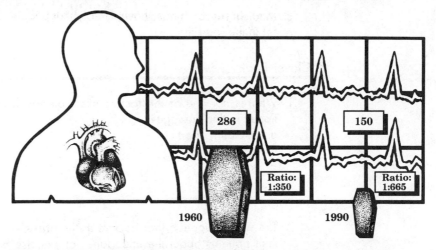

Figure 1. Deaths from heart disease in the United States, 1960–90 (per 100,000 residents). Heart disease is still a major cause of death in the United States. However, since reaching a high in the 1950s, the death rate from cardiovascular disease has been falling because of better diagnosis and treatment, and more importantly, because of better prevention. (*Source:* National Center for Health Statistics, *Health, United States 1991* [Hyattsville, MD: Public Health Service, 1992].)

15   health. Today many people are changing their dietary habits and eating food with less fat and cholesterol. Many are paying more attention to reducing stress in their lives. The number of smokers in the United States is now far below the level of twenty years ago as many people succeed in breaking the habit and as fewer people
20   take it up. More and more are aware of the benefits of regular exercise like walking, running, or swimming; some have begun to walk or ride bicycles to work instead of driving. Millions have become members of health clubs and have made health clubs one of the fastest growing businesses in the United States today. And
25   now the beneficial effects of these changing attitudes and behaviors are beginning to appear (see Figure 1): an encouraging decrease in deaths from heart disease.

Main Idea Check

Choose the sentence that best expresses the main idea of the passage.

a. As a result of medical evidence about the causes of heart disease, more and more people are changing the way they live.

b. The number of health clubs in the United States is increasing rapidly.

    c. Medical research has shown clearly that people should reduce the amount of fat in the food they eat.

A Closer Look

1. What is *not* one of the factors associated with heart disease that are mentioned in this passage?
   a. unhealthy food
   b. cigarettes
   c. poverty
   d. pressure
   e. no regular exercise

2. The writer suggests that doctors in the past did not always inform their patients about the importance of exercise and good nutrition for their health.   T F

3. If you don't smoke, if you exercise regularly, if you reduce the fat in your food, the risk of heart disease
   a. increases.
   b. decreases.
   c. remains the same.

4. What change in attitude does the writer describe in this passage?
   a. More and more people are realizing that medical science can cure heart disease.
   b. More and more people are realizing that they should take better care of their bodies.
   c. More and more Americans are dying of heart disease.

5. Today an increasing number of people are driving to work instead of walking.   T F

What Do You Think?

Do you think that there are other factors that increase or reduce a person's chance of getting heart disease? What could these factors be? This passage, for example, doesn't mention poverty as a possible factor. Do you think it could be? If so, how could poverty possibly be associated with heart disease?

READING PASSAGE 1.2

Read this passage as many times as you need to. However, during your first reading, you should:

1. Stop reading at the end of each sentence that contains boldface words, and complete the Comprehension Building Task in the left margin. Then continue with your reading.

2. Try to identify the most important idea the writer wants to communicate to you in this passage.

Heart Disease: Treat or Prevent?

One of the greatest killers in the Western world is heart disease. The death rate from the disease has been increasing at an alarming speed for the past thirty years. Today in Britain, for example, about four hundred people a day die of heart disease. Medical experts know that people can reduce their chances of getting heart disease by exercising regularly, by not smoking, and by paying attention to their diet, but Western health-care systems are still not paying enough attention to the prevention of the disease. There is an urgent need for more programs to educate the public about the causes and prevention of heart disease. Instead of financing such programs, however, the U.S. health-care system is spending enormous sums of money on the surgical treatment of the disease after it develops.

What is the meaning of this emphasis on treatment? *Check previous sentences.*

This emphasis on treatment is clearly associated with the technological advances that have taken place in the past ten to fifteen years. In this time, modern technology has enabled doctors to develop new surgical techniques and procedures. Many operations that were considered impossible or too risky a few years ago are now performed every day in U.S. hospitals. The result has been a massive increase in heart surgery.

Although there is no doubt that a large number of people benefit from heart surgery, critics of our health-care systems point out that the emphasis on the surgical treatment of the disease has three clear disadvantages. First, it attracts interest and financial resources away from the question of prevention. Second, it causes the costs of general hospital care to rise. After hospitals buy the expensive equipment that is necessary for modern heart surgery, they must try to recover the money they have spent. **To do this,** they raise costs for all their patients, not just those patients whose treatment requires the equipment. The third disadvantage is that doctors are encouraged to perform surgery—even on patients for whom an operation is unnecessary—because the equipment and surgical expertise is available. A federal government office re-

What is the meaning of to do this?
a. *to help people with heart disease*
b. *to buy new equipment for the treatment of heart disease*
c. *to get back the money that has been spent for equipment*

35 cently concluded that major heart surgery was often performed even though its chances of success were low. In one type of heart surgery, for example, only 15 percent of patients benefited from the surgery. However, more than 100,000 of these operations are performed in the United States every year.

Main Idea Check

Choose the sentence that best expresses the main idea of this passage.

a. People can reduce their chances of heart disease by exercising regularly, by not smoking, and by paying attention to good nutrition.

b. Modern technology is allowing doctors to perform new types of surgery on people who are suffering from heart disease.

c. In the West, especially in the United States, we tend to emphasize the surgical treatment of heart disease; this has a number of clear disadvantages.

A Closer Look

1. Everyone is satisfied with the way Western health-care systems are attacking the problem of heart disease.   T F

2. Western health-care systems are spending too much money to educate people about the causes of heart disease.   T F

3. According to the critics of the U.S. health-care system, where does more emphasis need to be placed?
   a. on preventing heart disease
   b. on treating heart disease
   c. on developing new surgical techniques for heart operations
   d. on buying high-technology equipment for heart surgery

4. What is *not* true about heart surgery in the United States?
   a. It helps some patients.
   b. It is now being performed more often than in the past.
   c. It keeps medical costs down.

5. What effect, or effects, is modern technology having on medicine?
   a. It is a factor in the rising costs of medical treatment.
   b. It has clearly helped save the lives of patients.
   c. It makes some operations impossible.

What Do You Think?

You are a government official responsible for deciding where public money should be spent. You have $2 million to give to a project that will lower the death rate from heart disease. One project that wants the money is a program of research to develop an artificial human heart. The other project is a program to inform people about the connection between heart disease and the way they live. Which project do you decide to support? Justify your decision.

VOCABULARY PRACTICE

Same or Different?

Writers sometimes express the same ideas in sentences with very different grammar and vocabulary. This exercise will help you identify such occurrences.

Read the two sentences in each example, and decide if they express the same ideas or different ideas. Choose *S* when the two sentences express the same idea; choose *D* when they express different ideas. *Remember:* You can express the same ideas with different words and different grammar!

1. a. The patient is now recovering from her illness.
   b. The patient is now getting better after her illness.   S D

2. a. Experts believe that we can bring down the death rate from heart disease if we emphasize that exercise is very important.
   b. By stressing the importance of exercise, according to experts, we can reduce the number of people who die of heart disease.   S D

3. a. John is going to have major surgery on Monday.
   b. John is going to perform major surgery on Monday.   S D

4. a. Many people are realizing that high-technology equipment can also have disadvantages.
   b. High-technology equipment can also have disadvantages. Many people are now becoming aware of this.   S D

5. a. Instead of merely increasing the money that it is spending for hospitals, the government is also attempting to improve the nutrition of its people.
   b. The government is not spending more money for hospitals. It is trying to provide better food for its people.   S D

6. a. The enormously high costs of health care can be reduced if we stress the prevention of disease more than we do now.

   b. We can bring down the extremely high costs of health care by putting greater emphasis on the prevention of disease.   S   D

7. a. Medical research has shown that stress, poor nutrition, smoking, and lack of exercise are all factors in heart disease.

   b. According to medical research, there is a clear association between heart disease and stress, poor dietary habits, cigarettes, and insufficient exercise.   S   D

8. a. After the operation, the patient's condition improved.

   b. In spite of the operation, the patient did not recover.   S   D

Making Connections

Each example in this exercise has a lead sentence and two sentences (*a* and *b*) that might or might not logically follow the lead sentence. Read the lead sentence, and ask yourself what kind of ideas you expect in the next sentence. Then read sentence *a*. Decide if it can follow the lead sentence and make good sense. Choose *Y* for "Yes" or *N* for "No." Do the same for sentence *b*. Can it follow the lead sentence and make good sense? *Remember:*

1. Look for the ideas that make a logical connection between each pair of sentences.

2. This is also a vocabulary learning exercise. If you have problems with any new words, check their meaning as you work.

1. Medicine is again beginning to emphasize the prevention of disease.

   a. For example, more and more doctors are stressing the importance of exercise and good nutritional habits.   Y   N

   b. Experience with diseases like AIDS and many forms of cancer has clearly shown that we should not rely only on drugs and surgery to fight disease.   Y   N

2. The new technology that is being introduced into hospitals has some major disadvantages.

   a. It makes operations safer and increases the patient's chances for a successful recovery.   Y   N

   b. It forces hospitals to raise the cost of their services in order to recover the costs of the expensive new equipment.   Y   N

3. Heart disease is clearly associated with the type of life that a person leads.

    a. Modern technology allows doctors to perform surgery on patients who are suffering from heart disease.   Y N

    b. A poor diet, lack of exercise, and stress are all factors that play a role in the development of this disease.   Y N

4. In the United States, there has been an enormous increase in the number of people who are becoming members of health and sports clubs.

    a. The increase indicates that more and more Americans are becoming aware of the importance of regular exercise.   Y N

    b. Most large U.S. companies have health-insurance plans that pay for any medical treatment their employees need.   Y N

5. Experts in health care believe that our health-care systems emphasize the treatment of disease too much.

    a. There is an urgent need, they say, to stress disease prevention.   Y N

    b. Merely reducing fat in people's diet, they claim, would reduce the death rate from heart disease more than all the heart surgery that is performed in the United States annually.   Y N

Text Study 2.
Recognizing Text Organization:
Cause and Effect

It is not difficult to understand the connection between the ideas of the first and the second sentence in this example:

> Our plane was two hours late taking off from New York. There was a heavy snow storm that morning.

There are no clear connecting words; however, with your knowledge of English and with your knowledge of the world, you are able to see that the second sentence explains why we were late leaving New York. In other words, the first sentence contains an *effect*; the second sentence contains the *cause*.

Often writers want to examine the causes of a situation or its effects, or both. In these cases, writers organize their ideas in ways that make clear the cause-effect relationships.

EXAMPLE

Now look at this example. What is the connection between the first sentence and the second sentence?

> The talks between the workers and the company have failed. The company is attributing the failure to the attitudes of the workers. According to the company, the employees refuse to accept that new technology must be introduced into their factories and that this technology will need fewer workers to operate it.

The second sentence contains a possible cause for the event in the first sentence. Probably you found this connection more difficult to see than the connection in the first example. The verb *is attributing* tells a native speaker to expect a cause-effect connection. However, perhaps this verb is not in your English vocabulary yet, and this caused you to have problems understanding the example.

In this lesson, you will be able to review cause-effect vocabulary and learn some new words and expressions that show you that the writer is examining causes and effects.

EXPLANATION: MARKERS OF CAUSE AND EFFECT

Sometimes a writer does not need to use a special word in order to show a cause-effect connection in a sentence or between sentences. (Look at the example at the beginning of this Text Study.)

However, often a writer uses vocabulary that shows readers that they should expect a cause-effect relationship. This vocabulary includes verbs, nouns, adverbs, and connecting words and phrases. We call these words and expressions *cause-effect markers.*

Here is list of cause-effect markers. Read through it carefully; review the words and expressions that you have learned already; pay special attention to any new words or phrases. If you need an example for a new word or expression, ask your teacher or look for it in the exercises that follow.

Nouns

cause	result
factor	impact
reason	consequence
origin	outcome
effect	relationship
connection	

Verbs

C causes E	C produces E
C results in E	C forces E
E results from C	C contributes to E
C brings about E	C plays a part in E
C creates E	to attribute E to C
C gives rise to E	to blame E on C
C leads to E	to blame C for E

Connecting Expressions

Inside Clauses

as a result of [+ Cause]   owing to [+ Cause]
because of [+ Cause]   on account of [+ Cause]
due to [+ Cause]   thanks to [+ Cause]

Between Clauses

because [+ Cause]   the more [+ Cause] . . . the
since [+ Cause]   more [+ Effect]
as [+ Cause]   so [+ Cause] . . . that [+ Effect]
so [+ Effect]   if [+ Cause] . . . main clause
                                    [+ Effect]

Between Sentences

As a result [+ Effect]   Thus [+ Effect]
Consequently [+ Effect]   Hence [+ Effect]
Therefore [+ Effect]   For this reason [+ Effect]

READING STRATEGIES

1. While you are reading, look for markers in the text that tell you that the writer is examining cause and effect.

2. Make simple notes (with arrow diagrams) about the causes and the effects that you see.

EXERCISES

Sentence Reading

Read the following sentences. If you see a *cause*, underline it once. If you see an *effect*, underline it twice. If you see a clear marker for cause-effect, draw a circle around it.

Example
    According to scientists, a great deal of pollution is caused by power plants which produce electricity by burning coal.

1. Because of a severe storm in the area, our plane was three hours late in taking off.

2. More and more women are interested in work as a career, not just as a way to increase family income; for this reason we can expect an increase in the number of women in medicine, law, and scientific research.

3. The prices of new cars are forcing people to keep their old cars longer than they used to.

4. On account of the bad weather, the baseball game has been canceled.

5. There are a number of possible factors that police have found to be connected with traffic accidents. The most common of these are alcohol, speed, and mechanical failure.

6. A lack of rain is creating problems for farmers. Their crops are not growing well.

7. If farmers did not use some chemical on their crops, the food we buy in the supermarket would be more expensive.

8. In the 1980s, world oil prices fell. This brought about an improvement in the economies of countries that have to import oil.

9. Although 100 percent proof is difficult to find, some human diseases have been associated with chemicals in the environment.

10. Two months ago, a large factory here closed down. This resulted in 1,500 people losing their jobs.

Paragraph Reading

Read the following paragraphs. The writer has organized them according to cause and effect. Look for cause-effect markers, and then read carefully to follow the lines of cause and effect. Complete the arrow diagrams to show the cause-effect connections.

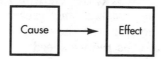

1. Fill in the arrow diagram with causes and effects from the list below the diagram. Write only the correct letter in each box.

In the 1970s, there was a rather large fall in the number of people who were killed in accidents on U.S. highways. According to some experts, the most important factor in the decrease was the 55-miles-per-hour speed limit. The original reason for the introduction of this speed limit was economic: it was to reduce the amount of gasoline that the country was using at a time when gasoline prices were very high.

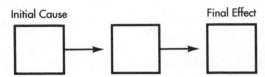

a. The country needed to reduce the amount of expensive gasoline it was using.
b. There was a large decrease in the number of deaths in traffic accidents on U.S. highways in the 1970s.
c. The 55 mph speed limit was introduced.

2. In this passage, there is one main, final effect and a number of connected causes. Fill in the arrow diagram with causes and effects from the list above the diagram. Write only the correct letter in each box.

In 1912, the *Titanic*, the largest and best equipped transatlantic liner of its time, hit an iceberg on its first crossing from England to America and sank. Of the 2,235 passengers and crew, only 713 survived.

Research has shown that a number of factors played an important part in the disaster. First, the *Titanic* carried only sixteen lifeboats, with room for about 1,100 people. This was clearly not enough for a ship of the *Titanic*'s size. In fact, the designer of the *Titanic* originally planned to equip the ship with forty-eight lifeboats; however, in order to reduce their costs for building the ship, the owners of the *Titanic* decided to give it only sixteen lifeboats.

A second factor was that the *Titanic*'s crew were not given enough time to become familiar with the ship, especially with its emergency equipment. As a result, many lifeboats left the ship only half-full and many more people died than needed to.

The third factor in the disaster was the behavior of the *Titanic*'s officers on the night of the disaster. In the twenty-four hours before the disaster, they received a number of warnings about icebergs in the area, but they took no precautions. They did not change direction or even reduce speed.

a. The *Titanic* did not have not enough lifeboats for all the passengers and crew.
b. The *Titanic* hit an iceberg in the North Atlantic and sank with the loss of 1,522 lives.
c. The *Titanic*'s officers did not pay any attention to warnings about icebergs near the *Titanic*.
d. The *Titanic*'s owners decided to save money by equipping the *Titanic* with sixteen lifeboats instead of the forty-eight that the ship's designer planned.

e. The crew were not very familiar with the ship and its emergency equipment.
f. Many lifeboats were only half-full of people when they left the *Titanic*.

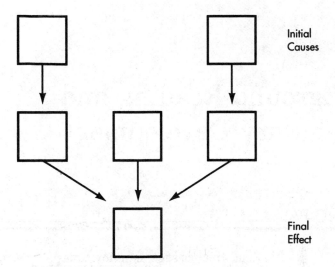

Background Reading and Vocabulary Development

Read this passage as many times as you need to. However, during your first reading, you should:

1. Stop reading at the end of each sentence that contains boldface words, and complete the Comprehension Building Task in the left margin. Then continue with your reading.

2. Try to identify the most important idea the writer wants to communicate to you in this passage.

Medicine and Genetic Research

Draw a simple cause-effect diagram while you read.

In recent years, there has been an enormous increase in inter- 1
est in and financial support for genetic research. **As a result,** a
great deal of progress has been made in this important area of
knowledge. For example, some years ago scientists successfully
5   identified the genes for a number of serious birth defects and diseases that children can inherit from their parents. On the basis of
Check back for the meaning of this ad-vance.
this advance, medical science has developed tests that enable doctors to discover a variety of genetic abnormalities in unborn
babies, abnormalities that are usually incurable and which often
10   result in death.

More recently, genetic researchers have begun to use their 2
knowledge not just to diagnose but also to develop treatment for
life-threatening genetic illnesses. For cases of diseases such as he-
mophilia, sickle-cell anemia, cystic fibrosis, and a number of im-

Check back for the meaning of such experimental treatments.

Draw a simple cause-effect diagram while you read.

15   mune-deficiency diseases, researchers are testing ways to introduce perfect genes into patients. Some of the early results of **such
experimental treatments** have been very promising. In one study, a
gene whose absence causes immune-deficiency has been introduced
into the white blood cells of two young immune-deficient children.
20   **As a result,** they are beginning to show the natural resistance to
diseases and infection that humans normally have. In other research, medical scientists are studying the effectiveness of a natural human protein that can now be produced in large quantities in
the laboratory, thanks to genetic engineering. The protein is being
25   given to patients who suffer from cystic fibrosis, a genetic disease
of the lungs that affects fifty thousand Americans and is often
fatal by the age of thirty.

Medical researchers are very excited about the possibility of   3
using techniques of genetic engineering to treat conditions like
30   cancer, diabetes, and heart disease. However, they caution that
such treatment is still years away. What is fully available today,
thanks to genetic research, is the possibility of eliminating a number of incurable genetic diseases. **We can begin to do this,** health
experts argue, by informing people who carry defective genes about

Check back for the meaning of this.
a. to identify defective genes
b. to eliminate some genetic diseases
c. to cure children with genetic diseases.

35   the health risks for any children they might have. This practice is
already quite common in the United States and in other industrial
countries. After tests have shown that they carry a genetic disease,
some people have decided not to have children. They don't want to
take the risk that a child of theirs will suffer from an incurable
40   mental or physical defect.

Up to now, has the passage discussed the medical benefits or problems of genetic research? What do you expect in this new paragraph?

However, progress in genetic research is also raising a num-   4
ber of important moral and ethical questions for the medical profession and for society in general. For example, we now have the
ability to produce human growth hormone by genetic engineering.
45   The hormone, of course, can be used to help people who are genetically lacking in it. But should it be made available to people who
are merely dissatisfied with their size and wish to be taller? A
more serious question is raised by our ability to identify defective
genes in unborn children and our wish to eliminate some genetic
50   diseases. If tests show that a baby will be born with some incurable
disease or abnormality, should the parents have the right to ask
for an abortion? Today in the United States and in many other
countries, abortions are legal in such cases. However, many people,
especially people with strong religious beliefs, disagree strongly

Check back for the meaning of this practice.

55   with **this practice.** For them abortion is morally wrong. In their
opinion, science must look for other ways than killing unborn
babies to eliminate genetic diseases.

Main Idea Check

Choose the sentence that best expresses the main idea of the passage:

a. Progress in genetic research has given us the hope of treating or eliminating genetic disease, but it is also causing moral and ethical problems.

b. Doctors can now identify people who perhaps will have children with genetic abnormalities.

c. Today, although abortion is legal in the United States, many people are opposed to it.

d. Medicine has benefited a great deal from the progress that has been made in genetic research in recent years.

A Closer Look

1. What are the names of some specific genetic diseases?

2. At the time this article was written, how much progress had been made by research in the genetic treatment of diseases?
   a. Research had made such great progress that some treatments were already becoming widely available.
   b. Research had been successful enough to give hope that genetic treatment would become available in the future.
   c. Failures and disappointments in the research had caused serious doubt that genetic treatment would ever be worthwhile.

3. How do health experts suggest that we begin now to solve the problem of some genetic diseases?
   a. By encouraging people with certain defective genes not to have children.
   b. By using technology to cure the diseases.
   c. By performing surgery on children with genetic defects.

4. Doctors never inform adults who carry defective genes about the danger that they will have children with serious mental or physical abnormalities.   T F

5. Everyone agrees that abortion should be available to women who are carrying unborn babies with incurable genetic diseases.   T F

6. There is a general chain of cause and effect that runs through Reading Passage 1.3. Fill in this cause-effect diagram with appropriate information from the list below the diagram. Write only the correct letter in each box.

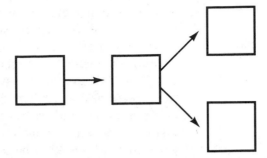

a. We now have the possibility of eliminating some genetic diseases.
b. Now there are important ethical questions that need to be answered.
c. Medical science is now able to identify some defective genes in adults and in unborn children.
d. Interest in and support for genetic research has been growing in recent years.

What Do You Think?

What is your opinion on the two specific moral and ethical questions that are mentioned in this passage? (1) Should people of normal size be able to use the products of genetic engineering (e.g., human growth hormone) to make themselves taller or stronger? (2) Should society allow abortions when an unborn child has a serious genetic defect?

READING PASSAGE 1.4

Read this passage as many times as you need to. However, during your first reading, you should:

1. Stop reading at the end of each sentence that contains boldface words, and complete the Comprehension Building Task in the left margin. Then continue with your reading.

2. Try to identify the most important idea the writer wants to communicate to you in this passage.

AIDS—Not Someone Else's Problem

By the early 1980s, a frightening new health problem was beginning to appear in the United States. Healthy young people, especially males, began to suffer from a number of infections that doctors had seldom needed to treat because the human immune   1

Check back for the
meaning of the infec-
tions.

5   system normally protects people from them. Without any effective
      treatment, **the infections worsened;** the patients weakened and
      ultimately died. The disease came to be named AIDS (acquired
      immuno-deficiency syndrome).

      The U.S. government was slow to recognize the seriousness of   2
10   the disease and at first made little financial support available for
      research into the disease. According to some critics of the govern-
      ment, there was no feeling of urgency because the population
      group that appeared to be most affected by AIDS was homosexual
      men. However, whatever the reason for the early lack of urgency,
15   it soon disappeared as the number of AIDS cases increased rapidly.
      Between 1984 and 1985, for example, there was a 100 percent rise
      in the number of people who were diagnosed as having AIDS.

      When governments made it a priority, research into AIDS,   3
      mostly in the United States and Western Europe, expanded

Check back for the
meaning of the dis-
ease.

20   greatly. Researchers were able to identify the cause of **the disease,**
      a virus that attacks the human immune system and which they
      named HIV (human immuno-deficiency virus). Further research
      has established that the virus is transmitted most frequently
      through blood-to-blood contact with a person who is infected with
25   the virus. The most common means of transmission are sexual con-
      tact or the use of hypodermic needles that are contaminated with
      the blood of an HIV-infected person. During the early years,
      smaller numbers of people were also infected with the virus when
      they received transfusions of infected blood in hospitals. Since
30   1985, however, supplies of blood and blood products to hospitals
      have been made almost 100 percent safe by the development of
      effective tests to identify the presence of HIV.

      Today AIDS is no longer a disease that is limited to a small   4
      section of the United States. Between 1984 and 1989, the number
35   of annual new cases of AIDS rose from 4,436 to 33,710, an enor-
      mous increase of 660 percent. Between 1989 and 1992, the number
      of American teenagers who were infected with the virus rose by 75
      percent.

      Although it first came to the public's attention in the United   5
40   States and Western Europe, AIDS is now truly a global problem
      (see Figure 1). It is spreading through sub-Saharan Africa, where
      the rate of infection in young heterosexual adults has reached cata-
      strophic levels in some countries. It has also reached Asia. It
      arrived late, but by 1992, for example, 40 percent of Thailand's
45   heroin users had AIDS and were passing the virus on to the gen-
      eral population through sexual contacts. In the same year, it was
      estimated that a full 1 percent of the Thai population was infected

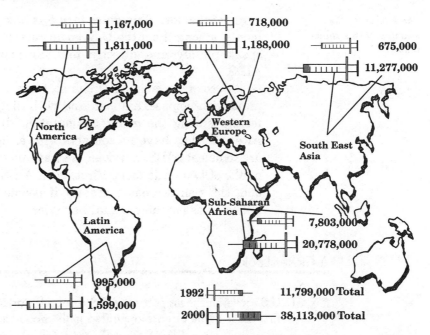

Figure 1. HIV infections: Estimates for 1992 and projections for 2000. The estimates of total HIV infections by 2000 suggest that the spread of HIV will have disastrous health and economic effects worldwide, especially in developing countries. (*Source:* J. M. Mann, D. J. M. Tarantola, and T. W. Netter, eds., *AIDS in the World* [Cambridge, MA: Harvard University Press, 1992].)

Check back for the meaning of this high transmission rate.

with the virus. If nothing is done to reduce **this high transmission rate,** experts are predicting that between 2 and 4 million
50 Thais could be infected with the AIDS virus by the year 2000.

How are we to solve the AIDS crisis? In spite of the massive 6 sums of money that are being spent for AIDS research, scientists warn that they are not close to finding an effective treatment for the disease. A vaccine is still years away; a cure may never come,
55 and the transmission rates show that we cannot afford to wait. However, we have a realistic answer—to emphasize prevention.

At first sight, the task of developing an effective AIDS pre- 7 vention program appears quite simple—for two reasons. First,

Check back for the meaning of this.

60 AIDS is always fatal. **This** is a fact that should give people all the incentive they need to avoid it. Second, we know how to prevent most cases of AIDS—by avoiding contact either through sex or through sharing a hypodermic needle with a person who might have the disease.

As you read, look for these two factors, and draw a simple cause-effect diagram.

However, the task is made much more complex by two 8
65 **factors.** First, people are often unwilling to speak openly about

Check back for the meaning of this reluctance.

sexual behavior. **This reluctance** is also shared by some governments, among them the U.S. government, which have been slow to speak plainly and directly to their populations about sex and AIDS.

70   Second, because AIDS is so often associated in the public's 9 mind with homosexual men and with illegal drug users, there is a feeling among the general population that they are not at risk. After all, they have no contacts with either of these groups. If we are to defeat AIDS, however, we have no choice but to convince the

75   public of two basic facts: First, with AIDS everyone is at risk; second, the risk decreases greatly if people avoid illegal drugs and follow rules for safer sexual behavior.

A Closer Look

1. U.S. government support for AIDS research started as soon as the first cases of the disease appeared in the population.   T   F

2. Identify the way or ways, according to the article, in which a person could have become infected with the AIDS virus in the early 1980s.
   a. through sexual contact with an infected person
   b. through a transfusion of infected blood
   c. through sharing a drug needle with an infected person
   d. through living in the same house as an infected person

3. Heterosexual sex carries no risk of AIDS.   T   F

4. According to the writer, developing a vaccine for AIDS may be easier than developing a cure for it.   T   F

5. Reread paragraphs 5–8. Then fill in this cause-effect diagram with information from the list that follows the diagram. Write only the correct letter in each box.

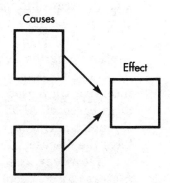

a. It becomes more difficult to convince people that they should protect themselves against AIDS.
b. People think that AIDS is a disease that attacks only homosexual men and illegal drug users.
c. People do not like to speak openly and plainly about sexual behavior.

What Do You Think?

How big a problem is AIDS now in the country where you were born? What are the health services there doing about AIDS? Do you agree with what they are doing?

Imagine you have a son or daughter. How would you go about protecting them from the danger of AIDS?

READING PASSAGE 1.5

Read this passage as many times as you need to. However, during your first reading, you should:

1. Stop reading at the end of each sentence that contains boldface words, and complete the Comprehension Building Task in the left margin. Then continue with your reading.

2. Try to identify the most important idea the writer wants to communicate to you in this passage.

Ethical Questions in Health Care

Draw a simple cause-effect diagram as you read this paragraph.

In the past ten years, advances in medical technology have enabled doctors to treat medical conditions that they were not able to treat before. For many patients, the new technology has brought new life and new hope. For the medical profession and for society, however, it has also created a number of very difficult ethical and moral problems. 1

Even with the new technology, doctors are often not capable of improving the condition of their patients; in these cases, the new machines merely prolong life instead of improving it. Sometimes conscious patients continue to live and suffer because they are kept alive by machines. There are also other patients in U.S. hospitals who have been unconscious for long periods of time because parts 2 of their brain are not functioning. They are kept alive by modern drugs and life-support systems, but there is often little or no

*Check back for the
meaning of* situations
like these.

15   chance of recovery. **Situations like these** are forcing us to reconsider our ideas about the goals of medicine. For example, is one goal to prolong life, regardless of the quality of that life? Alternatively, are there circumstances where doctors can stop treatment and allow the disease to reach its natural end—often the death of

20   the patient?

What is this second
question? *Check back.*

Many people in the United States answer **this second question** with a definite "Yes." They believe that a patient's survival regardless of the circumstances is absolutely not the goal of medicine. Many state legislators agree, and many states now define

25   death in a way different from the traditional way. According to the law in these states, a patient is dead when certain parts of the brain stop functioning, not when the heart stops. And in more than twelve states, patients can now request their doctors not to prolong their lives if they have no hope of recovery.

*Check for the meaning
of* these developments.
a. *allowing incurably
ill patients to die if
they wish*
b. *changing the definition of death*
c. *both (a) and (b)*

30   However, other people fear that **these developments** will contribute to the growth of a society that places less importance on human life. They point out that already in some cases, babies with massive brain damage are not given treatment for some other unconnected illness. They have been allowed to die because it was

35   decided that they had no chance of living a normal human life. In the case of other patients who are unconscious and incapable of deciding for themselves, the critics ask, who will make the decisions about stopping or continuing treatment? Do we really want, they ask, a society where someone else can decide whether we live

40   or die?

3

4

Main Idea Check

Choose the sentence that best expresses the main or central idea of the passage:

a. There is disagreement in the United States about a question that is raised by modern medical technology: Should we prolong life in all circumstances?

b. Although medicine has benefited greatly from modern technological advances, doctors are still not capable of improving the condition of all their patients.

c. A lot of people in the United States believe that it is always wrong to stop giving treatment to incurably ill patients.

A Closer Look

1. Technology has brought considerable benefits to medicine.   T F

2. In your own words, complete this cause-effect diagram to show the cause-effect relationships that are examined in the first paragraph of the passage.

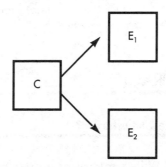

3. Everyone agrees that one goal of medicine is to prolong life in all circumstances.   T F

4. According to the traditional definition of death, a person is dead
   a. when the heart stops beating
   b. when certain parts of the brain stop functioning
   c. when the patient has no hope of recovery

5. The writer describes the different opinions of two groups of people. What is the opinion of the first group of people the writer mentions in the passage?
   a. There are circumstances in which a patient can be allowed to die without more treatment.
   b. The duty of a doctor is to prolong a patient's life, regardless of the circumstances.
   c. It is dangerous to give people the right to decide that a patient is not to receive any more treatment.

6. What side does the writer support in the discussion that is described in paragraphs 2, 3, and 4 of this passage?
   a. The writer clearly agrees with the people who believe that patients must be kept alive in all circumstances.
   b. The writer does not make his opinion clear.
   c. The writer clearly agrees with the people who believe that incurably ill patients have the right to ask for their treatment to be stopped.

What Do You Think?

1. Do you think that an incurably ill person should have the right to ask for an end to treatment that keeps him or her alive? If so, do you think that anyone

else has the right to make the decision for the patient if the patient is unable to communicate his or her wishes?

2. Imagine you are working in a health-care system with very limited resources. You have two patients who are suffering from incurable kidney disease. One is a twenty-year-old female student who is studying biology. The other is a fifty-five-year-old female biology researcher. Finally you have available one kidney that is suitable for transplanting into either patient. What do you decide, and why?

VOCABULARY PRACTICE

Same or Different?

Writers sometimes express the same ideas with very different grammar and vocabulary. This exercise will help you identify such occurrences.

Read the two sentences in each example, and decide whether they express the same ideas or different ideas. Choose *S* when the sentence expresses the same idea; choose *D* when they express different ideas. *Remember:* You can express the same ideas with different words and different grammar!

1. a. In spite of the considerable advances that have been made in medicine in the last thirty years, we still have not eliminated a number of infectious diseases.
    b. Many infectious diseases have now disappeared because of the great progress that has been made in medicine during the last thirty years.   S   D

2. a. The patient recovered consciousness an hour after the operation.
    b. After the surgery, the patient remained unconscious for only an hour.   S   D

3. a. Sometimes doctors can save the life of a patient if the latest high-technology equipment is available to them.
    b. The latest high-technology equipment sometimes enables doctors to prevent a patient's death.   S   D

4. a. The number of women who die from lung cancer every year has been rising in recent years.
    b. In recent years, among females there has been an increase in the annual death rate from lung cancer.   S   D

5. a. In the United States, abortions are available to pregnant women who are carrying babies with serious genetic defects.

b. In the United States, if a serious genetic abnormality is discovered in an unborn child, the mother can request and receive an
abortion.   S   D

6. a. Polio is a very infectious disease.
   b. There is a very effective vaccine for polio.   S   D

7. a. The number of cases of infectious diseases in the Third World
      could be greatly reduced if better sanitation were provided.
   b. By improving sanitation in developing countries, we could
      achieve a considerable reduction in the number of people who
      catch infectious diseases.   S   D

8. a. Medical science still knows very little about mental illness.
   b. Medical science still has a very poor understanding of genetic
      diseases.   S   D

9. a. Mass immunization programs cost a great deal to carry out.
   b. It is very expensive to immunize large populations of people.   S   D

10. a. New and safer vaccines are being developed by medical sci-
       ence for certain diseases.
    b. Medical scientists are developing new and safer drugs for the
       treatment of certain diseases.   S   D

11. a. Providing adequate sanitation and clean water are the two top
       priorities for the health-care systems in many developing coun-
       tries.
    b. In many Third World countries, the lack of adequate sanitation
       and clean water are the two most urgent problems for the
       health-care systems.   S   D

12. a. Advances in genetic research and medical technology are forc-
       ing the medical profession to answer difficult ethical questions.
    b. Because of the progress that has occurred in the area of ge-
       netic research and medical technology, the medical profession
       is having to make some difficult ethical decisions.   S   D

Making Connections

Each example in the exercise has a lead sentence and two sentences (*a* and *b*)
that might or might not logically follow the lead sentence. Read the lead sentence, and ask yourself what kind of idea you could expect in the next sentence.
Then read sentence *a*. Decide whether it can follow the lead sentence and make
good sense. Choose *Y* for "Yes" or *N* for "No." Do the same for sentence *b*
Remember:

1. Look for the ideas that make a logical connection between each pair of sentences.

2. This is also a vocabulary learning exercise. If you have problems with any new words, check their meanings as you work.

1. In industrial countries, mass immunization has made it possible to almost eliminate certain infectious diseases.

   a. In the United States, for example, there have been very few cases of polio since the polio vaccine became widely available in the 1950s.   Y N

   b. Influenza, for example, still causes ten thousand deaths in the United States annually.   Y N

2. According to the Centers for Disease Control in Atlanta, an annual shot of influenza vaccine would especially benefit older people with heart and lung problems.

   a. If all members of this section of the population received flu shots, a considerable number of lives would be saved every year.   Y N

   b. These people often do not have the physical strength to recover from an attack of flu that would be unpleasant but not fatal for a younger person.   Y N

3. An enormous number of people in the world's poorest countries do not have clean drinking water or adequate sanitation facilities.

   a. In these countries, the annual death rate from preventable diseases like simple diarrhea is extremely high.   Y N

   b. So in these countries, the first priority of the health-care systems is to build more hospitals.   Y N

4. In 1976, an official report concluded that the health service in Cuba was not paying sufficient attention to the prevention of health problems.

   a. The report suggested that more of the latest drugs and medical technology should be made available to hospitals for the treatment of their patients.   Y N

   b. This lack of attention, the report concluded, contributed to the failure of the health-care system to effectively solve the country's health problems.   Y N

5. Recent advances in genetic research have caused ethical problems for the medical profession and for society in general.

a. For example, scientists are hoping ultimately to be able to use genetic engineering to produce new and safer vaccines for human use.   Y N

b. For example, we may be able to successfully treat some genetically inherited diseases.   Y N

6. It seems that the new drug the doctors are using in this patient's case has been very effective.

   a. He is now completely incapable of any physical movement.   Y N

   b. The infection is disappearing and he is now conscious.   Y N

7. Some doctors are completely opposed to the idea that incurably ill patients should be allowed to die if they want to.

   a. They cannot imagine any circumstances where they would be willing to turn off life-support equipment.   Y N

   b. If you give expensive treatment to people like these, the doctors argue, you are wasting money and resources that are urgently needed for other cases.   Y N

8. According to many people, we cannot force people who are carrying a serious genetic disease not to have children.

   a. To do this would be unethical and inhuman.   Y N

   b. However, we can encourage them not to have children by informing them of the possible mental or physical abnormalities that their children could be born with.   Y N

Synonyms and Paraphrases

Review the meanings of the words to the left of each paragraph below. Find out how to use these words by studying examples from the Vocabulary Study and from the reading passages of this unit. Then read each paragraph for its details. Replace the words in boldface with the correct new words. Sometimes you will need to change the grammar of the sentence so that the new word or expression fits into it correctly.

to infect
to become aware
rate

1. Since the late 1980s and early 1990s, AIDS has spread through different countries of the world at a **speed** (1) **that is causing great concern** (2). However, it is at present very difficult to prevent or even slow its **spread**—for a number of

to be infected
alarming
transmission

reasons. The first of these is that clear symptoms of the disease are often very slow to appear. People may **carry** HIV, the virus that causes AIDS, for more than ten years without **realizing** it. During this time, however, such people will probably **pass the virus on to** others.

mass
reliable
expertise
circumstances
capable
to diagnose
threat
to perform

2. If we wait until we can clearly **identify** AIDS in a patient, we cannot hope to stop its spread. We clearly need to identify those who are infected with HIV and who are therefore a **danger** to others in certain **situations.** There are blood tests **that can be trusted** to show if an individual is carrying the AIDS virus. However, here we run into a number of other problems. First, some **knowledge, skill, and experience are** necessary if the test is to be **conducted** correctly. Second, the tests are not cheap. Most developing countries will **not be able** to support HIV-testing programs **for large numbers of people.**

to transmit
priority
to consider
to become infected
to be reluctant
to attempt

3. One possible solution would be to **try** to identify those people who are **thought** to be in greatest danger of **getting** the AIDS virus. Testing these people would then be **the thing we want to do before testing others.** Even here, of course, we face serious problems. Possibly the most important of these is that people in general **do not like** to talk honestly and openly about sexual behavior—the main way in which the HIV virus **spreads.**

estimated
resource
ultimately
to finance
impact
catastrophe
incentive
regardless of
immunity
alternative

4. **At the end of a long process of research,** scientists may be able to develop a vaccine that will provide some **protection against** AIDS. In the meantime, however, we need to use **all that is available to help ourselves** in order to slow the infection rate for HIV. We have no **other choice.** To do less would be to accept a world health **disaster** that in its **effect** could equal the Black Death of history, the bubonic plague which killed **about** 25 million Europeans (about one-quarter of the population) in the fourteenth century. This horrifying possibility should be the **encouragement** we need to develop and **provide money for** programs of HIV-testing and AIDS education **no matter** how much they cost.

Using New Vocabulary

Review the meanings of the following verbs. Use the examples in the Vocabulary Study to learn how to use the verbs in sentences.

to consider/reconsider	to threaten
to be/become aware	to eliminate
to contribute	to be reluctant

Now finish each of the following sentences in a way that seems appropriate and interesting to you. You may want to use ideas from your readings in this section.

1. Many U.S. companies have begun to consider . . .

2. As we will not have sufficient funds, we will need to reconsider . . .

3. Today many more people are aware . . .

4. After I studied English for a while, I became aware . . .

5. Alcohol is another factor that contributes . . .

6. AIDS threatens . . .

7. The health authorities are hoping to eliminate . . .

8. The U.S. government is reluctant . . .

Main Reading

DEALING WITH UNKNOWN VOCABULARY

In every text you read, you will probably meet words that are unfamiliar to you. You need effective strategies for dealing with this unknown vocabulary. What you should *not* do is immediately run for your dictionary and look up every word you don't know. The problem with that strategy is that it interrupts your reading and therefore makes it more difficult for you to get a general idea of what the writer wants to communicate. Dictionary work is useful, but you should try to delay it until after you've read the passage at least once.

Have a look at these examples. The words in italics may be new for you; however, the sentences should be understandable—after you think a little about them.

1. The successful treatment of some diseases depends on the availability of *sophisticated*, modern, high-tech equipment.

Omit the word *sophisticated* from the sentence, and read the remaining words. Probably you will understand the sentence completely. *Sophisticated* adds something to the sentence, but without it, the basic meaning of the sentence remains clear. *You can deal with some unknown vocabulary by omitting it.*

2. A new system of community health centers is being started in some Third World countries. The *funds* to finance these centers will be mainly provided by the World Bank.

Look at the other ideas in the two sentences (i.e., the context). Think especially about the word *finance*, which means "to pay for something." This suggests strongly that *funds* must mean something like "money." *You can deal with some unknown vocabulary by using the context and thinking.*

3. *Dieticians* warn us that we risk losing a lot of the *nutrients* in vegetables if we boil them.

Again look at the context—the other ideas in the sentence. Then look at the two new words, *dieticians* and *nutrients*. You can recognize the similarity between the new words and words you have learned in this unit—*diet* and *nutrition*. This suggests that *dieticians* are people, maybe experts, who study diets; *nutrients* are the things in food that give us what we need from food. *You can deal with some unknown vocabulary by using the context and by using your knowledge of word families.*

4. After their *abortive* attempt to enter the building, they decided to leave.

You know some of the word family of *abortive;* you know *abortion.* However, this may hurt you rather than help you. *Abortive* has nothing to do with abortions; it means "unsuccessful." The context really doesn't make anything clearer for you. This example shows that *there are dangers and limitations in guessing vocabulary from context and word families. However, in this sentence, you could omit the unknown word and still understand the main part of the sentence.*

READING STRATEGIES

1. Try to read and understand the text *without* the unknown words.

2. Think about the context (the ideas in the sentences around the unknown word), and try to guess a general meaning that "fits" the context.

3. Use your knowledge of word families if you see a similarity between the unknown word and a word you already know.

4. Be careful! Don't expect 100 percent success from strategies 1–3.

5. After you stop reading, use your dictionary to check the meanings of unknown words. Start to learn the words that you feel will be useful to you.

EXERCISE: VOCABULARY IN CONTEXT

In this exercise, try to find the meaning of new words. Do not use your dictionary. Look for help from other words and ideas in the sentence (the context).

Read each example to the end. Do *not* stop when you see the new word (in *italics*). Then choose the best meaning for the new word.

1. Good nutrition and exercise are *essential* for health. Without them, a person runs a much greater risk of developing heart disease.
   Essential means a. very important and necessary.
                      b. very popular with the public.
                      c. harmful or damaging to someone.

2. The government's birth-control program failed because there was no *publicity* about it. There were no reports in the newspapers, on the radio, or on television. Few people were aware that the program even existed or what its benefits would be.
   Publicity means a. things that belong to the public, not to one person.
                      b. information that is given to people about something.
                      c. a general word for newspapers, radio, and television.

3. The people who conducted the inquiry into the air disaster last year *recommended* that the aircraft equipment law should be changed. All aircraft should carry a device that would warn the pilot if another plane were dangerously close. The government accepted the *recommendation* and changed the law.
   To recommend X means a. to say that it would be good to do X.
                          b. to criticize X.
                          c. to order someone to do X.

4. Americans are so used to things like safe water, adequate sanitation, and good medical care that they *take them for granted*. In some countries, however, these things are not available. When Americans first come to these countries, they are often very shocked.
   To take for granted means a. to not like something or someone.
                               b. not to appreciate the value of something or someone that is very familiar to you.
                               c. to buy something that is available.

5. It is often difficult to prove 100 percent that humans will develop cancer from exposure to a certain chemical. However, many people believe that if we can find a *link* between a certain chemical and cancer in test animals, then we should ban the use of that chemical.
   Link means a. a connection.
                b. a cause.
                c. a reason.

PREREADING THE ARTICLE: WHAT CAN YOU EXPECT? _____

When you begin to read an article, it helps if you already have some ideas about what you will read before you begin. We'll call these ideas *expectations*. You are going to develop some expectations for the main article of this unit.

Turn to page 44, and read the title of the article carefully. Now use the ideas from the title to answer the expectation questions below. Some of them express ideas that you can expect in the article; others contain ideas that you don't really expect. Choose *Y* for "Yes" or *N* for "No" for each idea.

1. The article will describe only the health-care system in the United States.   Y N

2. The article will discuss some of the problems of health care systems.   Y N

3. The article will suggest no solutions to the problems of health-care systems.   Y N

4. The article will mainly discuss the different systems of government in the world.   Y N

5. The article will discuss medical questions that concern both wealthy and poor countries.   Y N

This article has a number of sections, and each section has its own title. Read the title of each section carefully. Then read the following ideas, and choose the section where you expect to find each idea.

6. Where do you expect to find information about the health-care systems of countries like Canada, Britain, Germany, and the United States?
   a. section 1
   b. section 2
   c. section 3
   d. section 4

7. Where do you expect to find information about the health-care systems in developing countries?
   a. section 1
   b. section 2
   c. section 3
   d. section 4

8. The article will show that industrial countries and developing countries have nothing in common in the area of health care.   Y N

9. The writer will show that health care is becoming too expensive in industrial countries.   Y N

10. The article will discuss only one main type of problem in the health-
    care systems of industrial countries.   Y N

Now go back to expectations 1–5. Do you want to change any of your earlier
answers?

MAIN READING

Read this passage as many times as you need to. However, during your
first reading, you should:

1. Stop reading at the end of each sentence that contains boldface
   words, and complete the Comprehension Building Task in the
   left margin. Then continue with your reading.

2. Try to identify the most important idea the writer wants to communicate to you in this passage.

3. Look for cause-effect relationships. Diagram them as you find
   them.

As you read each section for the first time, complete the Main Ideas
Check. After your first reading, answer the questions in A Closer Look.
You may find that you need to scan and read parts of the passage again.
This is normal. Remember that this is a reading exercise, not a memory
test.

Better Health for Everyone:
Health Care in the Industrial
and Developing Worlds

1. One Earth—Two Worlds of Health

"How can we provide the best health care for our people?"   1
This is a question that every responsible society and government is
attempting to answer. In the wealthy industrial nations, advances
in drugs and medical technology have made possible new treatments for diseases that medical science could not hope to cure ear-   5
lier this century. **In these countries,** doctors and patients expect
the latest drugs and technology, regardless of cost. If they are not
available to patients, angry protests are heard. In the countries of
the Third World, however, the health problems that have priority
are very different. Here over 9 million children die annually from   10

Check back for the
meaning of in these
countries.

15

treatable respiratory infections, from common, curable diarrhea, and from infectious childhood diseases like measles and whooping cough, diseases that have almost completely disappeared in the industrial countries. In the same Third World countries, it is believed that about 80 percent of all cases of illness are the result of contaminated water and inadequate sanitation.

Look for more differences as you read this paragraph.

20

25

30

It seems, therefore, that there are two worlds of medicine and that these two worlds have nothing in common with each other. The first world is concerned about diseases like heart disease and cancer, diseases that are often still incurable; the other world is concerned about diseases that would disappear if basic health programs could be afforded. The first world wants to provide the latest drugs and technology for that small section of the population who are ill; the other world needs to provide for the majority of its people the things the industrial world takes for granted— clean drinking water and a sufficient supply of essential drugs and basic vaccines. The immediate problems that face these two worlds seem very different. However, if we examine the problems and possible solutions, we will see certain similarities as well as clear differences.

2

2. Increasing Costs and Ethical Choices: Health Care in the Industrial World

Follow the cause-effect relationships here. Draw a diagram while you read.

35

40

45

Although industrial countries have made great advances in health care, today their health-care systems are experiencing some serious problems. By far the most urgent of these problems is financial: medical costs are rising faster than prices in most other areas of the economy. In the United States, for example, nearly $2 billion is spent every day for health care, and this amount is increasing at an annual rate of 12 percent. **As a result of these increasing costs,** access to good health care is being reduced rather than expanded. In Britain, a country with public health insurance, economics has forced the government to reduce the number of hospital beds, to cut back purchases of new equipment, and to employ fewer doctors and nurses. Today certain expensive treatments are not available to every patient who might need them. Other patients must wait for up to two years for some types of nonemergency surgery. In the United States, a country with a system of private health insurance, employers are finding it difficult to provide the same level of health insurance for their workers as they used to. Many are reducing or even eliminating health bene-

3

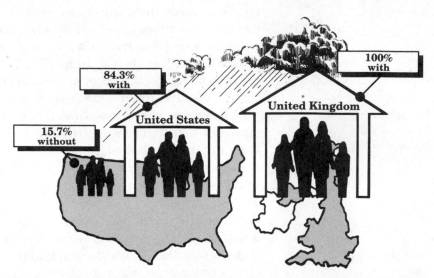

Figure 1. Health insurance coverage in the United States and United Kingdom, 1989. By 1989, about 37 million Americans were without medical insurance. The causes included rapidly rising health-care costs, employers who could not afford to buy health insurance for their employees, and lack of a national plan to provide coverage for those without private health insurance. Contrast this with the situation in the United Kingdom, where, although there are other problems with the health-care system, everyone is insured through the National Health Service. (*Source:* National Center for Health Statistics, *Health, United States 1991* [Hyattsville, MD: Public Health Service, 1992].)

fits for their employees. In 1992, for example, it was estimated that
50   37 million Americans were without health insurance (see Figure 1).

The problem of increasing costs is partly due to the expensive new technology that has been introduced into health care. This technology allows doctors to treat a variety of conditions that were incurable and often deadly some years ago. However,
55   the use of the new technology also increases medical costs enormously. The costs of purchasing, maintaining, and operating modern medical technology are extremely high. These are costs the health-care providers need to recover; as a result, the costs are passed on to the consumers—the patients—in higher charges for
60   all treatment. For example, a CAT scanner, a machine that enables doctors to discover abnormal growths inside a patient's body without operating, costs $1 million to buy and $100,000 a year to operate. A renal dialysis machine, which performs the same functions as a patient's kidneys, costs over $35,000 a year to operate for
65   each patient.

As you read the rest of the paragraph, look for an explanation of the general cause-effect relationship in the first sentence.

4

Check for the meaning
of for this purpose.
a. to treat diseases
b. to train doctors
c. to develop new
   technology

Follow the cause-effect
relationships here.
Draw a diagram
while you read.

Check back for the
meaning of these de-
velopments.

For some critics of our health-care systems, a more basic fac- 5
tor in rising health-care costs is this: Our health-care systems
place too much emphasis on the treatment of diseases after they
occur. Doctors are trained and hospital facilities are built mainly
for this purpose. In Britain, for example, 70 percent of the funds
for the National Health Service goes to hospitals. According to the
critics, the traditional attitude of our health authorities means
that we tend to ignore the fact that it is often more expensive and
less effective to try to solve medical problems after they occur than
to prevent them from occurring. The great infectious diseases of
history, these critics point out, were not eliminated by better medical treatment. They ultimately disappeared because there were
great improvements in housing and sanitation and because of immunization.

Today the great killers of the industrial world, for exam- 6
ple, heart disease and cancer, are diseases that are clearly
associated with our environment and with the way we live.
Tobacco, alcohol, poor nutritional habits, lack of exercise, stress,
and environmental pollution can all be factors that contribute to
the development of these diseases. Our health-care systems, however, use a large part of their resources for the treatment of the
diseases, treatment that is extremely costly and often not very effective. The critics of our health-care systems argue that there
needs to be a better balance between prevention and treatment.
Some of the money that is now spent for treatment would be better
spent for the prevention of these diseases. Prevention is always
better than cure, they argue; and usually it is cheaper!

There are, however, some indications that attitudes toward 7
health care are changing. Health-care providers are beginning to
emphasize healthy living. The general public, as a result of publicity about the causes of heart disease and cancer, for example, is
becoming aware of the link between disease and the way they live.
As a result, many people are changing their habits. They are taking regular physical exercise, cutting out cigarettes, and being
much more careful about their diet. **These developments are**
welcome, but more needs to be done before we can achieve a good
balance between preventative medicine and curative medicine.

Economic problems are not the only problems that are created 8
by the use of new drugs, new surgical techniques, and new medical
technology. Modern medicine has raised a number of serious ethical questions that have not yet been answered in a satisfactory
way. One central question is this: Should we prolong life if we can,
regardless of the quality of that life? With new drugs and new

technology, we are often capable of keeping a patient alive but in-
110   capable of improving that patient's condition. In some cases, the
patient remains unconscious, incapable of thought or feeling; in
other cases, the patient is conscious and suffers terribly while modern medicine keeps him or her alive. What should be done **in
such circumstances?**

*Check for the meaning
of in such circum-
stances.*

115   If a conscious patient says that he or she wishes to be allowed   9
to die, some doctors will agree to stop treating the patient. However, it is a very difficult decision. The problem is even more difficult when the patient is unconscious or is a baby. **In these circumstances,** who takes the decision about life or death for the
120   patient? The doctor? The parents? The relatives? The government?
And what should that decision be? If we decide to keep an incurably ill person alive, will that use up medical resources that could
be used to treat patients with curable diseases? If we allow people
to decide about the life or death of others, how can we be sure that
125   the decisions are best for the patient and not merely for the benefit
or convenience of the person who is making the decision?

*Check for the meaning
of in these circum-
stances.*

**Other ethical problems are raised by progress in genetic   10
research.** Doctors are now able to identify genes that carry serious
and fatal genetic diseases. Amniocentesis and chorionic villus sam-
130   pling, tests that are performed on women during early pregnancy,
are enabling doctors to discover a number of these genetic diseases
in babies before they are born. Already women are asking for and
receiving abortions after the tests have identified serious genetic
defects in their babies. However, is **this practice** ethically right?
135   Should medicine attempt to solve the problem of genetic disease
through abortions? And if abortions become more and more acceptable as a way to avoid giving birth to a severely handicapped child,
how long will people have the freedom to choose or not to choose an
abortion? There are already influential people who argue that we
140   should not permit people with defective genes to have children.
Will there come a time when people are forced to have abortions in
order to eliminate new carriers of a genetic disease? These then are
some of the problems and questions that modern medicine is forcing us to consider.

*In this sentence, check
for an idea that re-
peats the general topic
of paragraph 9.*

*Check back for the
meaning of this prac-
tice.*

3. A Question of Priorities: Health Care in
the Third World

145   At first glance, the health concerns of developing countries   11
seem very different from those of the industrialized world. Infectious diseases and child health care, for example, are clearly much

greater concerns for developing countries than they are for the industrialized world. In 1985, diarrhea, tuberculosis (TB), respiratory infections, and other preventable or treatable diseases caused 44 percent of the total number of deaths in developing countries. In the same year, only 5 percent of deaths in the industrial world were due to these infectious diseases. In the mid-1980s in developing countries, almost 37 percent of those who died were children below the age of seven. In the industrial world, child deaths were only 3 percent of the total.[1]

Quickly look forward through the text. Identify and mark these three areas. Then come back and begin reading again in more detail.

In three other areas, however, the health-care concerns of   12
developing and industrialized countries have a great deal in common. First, AIDS, which was first identified as a major problem in the United States, is spreading rapidly in many developing nations (see Figure 2). It now threatens the physical health of millions and the economic health of many developing countries. Second, cardiovascular diseases (diseases of the heart and circulatory system) are increasing in many developing countries as these countries modernize and life expectancy rises. In Singapore, for example, between 1940 and 1979, deaths from infectious diseases fell from 40 percent to 12 percent of total deaths, while life expectancy rose from forty to seventy years. At the same time, however, deaths from cardiovascular diseases rose from 5 percent to 32 percent of all deaths.[2]

The health-care systems of industrialized and developing   13
countries have one further area of common concern: their emphasis on treatment. Developing countries have inherited the Western emphasis on treatment. Although they have less money to spend for health care, it is clear that their systems also give priority to curative medicine. Recent statistics show that about 80 percent of health-care funds in developing countries is spent to train doctors and to build hospital facilities.

Quickly look forward and identify in the text where to find these two reasons. Then come back and start reading in more detail.

There are perhaps two reasons for this emphasis on   14
treatment and curative medicine. First, many Third World doctors have received their medical training in Western industrial countries, or in systems that follow Western traditions. As a result, they tend to have the attitudes that are typical of Western medicine. Naturally, the type of system that they want for their own countries is the type of system that seems to be so successful in

[1]Except where otherwise noted, the figures in this section are those compiled from various sources by the World Resources Institute, *World Resources 1991–1992* (New York: Oxford University Press, 1992) pp. 78–84.
[2]Figures from P. Ozorio, Heart attacks: developing in developing countries. *World Health* (January–February 1992), pp. 26–27.

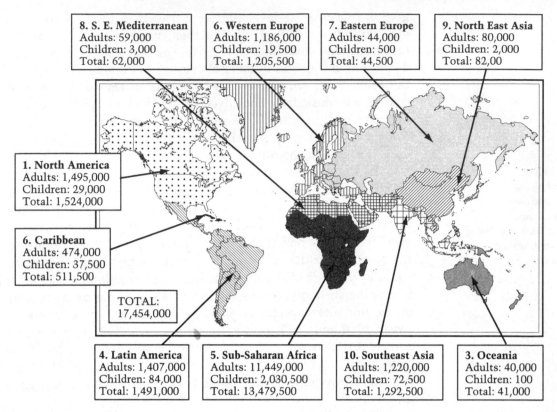

8. S. E. Mediterranean
Adults: 59,000
Children: 3,000
Total: 62,000

6. Western Europe
Adults: 1,186,000
Children: 19,500
Total: 1,205,500

7. Eastern Europe
Adults: 44,000
Children: 500
Total: 44,500

9. North East Asia
Adults: 80,000
Children: 2,000
Total: 82,00

1. North America
Adults: 1,495,000
Children: 29,000
Total: 1,524,000

6. Caribbean
Adults: 474,000
Children: 37,500
Total: 511,500

TOTAL:
17,454,000

4. Latin America
Adults: 1,407,000
Children: 84,000
Total: 1,491,000

5. Sub-Saharan Africa
Adults: 11,449,000
Children: 2,030,500
Total: 13,479,500

10. Southeast Asia
Adults: 1,220,000
Children: 72,500
Total: 1,292,500

3. Oceania
Adults: 40,000
Children: 100
Total: 41,000

Figure 2. Total estimated number of HIV infections by 1995 in different areas of the world. These estimates show how the deadly virus is spreading rapidly around the globe. Especially alarming for the developing countries is the total of HIV infections for Sub-Saharan Africa. Even more catastrophic may be the total for Southeast Asia, which represents an increase of about 66 percent from the 1992 total. (Reprinted by permission of the publishers from *AIDS in the World* by J. M. Mann, D. J. M. Tarantola, and T. W. Netter, eds., Cambridge, MA: Harvard University Press. Copyright © 1992 by the President and Fellows of Harvard College.)

As you read, draw a cause-effect diagram that includes information from this paragraph and the previous paragraph.

Western industrial countries. Thus, they support a curative health-care system even though it may not be the most realistic answer to the health problems in their own countries.

190   **There is a possible commercial reason for the emphasis**   15
on treatment and curative medicine in Third World coun-
tries. It is encouraged by the industries that produce the drugs and equipment for modern medicine. Curative medicine in the Third World gives companies, often from Western countries, a larger market for their products and opportunities for bigger profits. Con-
195   sequently, they often offer financial incentives to support the de-velopment of curative health-care systems in Third World coun-tries.

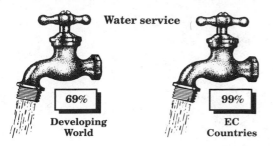

Figure 3. Access to water and sanitation services, 1990. The lack of safe water and adequate sanitation facilities is one of the main reasons why infectious diseases remain a major problem in the developing world. (*Source:* World Health Organization and D. A. Okun, "A Water and Sanitation Strategy for the Developing World" *Environment* 33.8 [1991]: 16–43.)

Use this sentence to refresh your memory of what you have just read.

For these two reasons, the health-care services of developing countries, like those of industrial countries, have developed into systems for the treatment, rather than the prevention, of disease. We have seen that this emphasis creates considerable problems for industrial countries. For developing nations, it has even more disastrous consequences. In the Third World, six children die of simple diarrhea every minute of the day, every day of the year. This diarrhea is caused by contaminated water (see Figure 3) and food. In addition, the so-called vaccine-preventable diseases (measles, whooping cough, diphtheria, tetanus, polio, and tuberculosis) killed 2.1 million Third World children in 1990.

Check back for the meaning of these health problems.

These health problems are not the same problems that face the industrial world today, but they are similar to the problems that faced them in the nineteenth century and first sixty years of the twentieth century (see Figure 4). They were solved then not by modern medical technology and expensive medical treatment. They were ultimately solved when safe water, adequate sanitation facilities, and mass immunization programs became available—in other words, by prevention.

In order to solve the most urgent health problems of developing countries, health experts recommend that priority should be given to primary health care. Primary health care emphasizes the prevention of disease by financing water and sanitation projects as well as mass vaccination programs. In addition, it includes health education programs that provide people with the information they need to improve their own health; for example, information about the link between malaria and mosquitoes or about the importance of nutrition, especially for pregnant women and young children.

16

17

18

200

205

210

215

220

225

This sketch records the 1866 cholera epidemic in London. Today cholera and other water-borne diseases are still a serious problem in many developing countries; in the industrialized world, however, they are no longer a major threat to a population that has complete access to safe water and adequate sanitation. (*Death's Dispensary*, George John Pinwell. Reprinted by permission of the Philadelphia Museum of Art. Purchased: SmithKline Beckman Corporation Fund.)

Primary health care is also designed to provide basic medical treatment for the general population instead of sophisticated and expensive treatment for a few wealthy people. Instead of building a few
230   expensive hospitals, governments would be given incentives to build community health centers. Here cases of illness would receive immediate attention from doctors and nurses who have an adequate supply of basic drugs. These local health centers would be

235 more accessible to people who need treatment than a few hospitals in the larger cities; since patients would receive attention sooner, their treatment would probably be more effective and more economical.

Check back for the meaning of this type of health care.

If developing countries stress **this type of health care,** the 19 health of their general populations will improve rapidly. A number 240 of developing countries have already shown that these primary health-care programs can be very successful. Cuba eliminated polio in 1972, even before the disease was eliminated in the United States. At the end of the 1970s, the World Health Organization began a program to immunize the world's children against vaccine-245 preventable diseases. By 1990, according to UNICEF (the United Nations Children's Fund), the program was preventing 2.5 million deaths per year. As the result of another program in one area of Nigeria, deaths from diarrhea fell by 82 percent after local health workers learned to use oral rehydration therapy (ORT), a simple 250 treatment for diarrhea that does not depend on sophisticated hospital equipment, medical expertise, or expensive drugs.[3] By 1990, according to UNICEF estimates, ORT was saving the lives of 1 million children annually.

4. Prevention—Often Better Than Cure

In conclusion then, health care in both the industrial world 20 255 and in the Third World would benefit if more attention were paid to prevention. In the industrial world, medical costs would fall, or at least increase less quickly than at present, because there would be less need for expensive drugs, equipment, and surgery. More importantly, people would enjoy better health. In the developing 260 world, a greater emphasis on prevention might stop the increase in cancer and cardiovascular disease that traditionally has been associated with rising standards of living. Certainly, however, clean water, adequate sanitation, vaccination programs, and basic medical care would eliminate or control the developing world's tradi-265 tional killer diseases. To provide these necessities for the entire population, of course, will require enormous supplies of vaccines, essential drugs, and basic equipment as well as building materials. Clearly many developing countries will not be able to afford these necessities without massive economic aid from wealthier countries. 270 This assistance, however, will not be a waste of money if it is spent

[3]Figures from Merson, M. H. 1986. Tackling diarrhoea on a world scale. *World Health* (April 1986), pp. 2–4.

for primary health care. Its results will soon become clear: a better standard of health for the great majority of the population.

WORKING WITH THE MAIN READING

1. ONE EARTH—TWO WORLDS OF HEALTH

A Closer Look

1. Developing countries and industrial countries have very similar
   health problems.   T F

2. Modern drugs and high-tech medical equipment are the way to
   solve the health problems of developing countries.   T F

3. What is not true about the health-care systems of industrial countries?
   a. Usually they need to serve only a small section of the population because only these people are ill.
   b. They cannot afford basic vaccination programs.
   c. They attempt to provide the most modern drugs and medical treatments.
   d. Cancer and heart disease are two of their biggest problems.

4. What is not true about the health-care systems of developing countries?
   a. Their most serious problems are diseases like heart disease and cancer.
   b. They do not have adequate supplies of vaccines and essential drugs.
   c. Their services are needed by enormous numbers of people.
   d. The most urgent health problems that face them are no longer real problems for the industrial countries.

Vocabulary in Context

Here are some words from section 1 that you may not have known. You either guessed their meaning from context or from your knowledge of word families, or you omitted the word and were still able to understand the sentence. Now check and learn the meanings of the words. Use your dictionary to help you.

diarrhea (line 11)
sanitation (line 16)
to have X in common (line 18)
to afford (line 22)

2. INCREASING COSTS AND ETHICAL CHOICES: HEALTH CARE IN THE INDUSTRIAL WORLD

Main Idea Check

Here are the main ideas for this section of the passage. Write the correct paragraph number beside its main idea.

_____ Modern medicine is forcing us to consider a number of difficult ethical questions.

_____ Our health-care systems can be criticized because they place too much emphasis on the treatment of disease.

_____ People disagree about giving abortions to women who have unborn babies with serious genetic defects.

_____ The large number of cases of heart disease and cancer show the need to spend more money on prevention.

_____ Modern technology has contributed to the considerable increase in the cost of health care.

_____ "Should we allow an incurably ill person to die?" There is no agreement about the answer to this question.

_____ Health-care systems in industrial countries are experiencing problems because of rapidly rising health-care costs.

_____ Although people are becoming aware of the importance of disease prevention, medicine still does not have a good balance between prevention and cure.

A Closer Look

1. Why does the writer use the example of Britain in paragraph 3?
   a. to show that increasing health-care costs are causing problems for the health-care systems of industrial countries
   b. to show that great advances have been made in health care in the industrial countries
   c. to show that the British health service is not as good as the health-care system in the United States

2. Why does the writer use the examples of the CAT scanner and the artificial kidney machine in paragraph 4?

     a. to show that modern medical equipment can save the lives of patients who are dangerously ill

     b. to show that some medical equipment is more expensive and more sophisticated than other medical equipment

     c. to show that modern technology is one of the causes of rising medical costs

3. What may be a more basic reason for the economic problems of our health-care systems?
   a. They tend to stress the prevention of certain diseases.
   b. They pay no attention to the treatment of certain diseases, like heart disease and cancer.
   c. They do not pay enough attention to the prevention of disease.

4. What is *not* mentioned as being a factor in the elimination of infectious diseases in the industrial countries?
   a. better sanitation
   b. better housing
   c. better drugs
   d. vaccines

5. The public has received no information about the connection between heart disease and the way people live.   T F

6. Find two possible reasons in the text that a person could use to argue that we should allow an incurably ill patient to die.

7. What is the writer's answer to the question "Should doctors attempt to prolong life regardless of the circumstances?"
   a. Yes. Doctors must do everything in their power to keep a patient alive.
   b. No. There may be circumstances where a person should be allowed to die.
   c. The writer does not give a clear answer to this question.

8. Some people believe that we should force people who carry serious genetic diseases not to have children.   T F

9. What is the writer's answer to the question "Is it right to abort babies who have serious genetic defects?"
   a. The writer does not give a clear answer to this question.
   b. The writer believes that abortions are wrong regardless of the circumstances.
   c. The writer believes that abortion should be permitted in these circumstances.

10. In this section, you can identify a number of cause-effect relationships that are connected with the high costs of health care. What causes health-care costs to increase? And what effects do these rising costs have? Read the relevant paragraphs again. Then fill in this cause-effect diagram with appro-

priate information from the list below the diagram. Write only the correct letter in each box.

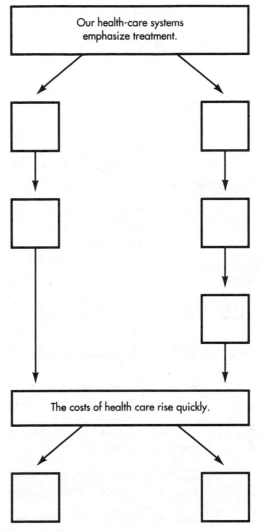

a. More people become ill and need expensive treatment.
b. In countries with private health insurance, employers begin to reduce or eliminate health insurance benefits to workers.
c. Health-care providers need to raise the costs of treatment for all patients.
d. In countries with public health insurance, governments begin to reduce the availability of certain types of treatment.
e. Health-care providers need to recover the costs of purchasing expensive modern equipment.
f. Health-care systems tend to ignore the prevention of diseases that are difficult and expensive to treat and sometimes incurable.
g. Health-care providers buy expensive new technology for new methods of treatment.

What Do You Think?

What type of health insurance do you have in your country? Is it public, private, or mixed? How could the health-care systems of your country and the United States be improved? Use your reading and your own experience for ideas.

Vocabulary in Context

Here are some words from section 2 that you may not have known. You either guessed their meaning from context or from your knowledge of word families, or you omitted the word and were still able to understand the sentence. Now check and learn the meanings of the words. Use your dictionary to help you.

access (line 38)   to maintain (line 56)
purchase (line 41)   to ignore (line 73)
nonemergency (line 45)   to cut out (line 99)
to purchase (line 56)   handicapped (line 137)

3. A QUESTION OF PRIORITIES: HEALTH CARE IN THE THIRD WORLD

Main Idea Check

Here are the main ideas for this section of the passage. Write the correct paragraph number beside its main idea.

_____ Experience shows that primary health care can benefit the populations of developing countries.

_____ The emphasis on treatment creates difficulties for the Third World because many of its special health problems cannot be solved by medical treatment.

_____ AIDS and cardiovascular disease are problems that industrialized and developing countries have in common.

_____ The medical training of Third World doctors is one reason for the emphasis on treatment in Third World health-care systems.

_____ Developing countries should provide primary health care, which stresses prevention and provides basic medical treatment.

_____ Developing and industrialized countries appear to have very different concerns and priorities in health care.

_____ Another reason for the emphasis on treatment in Third World health-care systems is the influence of the drug and medical equipment industries.

_____ There is also an emphasis on the treatment of disease in the health-care systems of the Third World.

_____ The special health problems of developing countries today are similar to problems that were solved by prevention in the industrial countries.

A Closer Look

1. Western industrial countries have influenced attitudes to health-care in the Third World.   T   F

2. Why does the writer use the statistic in lines 176–78? (Before you answer this question, think about the main idea of paragraph 13.)
   a. to show that developing countries spend a great deal of money for health care
   b. to show that treatment is considered more important than prevention by health authorities in the Third World
   c. to show that developing countries are attempting to improve their health care systems

3. In lines 203–09, why does the writer mention the great numbers of children who die of diarrhea and infectious diseases in the Third World? (Before you answer this question, think about the main idea of paragraph 16.)
   a. to show how enormous the health-care problems of Third World countries really are
   b. to show that better hospital facilities are a priority if the most urgent health-care problems of the Third World are to be solved
   c. to show that many of the worst health problems of the Third World could be prevented

4. What is *not* suggested as a solution to the principal health problems of developing countries?
   a. mass immunization
   b. health education
   c. clean water
   d. expensive hospitals
   e. better sanitation
   f. community health centers

5. The writer suggests that the health-care systems of the Third World tend to serve only a wealthy minority of the population.   T   F

6. In developing countries, large modern hospitals with the latest medical technology would be a better solution to the health problems than community health centers.   T   F

7. Why does the writer use the examples of Nigeria, Cuba, and UNICEF in para-

graph 19? (Before you answer this question, think about the main idea of paragraph 19.)

    a. to show that primary health-care programs can be very effective in developing countries

    b. to show that developing countries are facing massive health problems

    c. to show that the prevention of disease is always better than cure, especially for developing countries

8. Primary health-care programs would pay no attention to the treatment of health problems.   T F

9. In this section, you can identify a number of cause-effect relationships that are connected with the fact that health-care systems in the Third World emphasize treatment and curative medicine. What are the causes and effects of this emphasis? Read the relevant paragraphs again. Then fill in this cause-effect diagram with appropriate information from the list that follows the diagram. Write only the correct letter in each box.

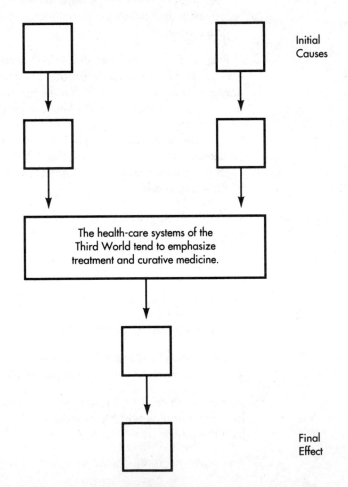

a. Third World doctors believe that health care should emphasize treatment.
b. Disease prevention and primary health care receive inadequate attention and financial support.
c. The drug industry and medical-equipment industry see the opportunity for profits in new health-care systems that emphasize curative medicine.
d. Millions die every year of simple, preventable diseases.
e. Many Third World doctors receive their medical training abroad, in systems that stress curative medicine.
f. Western companies support the development of health-care systems that are designed to treat disease.

What Do You Think?

You are the health minister of a developing country with health-care problems similar to those that are described in section 3. You have only limited funds for health-care programs, and you need to set priorities. Here is a list of areas that, according to different experts, need your attention. Choose six priority areas for funding, and explain your decisions.

HIV testing

building urban hospitals

training specialist doctors

providing safe water

health-education programs

birth-control programs

training health-care workers

child immunization (polio, DTP, measles, and TB)

making basic drugs (e.g., antibiotics) available

purchasing the latest high-tech equipment for diagnosis and treatment

developing expertise in treating heart disease

Building community health centers

Vocabulary in Context

Here are some words from section 3 that you may not have known. You either guessed their meaning from context or from your knowledge of word families, or you omitted the word and were still able to understand the sentence. Now check and learn the meanings of the words. Use your dictionary to help you.

facilities (line 178)
curative (lines 176, 180, 186, 196)
realistic (line 187)
commercial (line 189)

profits (line 194)
sophisticated (lines 228, 250)
accessible to (line 234)
rapid(ly) (line 239)

4. PREVENTION—OFTEN BETTER THAN CURE

A Closer Look

1. What would happen if industrial countries paid more attention to the prevention of disease?
   a. Third World countries would benefit.
   b. Medical costs would rise.
   c. The general health of the population would improve.

2. What do the health-care systems of the industrial world and the Third World have in common?
   a. They are facing identical threats to the health of their populations.
   b. They both would benefit from disease prevention.
   c. They both need to improve the quality of their water.

3. What are the killer diseases (line 265) that could be prevented by primary health care in the Third World?
   a. serious genetic diseases
   b. diseases like heart disease and cancer
   c. diseases like diarrhea, polio, and measles

4. Many developing countries are not capable of financing primary health-care programs themselves.   T   F

5. One advantage of primary health care programs is that they are cheap.   T   F

6. Choose the sentence that best expresses the central idea of the whole article.
   a. While heart disease and cancer are the diseases that most concern doctors in industrial countries, doctors in developing countries still have to solve the problem of diseases like diarrhea, diphtheria, and measles.
   b. Despite different health problems, the health-care systems of both the industrial world and the Third World would benefit if they placed a greater emphasis on the prevention of disease.
   c. The industrial world and the Third World are facing very different health problems, which need very different solutions.

Vocabulary in Context

Here are some words from the passage that you may not have known. You either guessed their meaning from context or from your knowledge of word families, or you omitted the word and were still able to understand the sentence. Now check and learn the meanings of the words. Use your dictionary to help you.

supplies (line 266)   aid (line 269)

Unit Two

The Challenge of Diversity

Text Study.
Identifying Main Ideas

Being able to determine the main idea of a paragraph is one of the most useful skills you can develop.

1. It will make you a better reader. Difficult paragraphs become easier to follow if you can identify the main idea; details are easier to understand if you have a main idea to which you can connect them.

2. It will also help you remember what you read: you can use main ideas to organize your memory of texts you have read. Research shows that this kind of organization improves a student's memory of what he or she reads. If you remember better, your performance on tests and examinations will also improve.

ENGLISH PARAGRAPHS AND MAIN IDEAS

A good English paragraph develops one main idea. This main idea is the central idea that most or all of the sentences of the paragraph support, describe, or explain. The main idea will be connected to all, or most, of the other ideas in the paragraph. It will therefore be *general enough* to include these ideas. However, it will also be *specific enough* to include the ideas of *only* that paragraph.

IDENTIFYING MAIN IDEAS: STRATEGY 1

The first and most useful strategy can be called *hypothesis formation and testing (HFT)*. A hypothesis is a "working idea" that a scientist develops in order to explain some phenomenon. In this lesson, your hy-

65

pothesis will be a working idea about what could be the main idea of the paragraph you are reading.

EXAMPLE

The best way to learn the HFT strategy is to use it and to see it being used in some practice paragraphs. Read the example paragraph one sentence at a time. Then look at what the reader is thinking while he or she reads the sentence (the paragraph following each sentence).

1. In the past thirty years, the number of divorces in the United States has been rising rapidly.

   My first hypothesis (H_1) is that this paragraph will be about how divorce is becoming more common in the United States.

2. According to many people, the breakup of the traditional American family by divorce is the primary cause of a number of extremely serious social problems.

   Wait a moment! The general topic is still divorce, but the focus is different. The writer has introduced a new aspect of divorce, i.e., people see divorce as a cause of serious social problems. My new revised hypothesis (H_2) is: Many people think that the increase in divorce is causing serious problems for U.S. society.

3. It clearly is one cause of poverty; a majority of the children who are living below the official poverty level are living with a divorced parent, usually their mother.

   Here's an example of a problem (poverty) that is linked to divorce. I can continue with the same revised hypothesis (H_2).

4. When marriages end in divorce and families break up, mothers often have to leave their children in inadequate care in order to go out and earn money to feed, clothe, and house themselves and their children.

   Here is the beginning of another bad effect of divorce—children in inadequate care. My revised hypothesis (H_2) is confirmed again.

5. Studies have shown that the chances are much greater that such children will fail or do poorly in school, experiment with alcohol or with illegal drugs, and get into trouble with the law.

   This sentence gives specific examples of the bad things that happen to children of divorced parents. I could describe these things as "serious social problems," so I don't need to change my present hypothesis (H_2).

6. Divorce, therefore, can be associated with increasing crime and the use of illegal drugs as well as with falling levels of education among America's young people.

This sentence describes specific social problems that are
divorce—serious problems. The ideas of this sentence th[e]
firm my revised hypothesis. The main idea of the parag[raph]
clearly my (H₂): The increase in divorce is causing serious pro[blems]
for U.S. society.

EXPLANATION

The HFT strategy has four steps:

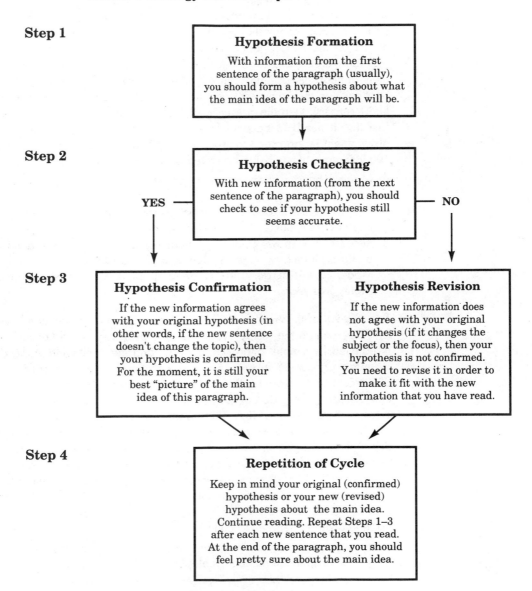

Step 1

Hypothesis Formation

With information from the first
sentence of the paragraph (usually),
you should form a hypothesis about what
the main idea of the paragraph will be.

Step 2

Hypothesis Checking

With new information (from the next
sentence of the paragraph), you should
check to see if your hypothesis still
seems accurate.

YES — NO

Step 3

Hypothesis Confirmation

If the new information agrees
with your original hypothesis (in
other words, if the new sentence
doesn't change the topic), then
your hypothesis is confirmed.
For the moment, it is still your
best "picture" of the main
idea of this paragraph.

Hypothesis Revision

If the new information does
not agree with your original
hypothesis (if it changes the
subject or the focus), then your
hypothesis is not confirmed.
You need to revise it in order to
make it fit with the new
information that you have read.

Step 4

Repetition of Cycle

Keep in mind your original (confirmed)
hypothesis or your new (revised)
hypothesis about the main idea.
Continue reading. Repeat Steps 1–3
after each new sentence that you read.
At the end of the paragraph, you should
feel pretty sure about the main idea.

EXERCISE

Use the HFT strategy when you read these paragraphs. Then choose the sentence that best expresses the main idea of each paragraph. To assist you in two of the paragraphs, we show in the right margin how many hypotheses you need to make.

1. Heart surgery, in spite of the enormous progress it has made in the last H_1 twenty-five years, still has a number of clear weaknesses as a general answer to heart disease. First, the exciting world of heart surgery attracts research and public interest away from the question of preventing heart disease. Second, it attracts money that could be used for more programs to educate the public on the factors that contribute to heart disease—smoking, a lack of regular exercise, and fat in our diet. Third, an emphasis on the surgical treatment of heart disease may cause doctors to perform unnecessary surgery. If a hospital has the equipment and the medical expertise that are needed for heart surgery, then the presence of that equipment and expertise—and the fact that it needs to be paid for—creates pressure to use it. A recent U.S. government report found that one type of heart surgery was performed over 100,000 times annually but benefited only 15 percent of the patients.

   a. Modern heart surgery is not a perfect solution to the problem of heart disease.
   b. Heart disease is one of the most serious problems that are facing the health-care systems of the Western world.
   c. Research has shown clearly that smoking, a lack of exercise, and fat in the diet are all factors in the development of heart disease.
   d. Modern heart surgery has made a great deal of progress in the last twenty-five years.

2. The survival of the African elephant in Kenya, where its numbers have fallen by 70 percent in the last ten years in spite of a ban on all hunting, is being threatened by simple ignorance, poverty, and the continuing world demand for ivory. Consumers in Asia, America, and Europe do not realize that about 80 percent of the ivory on the market today is from elephants that have been killed illegally. They do not realize that they are helping to kill off the African elephant by buying this ivory. Their ignorance, of course, creates conditions in which the demand for ivory can continue. In the past ten years, the continuing demand has caused the price of ivory to rise more than 200 percent to an attractive $80 a pound. The widespread poverty in this part of Africa means that a poacher in northern Kenya or in Somalia can earn much more by killing one elephant than he would normally earn in one year. The same poverty also means that some governments are willing to participate in the illegal ivory trade in order to help their economies.

   a. Poverty, ignorance, and the demand for ivory are the reasons for the dangerous drop in the number of elephants in Kenya.

b. About 80 percent of the ivory that is sold today comes from elephants that have been killed illegally.

c. The high price of ivory causes poor people in Kenya and Somalia to be willing to kill elephants illegally.

d. As a result of illegal hunting by poachers, the number of elephants in Kenya has fallen by 70 percent in the last ten years.

3. In recent years, interest in and financial support for genetic research have H_1 increased enormously. As a result, a great deal of progress has been made in H_2 this important area of knowledge. For example, scientists have successfully identified the genes for a number of serious birth defects and diseases that children can inherit from their parents. Medical science has developed amniocentesis, and more recently, chorionic villus sampling, tests that can be performed on pregnant women. These tests allow doctors to discover a variety of genetic abnormalities in unborn babies, abnormalities that are usually incurable and which often result in death.

a. Recent years have seen a great increase in interest in and financial support for genetic research.

b. Modern tests like amniocentesis and chorionic villus sampling can identify genetic problems in babies before they are born.

c. Because of increased interest and financial support, genetic research has made a great deal of progress in recent years.

d. Medical science has succeeded in identifying the genes for a number of serious birth effects and diseases.

4. Annually about 12 million children in Third World countries die before their first birthday from diseases like diphtheria, measles, whooping cough, and simple diarrhea. The health-care systems of developing countries could save many, if not all, of these children if they were to emphasize the prevention and not the treatment of disease. Some of the diseases that kill so many Third World children are diseases for which preventative vaccines are available. Using the vaccines is simple and effective: after a small number of doses, the patient has a natural protection against the disease. On the other hand, treating the diseases after they occur is often not effective; it is always very expensive and difficult and requires drugs, facilities, and medical expertise that Third World countries often cannot provide. Other killer diseases, such as simple diarrhea, are closely associated with poor and unhygienic living conditions and can easily be prevented if clean water and adequate sanitation facilities are provided.

a. If the health-care systems of developing countries emphasized disease prevention, they could save many of the 12 million children who die every year.

b. In Third World countries, 12 million children die in their first year of life from diphtheria, whooping cough, polio, measles, and diarrhea.

    c. Vaccines are very effective against many of the diseases that kill children in the Third World.

    d. Diseases like diarrhea are no longer a serious problem in the industrial world because of new drugs and other improvements in medical treatment.

IDENTIFYING MAIN IDEAS: STRATEGY 2

EXPLANATION

If the main idea of one paragraph of an article is unclear, read the first sentence of the next paragraph. Writers often use the first sentence of a paragraph as a connecting sentence and repeat important information from the previous paragraph in this connecting sentence. The repeated information may help you understand the previous paragraph better; it can clarify the previous main idea for you, or it can help confirm the previous main idea and remind you of it.

EXERCISE

Use the HFT strategy while you read the following paragraphs for their main idea. (They are all based on paragraphs in Unit 1.) Then read the first sentence of the next paragraph. Use this sentence to help clarify or confirm your choice of main idea answer.

1. Why then do diseases like measles, diphtheria, and even common diarrhea still create such terrible problems for Third World countries? The first reason is clearly economic: Third World countries spend much less money for health care than industrial countries. They simply cannot afford to spend more. Their health-care systems already depend on the economic assistance they receive from wealthier countries.

      However, there is a second and perhaps more complex reason for the enormously high death rate from these childhood diseases.

    a. Diseases like diphtheria, measles, and diarrhea still cause enormously serious problems for Third World countries.

    b. One reason why diphtheria, measles, and diarrhea are a major problem is that developing countries have little money to spend for health care.

    c. Third World countries cannot solve their health-care problems without economic assistance from wealthier countries.

2. Although industrial countries have made great advances in health care, today their health-care systems are experiencing some serious problems. By far the most urgent of these problems is financial: medical costs are rising faster than prices in most other areas of the economy. In the United States, for example, nearly $2 billion is spent every day for health care, and this amount is increasing at an annual rate of 12 percent. These increasing costs are causing considerable problems. In Britain, a country with public health insurance, economics has forced the government to reduce the number of hospital beds, to cut back purchases of new equipment, and to employ fewer doctors and nurses. Today certain expensive treatments are not available to every patient who might need them. Other patients must wait for up to two years for some types of nonemergency surgery. In the United States, a country with a system of private health insurance, employers are finding it difficult to provide the same level of health insurance for their workers as they used to. Many are reducing or even eliminating health benefits for their employees. In 1992, for example, it was estimated that 37 million Americans were without health insurance.

   The problem of increasing costs is partly due to the expensive new technology that has been introduced into health care.

   a. Increasing costs is a major problem for the health-care systems of industrial countries.
   b. In 1992 in the United States, 37 million people were without health insurance because their employers could not afford to provide health-care benefits.
   c. In spite of great progress, the health-care systems of industrial countries are experiencing serious problems.

3. Developing countries are not yet facing some of the problems that modern medicine has created for the industrial countries, but they have inherited the Western emphasis on treatment. Although less money is spent for health care in the Third World, it is clear that their systems also give priority to curative medicine. Recent statistics show that about 80 percent of funds are spent to train doctors and to build hospital facilities.

   There are perhaps two reasons for this emphasis on treatment and curative medicine.

   a. The health-care systems of developing countries do not have to solve the same problems as the health-care systems in industrial countries.
   b. The health-care systems of developing countries also emphasize the treatment of disease.
   c. Developing countries spend most of their health-care funds to train doctors and build hospitals.

4. There are perhaps two reasons for this emphasis on treatment and curative medicine. First, many Third World doctors have received their medical training in Western industrial countries, or in systems that follow Western tradi-

tions. As a result, they tend to have the attitudes that are typical of Western medicine. Naturally, the type of system they want for their own countries is the type of system that seems to be so successful in Western industrial countries. Thus, they support a curative health-care system even though it may not be the most realistic answer to the health problems in their own countries.

There is a second possible reason for the emphasis on treatment and curative medicine in Third World countries.

a. Most Third World doctors receive their medical training in industrial countries.

b. One reason for the emphasis on treatment in Third World health care is that doctors there receive Western-style training.

c. There are two reasons for the emphasis on treatment in the health-care systems of the Third World.

Background Reading and Vocabulary Development

READING PASSAGE 2.1

Read this passage as many times as you need to. However, during your first reading, you should:

1. Use the strategies you have learned for dealing with unknown vocabulary.

2. Stop reading at the end of each sentence that contains boldface words, and complete the Comprehension Building Task in the left margin.

3. Use the strategies you have learned for identifying main ideas. After each paragraph, stop and choose its main idea from the sentences in the Main Idea Check.

Living in a New Culture

You feel generally depressed and unable to concentrate. Your pattern of daily activity may change: you find yourself awake and active in the middle of the night; you sleep late into the day, when most others are working. You stay in your room and have little contact with people except with those who speak your language. In your mind, you criticize the people around you—they are rude, loud, unfriendly, uninformed, concerned with insignificant things, even stupid; you complain about them to any friends you have. You become frustrated when you can't go into a restaurant and order

10   the type of food you really like; you get angry when the TV news contains mostly U.S. news and very little about events that are important to you. You are constantly making comparisons between life here and the perfect life back home. **Above all, you are homesick almost all the time.**

Read the first sentence of paragraph 2 before you choose the main idea of paragraph 1.

15   If you ever find yourself behaving in ways similar to these, you are probably suffering from culture shock. Culture shock is a psychological condition that sometimes has physical effects. It affects people who have moved away from an environment where they know how to live into a new environment where much is un-
20   familiar to them—the food, the weather, the language, and especially **the unwritten rules for social behavior that few people are consciously aware of.**

2

This idea may be difficult to understand. Look for an explanation of it as you continue reading.

Culture shock is caused, therefore, by a lack of familiarity with the system of rules that the new society uses for everyday
25   living. Language is an obvious example of one type of these rules. If your level of linguistic knowledge is low, even the simplest task can suddenly become immensely difficult for you and cause you to feel inadequate. However, knowledge of the language does not make you immune to the effects of culture shock, as many Britons
30   in the United States and many Americans in Britain will confirm. Most people are unaware that each culture has its own rules for social behavior; they take it for granted that polite, civilized people behave the same way in all cultures. **This mistaken belief** will cause you to behave and to judge the behavior of others according
35   to the rules you automatically learned as a member of your own culture. If the rules are different, (and there are sure to be significant differences) then people will misinterpret your behavior, and you will misinterpret theirs.

3

Check back for the meaning of this mistaken belief.

How can you deal with culture shock? First, you need to real-
40   ize that every newcomer suffers some culture shock. You're not the only case. Second, remember that culture shock is curable. The process of recovery will start as you begin to make the adjustment to the new culture. Of course, learning the language will help remove **the obstacles to communication** and will ease the job of
45   making friends with people. Recognizing and learning the new cultural rules of behavior, however, may be just as important. You'll still have emotional reactions to unfamiliar situations, but you'll find yourself making jokes about them rather than condemning the entire society as "stupid." The jokes are a good sign: they show that
50   you are recovering.

4

Use the context to find a meaning for obstacles.
a. things that make a task easy
b. things that make a task enjoyable
c. things that make a task difficult

Main Idea Check

Here are the main ideas for this passage. Write the correct paragraph number beside its main idea.

_____ the causes of culture shock

_____ some symptoms of culture shock

_____ the cure for culture shock

_____ a definition of culture shock

After you finish reading the passage for the first time, answer the questions in A Closer Look. You may find that you need to read parts of the passage again. This is normal. Remember that this is a reading exercise, not a memory test.

A Closer Look

1. The passage suggests that culture shock makes life back in your country appear much better than life in the new country.   T F

2. According to the passage, a good knowledge of the language of the new country will prevent you from suffering culture shock.   T F

3. According to the passage, the social rules for polite, civilized be-havior are international.   T F

4. If you have a perfect knowledge of their language, you will never be misunderstood by people from that culture.   T F

5. What can you conclude when you find yourself making jokes about features of the new culture that you find strange instead of complaining about them?
   a. You are in the process of recovering from culture shock.
   b. You have completely recovered from culture shock.
   c. You never suffered from culture shock.

What Do You Think?

Can you think of any examples of differences between U.S. culture and your culture in the rules for polite behavior? In the rules for polite speaking?

Vocabulary in Context

Here are some words from the passage that you may not have known. You either guessed their meaning from context or from your knowledge of word families, or you omitted the word and were still able to understand the sentence. Now check and learn the meanings of the words. Use your dictionary to help you.

lack (line 23)   obstacle (line 44)
linguistic (line 26)   to ease (line 44)
immensely (line 27)

READING PASSAGE 2.2

Read this passage as many times as you need to. However, during your first reading, you should:

1. Use the strategies you have learned for dealing with unknown vocabulary.

2. Stop reading at the end of each sentence that contains boldface words, and complete the Comprehension Building Task in the left margin.

3. Use the strategies you have learned for identifying main ideas. After each paragraph, stop and choose its main idea from the sentences in the Main Idea Check.

The Age of Immigration

European immigration to the United States has been continuous since 1606, but the most significant period of European immigration occurred between 1820 and 1930. During this time, a total of 32 million immigrants arrived in the country in successive waves. As shown in Figure 1, for the first seventy years, almost all came from the countries of northwest Europe, especially from Britain, Ireland, Scandinavia and Germany. **Then as the flow of immigrants from these countries declined somewhat, large numbers of people began to make the journey across the Atlantic from Italy, Hungary, Poland, Russia, Greece, and other countries of southern and eastern Europe.**

There was a variety of factors behind these waves of Euro-

Read the first sentence of paragraph 2, and look for a repeated idea. Then choose the main idea of paragraph 1.

5

10

1

2

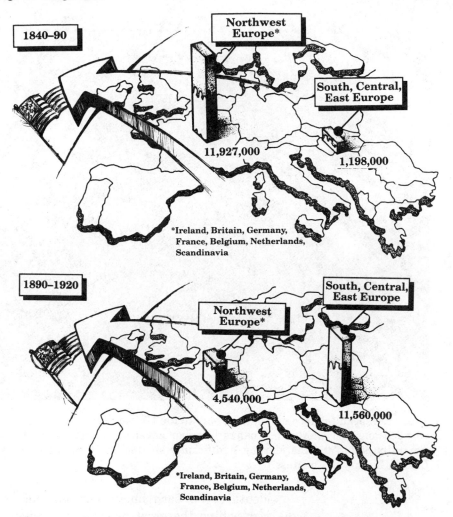

Figure 1. Changes in European immigration to the United States, 1840–1920. (*Source:* Immigration and Naturalization Service, *Statistical Yearbook,* annual.)

pean immigration. Some people were attempting to escape from political oppression in their native lands. Some, especially in Britain and Germany, had acquired technical skills that industrialization allowed them to sell on the open market. The period of great Irish immigration is associated with a disease that destroyed the potato crop and caused starvation throughout Ireland. **The Jews of eastern Europe saw America as a way to escape widespread anti-Jewish prejudice and violence in which thousands of them were murdered.**

Although a specific combination of circumstances could be   3

Read the first sentence of paragraph 3, and look for a repeated idea. Then choose the main idea of paragraph 2.

These European immigrants on their way to the United States in 1910 found conditions on board ship crowded and uncomfortable. Thanks to major advances in shipbuilding, however, life on board was generally better and the journey significantly shorter for them than for earlier immigrants. (Edwin Levick, Library of Congress.)

identified for each immigrant, one factor—economic hardship—was behind the great majority of decisions to leave home for an
25 uncertain future in America. Nineteenth-century Europe was a continent in economic transition: the old agricultural system was disintegrating, and unskilled laborers were being forced to look elsewhere for work. The population was increasing and crowding into the towns and cities that industrialization was creating. This
30 economic transition created living conditions in which poverty, unemployment, and ill-health were the features of normal life for masses of people, conditions that led many to consider making a new life elsewhere.

Pay attention to the
word however *when*
you look for the main
idea of the paragraph.

The immigrants thus came from a variety of language and   4
35 educational backgrounds. **However,** whether educated or illiterate, skilled industrial worker or unskilled farm worker, teacher or lawyer, most immigrants had two characteristics in common:

Living conditions for new immigrants were often very bad, with whole families often sharing a single room in a dirty, crowded building. (Lewis Hine. Courtesy George Eastman House.)

first, they had the energy of youth—most were between fifteen and thirty-five years of age. Second, they were willing to make sacri-
40 fices for their future in a country that they all considered the "land of opportunity."

And they made considerable sacrifices: They left home and 5 language with little more than a suitcase to carry their posses- sions; both men and women worked long hours for low wages. They

45 lived in unhealthy conditions in the overcrowded immigrant neighborhoods of the large cities of the Northeast, Great Lakes, and Midwest states (see photo on page 79). They suffered widespread discrimination as each wave of immigrants from a new country met the prejudice and fears of Americans and earlier immigrants.
50 Not many managed to achieve for themselves the prosperity that was the dream of every immigrant.

However, what these immigrants did achieve becomes visible 6 when you consider later generations. Within three generations, non-English-speaking immigrant families had acquired a new na-
55 tive language. The children and grandchildren of immigrants who spoke Swedish, German, Italian, and more than twenty other languages became native English speakers. This process of language shift is one of the most significant features of immigrant history in the United States. **While it did not guarantee that the new gen-**
60 **erations would advance economically, it was certainly essential for economic advancement and integration into the mainstream of U.S. society.**

The shift to English was accompanied by another change that 7 took place in the immigrant communities. While the first-generation
65 immigrants continued to think of themselves as Irish, English, Italian, or German, their children and grandchildren were clearly American. A story that was told by an English immigrant symbolizes a process that must have taken place in most immigrant households. One day the immigrant's son came home from school,
70 where his class had been learning about the American Revolution. He explained to his father what had happened in words similar to these: "You had the king's army, and we had only a bunch of farmers, but we beat you anyway."[1] Out of the diversity of more than thirty countries and almost as many languages, a generation
75 developed that felt itself to be true natives of the United States.

What is the main idea of this paragraph? Use the repeated idea in the first sentence of the next paragraph to help you.

Main Idea Check

Here are the main ideas for this passage. Write the correct paragraph number beside its main idea.

_____ Immigrants had a number of different reasons for wanting to leave home.

_____ Immigrant families made the important shift to English within three generations.

1. Charles W. Stubbs, *Some impressions of America*, *Outlook 65* (1990), p. 448.

_____ The great majority of the immigrants were young and ready to make sacrifices for a better future.

_____ The second and third generations of immigrant families no longer thought of themselves as from Europe; they were Americans.

_____ In the United States, the lives of many immigrants were very difficult.

_____ Difficult economic conditions at home was the main reason why people decided to emigrate to America.

_____ Thirty-two million immigrants came to the United States from all over Europe between 1820 and 1930.

After you finish reading the passage for the first time, answer the questions in A Closer Look. You may find that you need to read parts of the passage again. This is normal. Remember that this is a reading exercise, not a memory test.

A Closer Look

1. The highest number of German, Irish, British, and Scandinavian immigrants arrived after 1890.　　　　　　　　　　　　　　　　　　　　T　F

2. Most immigrants left their home countries in Europe because of political oppression there.　　　　　　　　　　　　　　　　　　　　T　F

3. What factor or factors brought about difficult economic conditions in Europe at the time these immigrants were leaving?
   a. an increase in the population
   b. the change to an industrial society
   c. the decline of traditional agriculture

4. What does the writer want to illustrate in mentioning the working conditions of immigrants in America, the prejudice they struggled against, and their unhealthy living conditions?
   a. the improvements that occurred in immigrants' lives in the United States
   b. the sacrifices that immigrants made in the United States
   c. the way Americans exploited the new immigrants

5. In the United States, the immigrants soon achieved the wealth and success that was their goal.　　　　　　　　　　　　　　　　　　　　T　F

What Do You Think?

Put yourself in the place of the English father in paragraph 7. How would you feel in similar circumstances? Would you react with happiness, with sadness, with anger, with mixed emotions? Why would you feel this way?

Vocabulary in Context

Here are some words from the passage that you may not have known. You either guessed their meaning from context or from your knowledge of word families, or you omitted the word and were still able to understand the sentence. Now check and learn the meanings of the words. Use your dictionary to help you.

to acquire (lines 15, 54)   to guarantee (line 59)
hardship (line 23)   mainstream (line 61)
characteristic (line 37)   to accompany (line 63)
shift (lines 58, 63)

VOCABULARY PRACTICE

Same or Different?

Writers sometimes express the same ideas with very different grammar and vocabulary. This exercise will help you identify such occurrences.

Read the first sentence in each example carefully. Then read each of the two following sentences to decide whether they are the same or different in meaning to the first sentence. Choose *S* when the sentence expresses the same idea as the first sentence. Choose *D* when it expresses a different idea.

1. The flow of immigrants into the United States from Europe declined significantly after 1925.

   a. After 1925, there was a considerable reduction in the number of European immigrants to the United States.   S   D

   b. After 1925, the level of European immigration to the United States declined considerably.   S   D

2. For some people, getting used to life in a different culture is immensely difficult.

   a. There are many obstacles that need to be overcome before anyone can feel completely at home in a new culture.   S   D

   b. The cultural adjustment necessary when you move to a new culture can be extremely difficult for some people.   S   D

3. Some immigrants believe that poor English is the main obstacle to prosperity.

   a. Prosperity prevents some immigrants from moving beyond their low level of English.   S   D

b. It is felt by some immigrants that their lack of English is the major factor that prevents them from becoming wealthy and successful.　　S　D

4. The process of integration into U.S. society took two or three generations for most immigrant families.

   a. It was two or three generations before immigrant families were completely accepted into American society.　　S　D

   b. European immigrant families disintegrated after two or three generations in the United States.　　S　D

5. After immigrants have acquired sufficient English, they are able to find better-paid jobs.

   a. Higher-paid employment is available to immigrants who have reached an adequate level of English.　　S　D

   b. Learning sufficient English will allow immigrants to take jobs with higher wages.　　S　D

6. How do you interpret these results?

   a. What do you think these results mean?　　S　D

   b. What results are you interpreting?　　S　D

7. A few European immigrants were unable to adjust to life in America and returned home.

   a. A small number of immigrants went back to Europe because they failed to make the transition to life in America.　　S　D

   b. A lack of prosperity caused a small number of European immigrants to return home from America.　　S　D

8. Complaining about the government was dangerous in many countries of Europe.

   a. In many European countries, people got into serious trouble if they expressed dissatisfaction with the government.　　S　D

   b. People's complaints about the government were misinterpreted in many countries of Europe.　　S　D

9. What are the possible obstacles to the success of our plan?

   a. What sacrifices might we need to make so that our plan is successful?　　S　D

b. What could cause our plan to fail?   S D

10. The transition to an industrial society caused great economic hardship in many parts of Europe.

   a. In many parts of Europe, the decline of industry brought about severe economic problems for people.   S D

   b. In many parts of Europe, there was great economic suffering during the change to an industrial society.   S D

Making Connections

Each example in the exercise has a lead sentence and two sentences (*a* and *b*) that might or might not logically follow the lead sentence. Read the lead sentence, and ask yourself what kind of idea you could expect in the next sentence. Then read sentence *a*. Decide whether it can follow the lead sentence and make good sense. Choose *Y* for "Yes" or *N* for "No." Do the same for sentence *b*. *Remember:*

1. Look for the ideas that make a logical connection between each pair of sentences.

2. This is also a vocabulary learning exercise. If you have problems with any new words, check their meanings as you work.

1. The independent experts who looked into the causes of the plane crash found their task very frustrating.

   a. In spite of the obstacles that the government placed in the way of their inquiry, they were able to conclude that the accident had been caused by an explosion, not by poor visibility.   Y N

   b. The aircraft had disintegrated at twenty thousand feet, and there was little physical evidence of what had happened.   Y N

2. European immigrants had to make sacrifices when they came to America.

   a. They worked long hours for low wages in miserable and un-healthy conditions.   Y N

   b. Many were escaping from political oppression in their native countries.   Y N

3. The transition from an agricultural to an industrial society had immense consequences in nineteenth-century Europe.

a. One of these was massive unemployment and declining prosperity in rural areas as farm workers lost their jobs.   Y   N

b. One result was a major shift of population, as large numbers of farm workers flowed out of the rural areas into the new industrial towns.   Y   N

4. In the nineteenth century, political oppression was widespread in many European countries.

a. It was a common reaction by rulers to the increasing demands for political changes from people who were suffering great economic hardship under their rule.   Y   N

b. People who merely complained about the government were often imprisoned or forced to leave the country.   Y   N

5. There may be significant differences between cultures in the rules that govern people's behavior and which others use to interpret this behavior.

a. These obstacles are very significant.   Y   N

b. For example, what is accepted as normal in one country might be considered very impolite in another.   Y   N

Background Reading and Vocabulary Development

READING PASSAGE 2.3

Read this passage as many times as you need to. However, during your first reading, you should:

1. Use the strategies you have learned for dealing with unknown vocabulary.

2. Stop reading at the end of each sentence that contains boldface words, and complete the Comprehension Building Task in the left margin.

3. Use the strategies you have learned for identifying main ideas. After each paragraph, stop and choose its main idea from the sentences in the Main Idea Check.

Who Are Today's Immigrants?

Today a new first generation of immigrants is pursuing its dream of a new life in the United States. This generation's background and experience are in some ways different from those of the typical European immigrant of the nineteenth and early twentieth centuries (see Figure 1). Contemporary immigrants come mostly from Asia and Latin America. In addition, some writers have claimed that a much greater proportion of the new immigrants are businesspeople, managers, and technicians, but this claim has been challenged and remains unproven. However, it is clear that many of the better-trained and more prosperous of these immigrants are

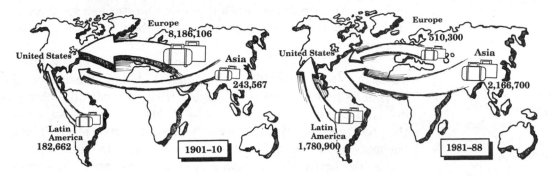

Figure 1. The changing face of U.S. immigration, 1900–88. (*Source:* Immigration and Naturalization Service, *Statistical Yearbook,* annual.)

Use the repeated information in the first sentence of paragraph 2 to help you choose the main idea of paragraph 1.

Pay attention to however when you decide the main idea of this paragraph.

moving not into their own ethnic neighborhoods but into middle-class suburbs. Last, the United States that they are experiencing is no longer a country that is expanding its industrial base. **It is no longer creating the numbers of new factory jobs that were available for the earlier immigrants.**

The differences between these modern immigrants and the earlier European immigrants cannot be ignored in any thorough analysis of the topic. The differences, **however,** should not be interpreted to mean that the behavior and experience of the modern immigrants is very different from those of their European predecessors. In fact, today's immigrants in many ways are following the patterns established by earlier immigrants.

Although some new immigrants live in white, middle-class suburbs, Asian and Latin ethnic neighborhoods are alive and well in cities across the United States. For many immigrants, these neighborhoods function in the same way that immigrant neighborhoods traditionally functioned for Europeans—as the place where they can find employment or start a business serving the ethnic community.

For those immigrants who don't live in distinct ethnic neighborhoods, the immigrant community remains an important part of their working and social lives. Each community, although its members may live some distance from one another, has organized itself to provide a network of connections and contacts similar to those that exist in ethnic neighborhoods. An ethnic community may not be identified with a specific neighborhood, but it functions as it has always functioned. It is a source of cheap labor for immigrant businesses and of financing for immigrants needing funds to establish such businesses. Also it is through the ethnic community that im-

Think about the meaning of sacrifice. *As you continue to read, look for things that you could consider sacrifices.*

40 migrants find employers willing to hire non-English speakers. It is with members of the community that they socialize and go to church.

Finally, the new immigrants are like those of one hundred years ago in the **sacrifices** they make. In their businesses, they 45 work long hours in order to compete with economically more powerful businesses. Some accept jobs of lower status than the jobs they had at home. Many, especially those who open stores in neighborhoods populated mainly by other ethnic and racial groups, have to face the hostility of Americans who perhaps resent their relative 50 economic success or even their mere presence in the neighborhood. For the new immigrants, as for their European predecessors, adjusting to life in the United States is not a bed of roses.

Main Idea Check

Here are the main ideas for this passage. Write the correct paragraph number beside its main idea.

____ The ethnic community is as important for the new immigrants as it was for earlier European immigrants.

____ New ethnic neighborhoods are functioning like the old European ethnic neighborhoods once did.

____ The immigrants coming to the United States today are somewhat different from the European immigrants of years ago.

____ Modern immigrants make sacrifices to live in the United States.

____ The lives of today's immigrants to the United States are similar in many ways to the lives of the European immigrants who came here in the nineteenth and early twentieth centuries.

After you finish reading the passage for the first time, answer the questions in A Closer Look. You may find that you need to read parts of the passage again. This is normal. Remember that this is a reading exercise, not a memory test.

A Closer Look

1. It is an established fact that there are more well-educated professionals among today's immigrants than there were among the earlier European immigrants.   T   F

2. In this passage, the writer is more interested in the similarities between today's immigrants and earlier European immigrants than in their differences.   T F

3. For what reason or reasons do modern immigrants meet other immigrants of the same national origin?
   a. to look for business loans
   b. to find employees for their businesses
   c. to spend free time
   d. to find work

4. Some of today's immigrants live in nonethnic neighborhoods.   T F

5. What experience or experiences do today's immigrants to the United States have in common with the immigrants of the nineteenth and early twentieth centuries?
   a. difficulty adjusting to life in the United States
   b. the support of immigrant communities
   c. their countries of origin
   d. the need to make sacrifices

What Do You Think?

According to the writer, what can make life difficult for modern immigrants? Can you think of any other factors that could cause problems?

Vocabulary in Context

Here are some words from the passage that you may not have known. You either guessed their meaning from context or from your knowledge of word families, or you omitted the word and were still able to understand the sentence. Now check and learn the meanings of the words. Use your dictionary to help you.

contemporary (line 5)   labor (line 37)
to expand (line 13)   status (line 46)
distinct/to distinguish   predecessor (line 51)
   (line 30)

READING PASSAGE 2.4

Read this passage as many times as you need to. However, during your first reading, you should:

1. Use the strategies you have learned for dealing with unknown vocabulary.

2. Stop reading at the end of each sentence that contains boldface words, and complete the Comprehension Building Task in the left margin.

3. Use the strategies you have learned for identifying main ideas. After each paragraph, stop and choose its main idea from the sentences in the Main Idea Check.

Cultural Diversity in Canada

Since the early 1970s, successive Canadian governments have supported the concept of cultural diversity for the nation. In the Multiculturalism Act of 1988, the government committed itself to maintaining the freedom of all members of Canadian society to preserve and share their cultural inheritance. It has also established a government Ministry for Multiculturalism with an annual budget of approximately $42 million. In immigration, the government has shifted from a policy that favored Europeans to a much more open policy. **In 1957, for example, 95 percent of immigrants were from Europe; thirty years later, 76 percent of immigrants were from Asia and elsewhere in the so-called Third World.**

What more general idea do the examples in this paragraph support?

Multiculturalism, however, is a controversial issue in contemporary Canada. The 1988 *Maclean's*/Decima public opinion poll found that approximately 60 percent of those responding were in favor of encouraging immigrants to adopt Canadian culture—in other words, to integrate. Only 38 percent disagreed and thought that immigrants should be encouraged to retain their own cultural ways. While support for assimilation was strongest (73 percent) among Canadians with low educational levels, it also existed among a 52 percent majority of university graduates.[1]

What results? Check back for the meaning of this phrase.

Some few people have suggested that **these results** are empirical evidence for widespread racism in Canadian society. Such an interpretation, however, appears unjustified. The same *Maclean's* poll also showed that a large majority (approximately 80 percent) of Canadians disapprove of selecting immigrants by their

1. The approximations are based on figures from the 1988 *Maclean's*/Decima Poll, as reported in Ann Walmsley, Uneasy over newcomers, *Maclean's*, vol. 102, no. 1 (January 2, 1989), pp. 28–29.

What is being explained here? Check back.

country of origin. This is hardly the position a racist nation would adopt. **A more likely explanation** is that many Canadians have realized in commonsensical fashion that a person cannot **retain**
30 100 percent of his or her culture while at the same time being a real member of a society that includes other cultural traditions. Some adaptation is essential and inevitable.

Use the repeated information in this sentence to confirm the main idea of the previous paragraph.

There is a second possible explanation for the finding 4
that Canadian opinion is divided on the issue of cultural di-
35 **versity.** Multiculturalism may not mean the same thing to everyone. To some, possibly many, European Canadians, it may mean that people should retain their own culture and should not **adapt** when they move to a new country. To others, many of whom are non-European immigrants, multiculturalism clearly means accept-
40 ing Canadian cultural ways for your public behavior while retaining your own culture in your private life. If multiculturalism were

In which way? Check back for the meaning of this phrase.

explicitly defined **in this way,** polls might reflect a greater acceptance of it. After all, assimilation in public and retention of native culture in private have characterized the lives of most American
45 first-generation immigrants. Later generations, however, have considered themselves fully assimilated Americans.

Main Idea Check

Here are the main ideas for this passage. Write the correct paragraph number beside its main idea.

_____ Canadians are against multiculturalism, not because of racism but because they think it's unrealistic to want to retain your native culture completely and be a Canadian at the same time.

_____ More people might accept multiculturalism if they understood that immigrants only want to retain their culture for their private lives, not their public lives.

_____ According to public opinion polls, a majority of Canadians is opposed to multiculturalism.

_____ Supporting cultural diversity in Canada is an official policy of the Canadian government.

After you finish reading the passage for the first time, answer the questions in A Closer Look. You may find that you need to read parts of the passage again. This is normal. Remember that this is a reading exercise, not a memory test.

A Closer Look

1. Look at the details in paragraph 1. Why did the writer choose to include these details?
   a. to show how expensive cultural diversity is for a society
   b. to show that the Canadian government approves of and encourages cultural diversity
   c. to show that Canada is becoming more culturally diverse

2. According to opinion polls, most Canadians agree with their government's multicultural policies.   T   F

3. Why does the writer believe that in general Canadians are not racists?
   a. Sixty percent of them are against encouraging immigrants to keep their own cultural ways.
   b. They themselves come from immigrant families.
   c. About 80 percent of them don't want country of origin to be a factor in deciding who is allowed to immigrate to Canada.

4. Everyone in Canada is in agreement on the meaning of the term *multiculturalism*.   T   F

5. Why does the writer introduce the topic of U.S. immigrants in the last paragraph?
   a. to show that multiculturalism does not prevent immigrant families from becoming assimilated into their new society
   b. to show that multiculturalism is different in Canada and in the United States
   c. to show that multiculturalism is a danger for society in general

What Do You Think?

Is it possible to belong to two cultures at the same time? Do you have any personal examples of this? For example, do you know anyone from your country who is "Americanized"? If you do, describe the ways in which this person is "American." Does this person behave like an American with you? Are you aware of any ways you have changed culturally since you've been away from home? Are there other ways you do not want to change?

Vocabulary in Context

Here are some words from the passage that you may not have known. You either guessed their meaning from context or from your knowledge of word families, or you omitted the word and were still able to understand the sentence. Now check and learn the meanings of the words. Use your dictionary to help you.

issue (line 13)   to select (line 26)
poll (line 14)   commonsensical (line 29)
approximately (lines 15, 25)   inevitable (line 32)
to adopt (lines 16, 28)   explicitly (line 42)
unjustified/to justify (line 24)

READING PASSAGE 2.5

Read this passage as many times as you need to. However, during your first reading, you should:

1. Use the strategies you have learned for dealing with unknown vocabulary.

2. Stop reading at the end of each sentence that contains boldface words, and complete the Comprehension Building Task in the left margin.

3. Use the strategies you have learned for identifying main ideas. After each paragraph, stop and choose its main idea from the sentences in the Main Idea Check.

The Nature of Prejudice

An introductory paragraph often begins with general ideas and then becomes more specific. This means that the most useful sentences for you may come toward the end of the paragraph.

Most people will admit that the relations between various ethnic and racial groups is a potential source of problems for a culturally diverse society such as the United States. Most rational people will also agree that prejudice plays an important role in the misunderstandings, intolerance, and even hostility that may develop and persist between such groups. If our objective is to minimize these problems, one necessary step is to address the issue of prejudice.   1

Research has clearly established that prejudice exists and that a person expressing a prejudiced view may be unaware that it is in fact biased. An interesting experiment, which is often cited in educational textbooks, was conducted in 1973 to determine the potential effects of prejudice on the judgments of future U.S. schoolteachers.[1] The researcher made videotapes of three children speak-   2

1. F. Williams, J. L. Whitehead, and L. M. Miller, Ethnic stereotyping and judgments of children's speech, *Speech Monographs* 38 (1971), pp. 166–70.

15 ing to an adult. The camera angle was such that the children's faces were not visible; however, it was obvious from the tapes that the children were speaking and that they were racially different (one was white; one was African American; the third was Mexican American). A soundtrack containing exactly the same conversation 20 in English with the same American voice was added to the tapes. Each tape was played to one of three groups of student teachers. **Their task was to judge the correctness of the speech of the child they had seen on the videotape.**

This paragraph has described the method of the experiment. What do you expect in later paragraphs?

The writer does not explain this idea, but you can understand it if you think back. What was the objective reality? What was the difference between this and the student teachers' perceptions?

Although they actually heard the same voice and conversa- 3 25 tion, the student teachers misjudged the language of the African-American and Mexican-American children and found it to be less like good Standard English than that of the white child (see Figure 1). These results may be interpreted as showing the existence and effect of prejudice in the student teachers. They were basing their 30 judgments on a previously formed opinion, namely that Mexican Americans and African Americans don't speak Standard English as well as white Americans. **In addition, this opinion was strong enough to affect their perception of objective reality.**

Your HFT strategy will be very useful in this paragraph. Pay attention to however.

Since prejudice is associated with insufficient knowledge, we 4 35 often assume that we can reduce it simply by replacing ignorance with knowledge. **However,** such an assumption is clearly unjustified. In the experiment described in the preceding paragraphs, prejudice successfully resisted change. In spite of hearing evidence that contradicted their previously held ideas, the student teachers 40 did not revise their prejudices. **Instead, they persisted with them and found the English on one tape to be superior to the same English on the other two tapes.**

Look for a repeated idea in the first sentence of paragraph 5. Use this to confirm the main idea of paragraph 4.

Thus, the real problem here seems not to be prejudice itself 5 but the persistence of prejudice. To address this problem rationally 45 and scientifically, we need answers at least to the following ques-

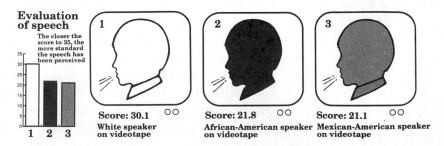

Figure 1. Ethnic prejudice and perceptions of children's speech. (*Source:* F. Williams, J. L. Whitehead, and L. Miller, "Ethnic Stereotyping and Judgments of Children's Speech," *Speech Monographs* 38 [1971]: 166–70.)

50 tions. Under what circumstances does prejudice resist change? Are there different kinds of prejudice, and if so, are some types more persistent than others? What types of experience can change prejudiced views? From these as yet unanswered questions, it is clear that the remedy for social prejudice will be more complex than merely providing objective information to those in need of it.

Main Idea Check

Here are the main ideas for this passage. Write the correct paragraph number beside its main idea.

_____ Reducing prejudice with correct information will not be easy because prejudice is difficult to change.

_____ We need research into why people revise their prejudiced opinions and why they don't.

_____ The writer describes an experiment investigating prejudice in future U.S. school-teachers.

_____ To lessen problems of racial intolerance and hostility, we need to understand prejudice.

_____ The student teachers showed the effects of unconscious prejudice when they misjudged the English of African-American and Mexican-American children.

After you finish reading the passage for the first time, answer the questions in A Closer Look. You may find that you need to read parts of the passage again. This is normal. Remember that this is a reading exercise, not a memory test.

A Closer Look

1. It is possible to be prejudiced and not realize that this prejudice is affecting your judgment.   T F

2. In the experiment described in paragraph 2, what were the student teachers asked to do?
   a. to say how good the child's English was
   b. to guess the racial background of the child
   c. to say what the child was talking about

3. On the videotapes, the three children had different accents.   T F

4. What conclusion(s) can be drawn from the results of the experiment?

    a. The student teachers were prejudiced.

    b. Prejudice can influence the way people see the world.

    c. Mexican Americans and African Americans don't speak Standard English as well as white Americans.

5. The writer believes that we can eliminate prejudice simply by providing the prejudiced person with the information that he or she does not yet have.   T F

What Do You Think?

The writer believes that we need to study the circumstances in which prejudice can or cannot be changed. What do you think could change prejudice? Is correct information enough? If not, what else will help? Do you have any personal experiences to illustrate your ideas?

Vocabulary in Context

Here are some words from the passage that you may not have known. You either guessed their meaning from context or from your knowledge of word families, or you omitted the word and were still able to understand the sentence. Now check and learn the meanings of the words. Use your dictionary to help you.

to admit (line 1)	obvious (line 16)
step (line 7)	actually (line 24)
to address (lines 8, 44)	ignorance (line 35)
biased (line 11)	remedy (line 50)

VOCABULARY PRACTICE

Same or Different?

Writers sometimes express the same ideas with very different grammar and vocabulary. This exercise will help you identify such occurrences.

    Read the first sentence in each example carefully. Then read each of the two following sentences to decide if they are the same or different in meaning to the first sentence. Choose *S* when the sentence expresses the same idea as the first sentence. Choose *D* when it expresses a different idea.

1. The government has committed itself to maintaining taxes at their present level.

   a. The government has stated publicly that it will need to raise taxes.   S D

   b. The government has promised not to raise taxes.   S D

2. Despite problems, governments of some Third World countries persist in developing health-care programs like those in Western countries.

   a. In spite of problems, developing countries continue to use the patterns established in Western countries for their own health-care systems.   S D

   b. Problems are forcing developing countries to pursue health-care policies that are distinct from those of Western nations.   S D

3. According to the latest poll, a large majority of people agree with the government's immigration policy.

   a. The most recent poll shows that most people are in favor of the government's policy on immigration.   S D

   b. The latest poll indicates approval of the government's immigration policy by a great majority of people.   S D

4. It is not likely that the views of prejudiced people can be changed merely by providing information that contradicts these views.

   a. People who are prejudiced do not like to be contradicted.   S D

   b. Just supplying information that shows their views are wrong will probably not be enough to make biased people change these views.   S D

5. Your willingness to accept and use different cultural rules determines how well you adapt to life in a new country.

   a. Successful adjustment to life in a new country depends on your being ready to adopt new cultural rules.   S D

   b. If you are determined to adapt to life in a new country, different cultural rules will not be an obstacle for you.   S D

6. Some people believe that ethnic tension and hostility are inevitable in a culturally diverse society.

   a. Some people believe that a multicultural society is capable of preventing ethnic tension and hostility.   S D

   b. It is thought by some that there is certain to be ethnic tension and hostility in a multicultural society.   S D

7. Abortion is a very controversial topic in contemporary U.S. society.

    a. There is widespread and deep disagreement in the United States today on the issue of abortion.   S D

    b. Modern American society disapproves strongly of abortion.   S D

8. Empirical research has shown clearly that immigration has a positive impact on the U.S. economy.

    a. There is proof provided by empirical research that the U.S. economy benefits from immigration.   S D

    b. Empirical research has challenged the claim that the U.S. economy is helped by immigration.   S D

9. The retention of the private behavior patterns of their native culture is typical of first-generation immigrants.

    a. Typically, first-generation immigrants continue to act in private in the same way as they did in their native culture.   S D

    b. In their private behavior, first-generation immigrants tend to retain the rules of their native culture.   S D

10. Studies show that immigrants and natives tend not to compete for the same jobs.

    a. According to researchers, there is little competition between immigrants and natives for the same jobs.   S D

    b. Research assumes that competition between immigrants and natives for the same jobs tends not to occur.   S D

11. The television program contained an objective analysis of the effects of the government's immigration policy.

    a. The television program's objective was to analyze the effect of the government's policy on immigration.   S D

    b. In the television program, there was an unbiased examination of the impact of the government's immigration policy.   S D

12. Over 50 percent of the students responding to the poll were in favor of retaining the president of the university.

    a. More than half of the students who took part in the poll supported the retention of the president of the university.   S D

    b. More than 50 percent of the students who answered the poll favored removing the president of the university.   S D

Making Connections

Each example in the exercise has a lead sentence and two sentences (*a* and *b*) that might or might not logically follow the lead sentence. Read the lead sentence, and ask yourself what kind of idea you could expect in the next sentence. Then read sentence *a*. Decide whether it can follow the lead sentence and make good sense. Choose *Y* for "Yes" or *N* for "No." Do the same for sentence *b*. *Remember:*

1. Look for the ideas that make a logical connection between each pair of sentences.

2. This is also a vocabulary learning exercise. If you have problems with any new words, check their meanings as you work.

1. Sometimes the presence of immigrants causes resentment in certain groups of the native population.

   a. This happens especially if immigrants are perceived to be using economic assistance that the natives feel would otherwise come to them.   Y N

   b. This is a pattern that was established in the nineteenth century and which still persists today.   Y N

2. A significant number of people disapprove of the government's policy of supporting cultural diversity.

   a. They believe it will have a positive impact on the society of the future.   Y N

   b. They challenge the government's claim that the policy will benefit society by helping immigrants to assimilate faster.   Y N

3. It is often assumed that the experiences of today's Asian immigrants are very different from those of their European predecessors.

   a. The differences, however, are less significant than the similarities.   Y N

   b. An analysis of each group's responses to life in the United States, however, suggests that this assumption is unjustified.   Y N

4. A recent analysis has shown that the economic impact of immigration on U.S. society is mostly positive.

   a. According to the study, immigrants are more likely than natives to become unemployed and to take money out of the economy in welfare payments.   Y N

    b. It does not confirm the common perception that immigrants make society less prosperous.   Y N

5. According to the U.S. government, bilingual education is designed to ease the immigrant family's transition to the new culture.

    a. Opponents claim, however, that it will ultimately strengthen rather than reduce ethnic and cultural divisions in the society.   Y N

    b. In bilingual classes, children learn better and faster; better educated people get better jobs and assimilate faster than those with less education and fewer skills.   Y N

6. In the early 1990s, some people felt that the U.S. government would soon adopt a national health-care system.

    a. Other political analysts considered such a step unlikely because of widespread hostility in the country to the idea of socialized medicine.   Y N

    b. They warned, however, that such a controversial move would be resisted by many people who wished to preserve the existing system of private medicine.   Y N

7. Ethnic neighborhoods and immigrant communities serve a very useful function.

    a. They can prevent the new immigrant from assimilating into the wider society.   Y N

    b. Through the network of contacts they make there, immigrants with little or no English are able to find work.   Y N

8. Scientists conducting empirical research into the nature of prejudice have obtained some interesting results.

    a. They have found, for example, that newly arrived immigrants do not have the same prejudices as the American community they move into.   Y N

    b. We need to reduce prejudice and ethnic hostility in our diverse, multicultural society.   Y N

Synonyms and Paraphrases

Review the meanings of the words to the left of each paragraph below. Find out how to use these words by studying examples from the Vocabulary Study and from the reading passages of this unit. Then read each paragraph for its details. Replace the words in boldface with the correct new words. Sometimes you will need to change the grammar of the sentence so that the new word or expression fits into it correctly.

address
controversial
obvious
challenge

1. In the late nineteenth and early twentieth centuries, one of the most **clearly visible** difficulties that teachers in New York schools had to face was how to teach children who did not speak English. Today's schools are facing a similar **problem** and are **attempting to solve** it by means of bilingual education—teaching children who are not native speakers of English through their own native languages and through English. Bilingual education, however, is a question **about which there is a great deal of heated discussion and disagreement** in today's American society.

assimilate
resent
have the potential
adapt
likely
persist
perceive
inevitable

2. Opponents **believe** that bilingual education **could** damage society. They argue that if students hear and use their native languages in school, it is **unavoidable** that they will have less reason to learn English. The more they keep using their native language, the less **probable** it becomes that these students will **become fully integrated members of** U.S. economic and social life. Moreover, we will cause additional problems if we **continue** to spend taxpayers' money on programs, like bilingual education, that discourage the learning of English. Ultimately, taxpayers will begin **to feel bitter and unfairly treated** because their money is being used to educate people who have little interest in **changing to fit into** American society.

preserve
empirical
actually
labor
contradict
be in favor of
hostility
respond to
cite
perception
compete
admit

3. Those who **support** bilingual education **answer** the criticism in two ways. First, they **agree and accept** that public support for bilingual education will disappear if **the belief** exists that it **maintains,** even increases, linguistic and ethnic divisions and **unfriendly behavior and feelings** in society. Second, however, they point out that the critics of bilingual education are not paying attention to a great deal of evidence **based on observation and experimentation** that bilingual education **in fact** helps children become productive members of society. They **point to** many studies that have established that children learn better and faster in bilingual education. Other studies have **completely disagreed** with the claim that bilingual education reduces children's willingness to learn English. This is not surprising; students in bilingual education feel they are acquiring skills that will allow them **to run against** others in the **job** market, a market in which they will clearly need English.

Using New Vocabulary

Review the meanings of the following verbs. Use the examples in the Vocabulary Study to learn how to use the verbs in sentences.

to assume   to perceive
to approve   to preserve
to adapt   to pursue
to determine   to be committed

Now finish each of these sentences in a way that seems appropriate and interesting to you. You may want to use ideas connected with your readings in this unit or in Unit 1.

1. I wrongly assumed . . .

2. According to the latest poll, only 25 percent of the public approve . . .

3. Few people find it easy to adapt . . .

4. No one has yet been able to determine . . .

5. Politicians are widely perceived . . .

6. Most people today feel it is important to preserve . . .

7. My friend has made up her mind to pursue . . .

8. According to the President, the government is committed . . .

Main Reading

PREREADING THE ARTICLE: GETTING A FIRST IDEA

Before you begin reading, you should try to develop your expectations for the article—an idea of what the article will be about.

Read the main title and section titles of the article carefully. Then read the sentences below. Choose *Y* for sentences expressing ideas that you can reasonably expect in the article. Choose *N* for sentences containing ideas that you can't really expect.

1. The article will be about U.S. society.   Y   N

2. The article will discuss immigration to the United States.   Y   N

3. The article will discuss the diverse cultures of the world.   Y   N

4. The article will suggest that cultural diversity can cause problems.   Y   N

5. The article will argue that some people have the wrong idea about
   immigration to the United States.   Y   N

Now remember what you know about introductions. Where in an introduction should you look first for clear, helpful information about the organization and ideas of the article?

Quickly look through the Introduction (paragraphs 1–5). Identify where the author outlines the article. Then review expectations 1–5, and complete expectations 6–8.

6. The article will show that everyone is happy that the United States is
   becoming so culturally diverse.   Y   N

7. The article will compare U.S. society with other societies.   Y   N

8. The article will discuss solutions to problems associated with diversity.   Y   N

MAIN READING _____

Read this article one section at a time. During your first reading, you should:

1. Use the strategies you have learned for dealing with unknown vocabulary.

2. Stop reading at the end of each sentence that contains boldface words, and complete the Comprehension Building Task in the left margin.

3. Use the strategies you have learned for identifying main ideas. After each paragraph, stop and choose its main idea from the sentences in the Main Idea Check.

After you finish reading each section for the first time, answer the questions in A Closer Look. You may find that you need to read parts of the passage again. This is normal. Remember that this is a reading exercise, not a memory test.

The Challenge of Diversity

1. Introduction

Today in the United States, a remarkable social experiment is   1
under way: the development of a truly multicultural society. In
California, for example, 90 percent of the immigrants settling in
Los Angeles are so-called visible minorities from the Third World.
5   The constant flow of new arrivals adds to the large communities of
Laotians, Cambodians, Mexicans, Koreans, Chinese, Guatemalans,
Iranians, Armenians, and others who already live there. **Eighty-
one languages, only a small proportion of which are European, are spoken in the elementary school system of the city.**

*Use the repeated in-
formation in the first
sentence of the next
paragraph to help you
identify the main idea
of paragraph 1.*

10   The increasing ethnic and racial diversity of the country is   2
associated with government policies. Washington's immigration
policy between 1965 and 1990 is the principal factor in the nation's
growing diversity today. The federal government's support for diversity is visible in legislation that requires school districts to offer

*Check back for the
meaning of it.*

15   bilingual education and which provides funding for it. **It can also
be seen in other laws that ban discrimination on the basis of race
or national origin and that encourage employers to hire minority
workers.**

Ethnic and cultural diversity will be an even more significant   3

20 feature of life in the United States of the twenty-first century. If recent U.S. immigration and population trends persist, the total population of so-called other races (i.e., nonwhite, nonblack) will rise from its present level of approximately 8.5 million to 19.5 million by the year 2025. This increase in numbers, because of the 25 much slower rates of population growth among whites and blacks, will also mean an increase in the percentage of the population represented by other racial groups. In 1990, other races represented 3.5 percent of the total population of the United States; in 2025, according to government projections, they will make up 6.5 percent 30 of the population.

Think about the idea of controversial. *It suggests two different points of view. Try to identify two different points of view while you read this paragraph.*

The U.S. experiment in multiculturalism, however, is 4 **controversial.** Its supporters point to the country's history as a nation of immigrants and argue that cultural diversity has always been a source of strength for American society. However, there are 35 many others who are opposed to the experiment. They feel that it will inevitably encourage the maintenance of social groups not interested in becoming part of the larger national community. The existence of such groups, according to the opponents of multiculturalism and diversity, could over time lead to social disruption 40 and the ultimate disintegration of U.S. society. To see the potential dangers of promoting cultural diversity, they argue, we need only look at what used to be Yugoslavia, where a multicultural society has been torn apart by ethnic hostility.

Check back for the meaning of this controversy. *Doing this should also help confirm the main idea of paragraph 4.*

Because of the emotions produced by **this controversy,** there 5 45 is a clear need for a rational analysis of the issue of ethnic and cultural diversity in the United States. As a first step toward providing such an analysis, this article will identify what has brought about the present level of ethnic and racial diversity. It will also examine the objections to pursuing policies that promote diversity

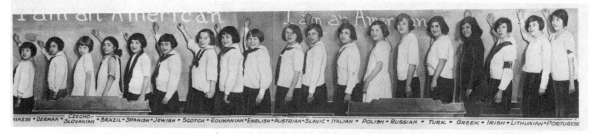

This photograph shows the diversity of ethnic and linguistic backgrounds present in the New York City public schools of 1926. Notice, however, the children are almost all from Europe, in contrast to the immigrant children attending U.S. public schools in the late twentieth century. (The Bettmann Archive.)

"What Happened To The One We Used To Have?"

Immigration policies between 1925 and 1965 were very restrictive and also biased against many ethnic groups and nationalities. Many Americans, including Harry Truman, the president in 1946, wanted fairer and more open immigration policies. (From the *Herblock Book* [Beacon Press, 1952]. Reprinted by permission.)

50   and attempt to identify the problems associated with such policies. Finally, it will offer some recommendations on how these problems might be addressed.

2. Origins of U.S. Cultural Diversity

From paragraph 5, you can expect this section to deal with the causes of diversity. As you read, draw simple diagrams of the cause-effect connections described by the writer.

The most obvious factor behind the growth of cultural diversity in the United States is the country's immigration policy. Immigration policy, in turn, reflects the political and social thinking of the period during which the policy came into existence.   55

6

Between 1921 and 1965, immigration was controlled by the National Quotas Acts of 1921 and 1924 and the Immigration and Nationality Act of 1952. Together these laws favored immigration from Europe by placing obstacles in the way of immigration from   60

7

elsewhere. They also restricted the annual number of immigrants
to 158,000, although, as has always been the case, the actual total
of immigrants who were admitted was always higher because refugees were not affected by the restriction. The result was a U.S.
65   population that was almost entirely European in origin.

*Check back for details
of the policy.*

      For forty years, **this immigration policy** was not effectively   8
challenged. However, in the early 1960s, many people in the
United States became aware of the discrimination that kept many
of their African-American fellow citizens without political or eco-
70   nomic power. As a result, politicians and the public realized that
the civil rights of all racial minorities needed legal protection, a
realization that led naturally to a reexamination of the contemporary immigration laws. In their clear preference for European immigrants, the laws were obvious examples of the legal racial dis-
75   crimination that was then being condemned inside the United
States. In 1965, Congress approved major changes in the Immigration and Nationality Act: The system giving preference to Europeans and discriminating against other nationalities disappeared;
the annual number of legal, nonrefugee immigrants was raised to
80   290,000; finally, the new law gave priority to admitting the relatives of recent immigrants and refugees and did not include them
in the new limit.

Notice the ideas vol-
ume *(How many?)*
and character *(What
type?) Continue read-
ing, and look for these
two different kinds of
impact.*

      The 1965 immigration law has had an immense impact   9
on the volume and character of immigration to the United
85   **States.** First, in the twenty-five years following the act, the proportion of European immigrants declined from 70 percent in the
first sixty-five years of the century to 11 percent in the 1980s. Second, at the same time, the proportion of immigrants from Latin
America and the Caribbean has climbed from 10 percent to 38 per-
90   cent of total U.S. immigration. Numerically, Latin American and
Caribbean immigration stands at 250,000 annually, a 110 percent
increase from the pre-1965 average. Yet even this increase is small
when it is compared with the enormous expansion of immigration
from Asia: Asians, who averaged 5 percent of all immigration be-
95   fore 1965, represented 46 percent of all immigrants to the United
States in the 1980s.

3. U.S. Immigration: Perceptions and Attitudes

      Throughout U.S. history, there has always been some degree   10
of hostility to each new wave of immigrants (see Figure 1). Some
section of public opinion, local or national, has at times been anti-
100   Catholic, anti-Irish, anti-German, anti-Jewish, anti-Chinese, anti-

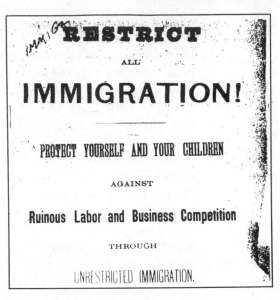

Figure 1. An 1885 leaflet appeals to traditional fears that immigrants will take jobs away from American workers or will ruin businesses that continue to employ more highly paid Americans. (Warshaw Collection of Business Americana, Archives Center, National Museum of History, Smithsonian Institution.)

Italian, anti-Swedish, anti-Arab, anti-Korean, anti-Vietnamese, anti-Cuban, or anti-immigrant in general. Opposition to immigration and the changes it brings about in U.S. society is therefore not new.

This paragraph contains two common charges made against immigrants. Charges can be true or false. Continue reading, and look for how these charges are answered.

105   One recurrent complaint is that immigrants immediately go   11
on welfare and remain dependent on welfare payments for a long
period of time. Thus, they take more out of the U.S. economy than
they ever contribute to it. This charge is often combined with the
allegation that immigrants take jobs from native workers, a belief

110   that is shared by a 53 percent majority of Americans, according to
a 1990 poll. **Since immigrants are willing to work for lower
wages, the charges go, employers dismiss native workers and
replace them with immigrants.**

Draw cause-effect diagrams as you discover how immigrants benefit the economy.

115   Research studies have shown these charges to be generally   12
unjustified. **In fact, on balance, the economy benefits from the
presence of immigrants.** First, immigrants on average pay considerably more in taxes during their lives than they receive in government benefits. Second, immigrants may actually help create
jobs. As additional consumers, they increase demand for the prod-

120   ucts and services of the U.S. economy; increasing demand causes
that economy to expand. Third, in those cases where immigrant

workers compete with native workers for jobs, they tend to do so within communities of recent immigrants or with unskilled workers. The competition may even pressure these unskilled
125 workers to acquire skills that would qualify them for more skilled jobs.

Another charge?
*Check back to refresh
your memory of ear-
lier charges.*

Another charge that is traditionally directed at immigrants   13
is that they are unwilling to assimilate and become part of U.S. society. As evidence for this, critics cite the tendency of immi-
130 grants to settle in their own ethnic neighborhoods—in the China-towns, Little Saigons, Manilatowns, and Koreatowns of today's major U.S. cities. A related charge is that they continue to use their native languages and are unwilling to learn English, a reluctance that is encouraged by the government's policy of bilingual educa-

*In the following para-
graphs, look for an-
swers to the criticism
of immigrants de-
scribed in this para-
graph.*

135 tion. By allowing people to be educated in their native language, the argument goes, we are removing the incentive to learn English. **In addition, we are ultimately encouraging the development of a society that will remain divided along ethnic, linguistic, and racial lines.**

140 It is true that new immigrants tend to settle in their own   14
ethnic communities. **However,** the social history of U.S. immigration since the mid-nineteenth century shows that this tendency did not prevent Italians, Germans, Swedes, European Jews, or any other immigrant group from assimilating into American society.

*Pay attention to the
word* however *in your
search for the main
idea.*

145 Indeed, there is evidence that strongly suggests that ethnic neighborhoods are a positive factor in immigrants' adjustment to life in the United States. These ethnic enclaves offer new immigrants opportunities, both social and economic, that may otherwise not exist for them in the larger U.S. society. They enable adult newcomers
150 to develop a supportive social life in the new country. Just as importantly, the ethnic enclaves offer economic support; through the network of contacts the newcomers make there, they will learn about the employment opportunities that will make them productive, contributing members of their new national society. The Eu-
155 ropean enclaves of the late nineteenth and early twentieth centuries helped their residents establish themselves here. In so doing, they supported the ultimate assimilation of immigrant families into the U.S. mainstream. **There is little reason to doubt that today's Asian and Latin enclaves will do the same for the**

*What charge or
charges against immi-
grants did this para-
graph answer? Check
back in previous para-
graphs.*

160 **new non-European immigrants.**

If the more recent immigrant communities were really less   15
willing than previous immigrants to learn English, it would be a matter of serious concern. Language is a powerful symbol of membership in a community. Immigrant communities that appear re-

165 luctant to learn English could be considered to be rejecting mainstream U.S. society. **However,** there is little or no evidence to
support the charge and much to contradict it. Linguistic and social
research has shown that immigrant communities typically take
three generations to shift from their native language to English.
170 Usually, first-generation adult immigrants acquire some English
but few, if any, master the language. Their children, educated
mostly in U.S. schools, are typically bilingual in English and the
native language of their parents, although their abilities in that
language may be limited. The third generation, the grandchildren
175 of the original immigrants, are typically monolingual English
speakers. **This is the pattern** followed by the non-English-speaking
European immigrants of the nineteenth and early twentieth centuries. In those communities of more recent immigrants where the
language behavior of three generations can be observed, evidence
180 of a similar pattern of language shift already exists. In the most
recent immigrant communities, of course, it may be too early to see
clear evidence of a shift to English. However, social scientists expect such communities to follow a pattern of language shift similar
to the pattern established by earlier immigrants.

185   All the available evidence, then, suggests that today's immi-   16
grant families are learning English and slowly assimilating to
mainstream U.S. society in similar fashion to the non-English-
speaking Europeans of yesterday. Although they have retained
part of their native culture, yesterday's European immigrant fami-
190 lies are now fully integrated into American society; and American
society has been changed and enriched by their being part of it.
Similarly, we can expect today's immigrant families to become part of
tomorrow's society and to add something of their own culture to it.

4. The Challenge

       The preceding discussion has demonstrated that many   17
195 **fears about modern immigration are the result of mispercep-**
tions. However, this does not mean that cultural diversity does not
cause problems. The truth is that immigration, as well as being of
long-term benefit to U.S. society, has the potential of creating its
own problems or exacerbating already existing ones. **It raises**
200 **complex issues that must be considered and brings real**
problems that must be addressed.
       One of these issues concerns the types of immigrant who will   18
be admitted into the United States. **In the late 1980s, a con-**

*Again, pay attention
to the word* however
*in your search for the
main idea.*

*Check back for the
complete meaning of
this. It includes the
ideas of more than one
sentence.*

*Use this sentence to
help you remember
the general idea of
section 3.*

*Quickly look forward
in the text. Identify
and mark where the
writer introduces these
issues. Then continue
reading paragraph 18.*

*As you continue read-
ing, identify and
count these reasons.*

205 **sensus developed in Congress that immigration policy
needed revision—for a number of reasons.** There was clear
statistical evidence that immigration policy from 1965 to 1990 was
in its effect biased against Europeans. There was also some evidence that immigrants during this period tended to have less education and lower levels of occupational skills than previously was
210 the case. In addition, the 1965 Immigration Act made it extremely
difficult to admit highly skilled or wealthy immigrants who would
be able to make an immediate significant contribution to the U.S.
economy. At the same time, the economy began to suffer the effects
of a lack of skilled workers in many fields.

215   A second issue, however, is raised by the suggestion that we   19
should solve the problems of the U.S. economy by importing skilled
workers from overseas. U.S. society already has large numbers of
people who are poorly educated, often illiterate, without any marketable skills, and, as a consequence, living in desperate poverty.
220 The desperation and resentment among this group, the so-called
underclass, will increase as they watch larger numbers of immigrants arrive and achieve what they cannot—success and acceptance in mainstream U.S. society. This desperation and resentment, sooner or later, will surely cause major social unrest in the
225 United States.

     A third issue concerns the tendency of new immigrants to set-   20
tle only in a few major urban areas of the United States. This
means that the cost of providing services to immigrants is not
shared equally among communities across the country. To cover
230 the costs of providing the additional services that are required, local governments of the affected communities respond in two ways:
They raise taxes or they lower the level of the services already
available to the community. Either solution has the potential for
causing resentment in the native community.

*Look back for exam-
ples of how immigra-
tion can cause these
reactions.*

235   **Finally, a more general issue is the obvious potential of**   21
**immigration to arouse hostility and resentment in the native
population.** In the past, such feelings have caused tension and
violence between native and immigrant groups, especially during
times of economic hardship. They have also reflected the racial

*Check back for the
meaning of* such feel-
ings.*

240 prejudice that seems to exist in most societies. In the future, **such
feelings** are likely to recur.

*As you read, identify
solutions, and check
back for the problems
they are designed to
solve.*

5. Responding to the Challenge

     This brief analysis of the problems associated with im-   22
migration suggests that at least three steps are necessary if

Now quickly look forward in the text. Identify and mark where the writer introduces these three steps. Then come back, and continue reading this paragraph.

there is to be a relatively smooth transition to a more diverse,
245 **multicultural society in the United States.** First, those who shape U.S. social policy must acknowledge that immigration, while historically beneficial to U.S. society in general, can cause potentially serious problems. They must attempt to minimize these problems.

250   Two of the problems we have identified have fairly obvious   23
solutions. To address the problem of a large underclass that is potentially resentful of the success of new immigrants, the federal government needs to offer effective programs of education and training to integrate as many members of this underclass as possi-
255 ble into American society. In this way, resentment against new immigrants will be minimized, and the potential for tension and violence between ethnic and racial groups will be significantly reduced.

          To ease the financial burden on those areas where immi-   24
260 grants settle, Congress should see to it that sufficient federal funds are directed to these areas to cover the costs of providing services to the new families. In this way, local native residents will not have grounds for complaining that their local tax dollars are being spent for the benefit of strangers.

265   A second necessary step is to develop a balanced new immi-   25
gration policy. **The policy must strike a balance among a number of potentially contradictory demands:** First, it should not be biased in favor of any racial or ethnic group. On the other hand, it must continue to recognize and satisfy the humanitarian need to
270 reunite new immigrants with their immediate families. It should also continue the country's tradition of offering freedom and opportunity to the poor and the oppressed of other nations. At the same time, the new policy must be flexible enough to respond to the changing needs of the U.S. economy for skilled employees and
275 leaders.

          The 1990 Immigration Act was a first attempt to strike **such** 26
a balance. By increasing the number of legal immigrants by up to 40 percent, it almost triples the number of immigrants who can be admitted because of their work skills. It also reserves 55,000 visas
280 for immigrants from countries that are not sending large numbers to the United States. Perhaps most significantly, the 1990 act recognized that immigration has significant, sometimes unpredictable, consequences for the United States. It has established an Immigration Commission that will study the effects of the 1990 law
285 and make recommendations for any necessary revisions to it in 1994 and 1997.

As you continue to read, identify these demands. How many are there?

What kind of balance needs to be achieved? Check back for what the writer has in mind.

If this is not the objective, what is? Look for it as you continue reading.

290   A third step is that both immigrant and native communities   27
must learn more about each other's cultural ways. **The objective here is not to force either community to change its ways of living and doing business.** Such changes will occur over time and will be relatively painless. Similar changes have occurred in the past, as successive generations of immigrant families were changed by U.S. society and as these immigrants themselves brought about changes in their new society. The objective rather is
295   to replace ignorance with knowledge and to substitute understanding for intolerance. **In this way,** we can create an atmosphere where the processes of assimilation and change can survive the inevitable downturns in the economy and the resulting local ethnic tensions. The result should be a productive and more fully inte-
300   grated society.

Check back for the meaning of this way.

WORKING WITH THE MAIN READING

1. INTRODUCTION

Main Idea Check

Here are the main ideas for the introduction. Write the correct paragraph number beside its main idea.

_____ U.S. government policies are a factor in the growth of cultural diversity in the United States.

_____ The article will examine the following aspects of cultural diversity in the United States: its historical causes, opposition to it, the problems it may create, and possible solutions to those problems.

_____ There is considerable public disagreement about multiculturalism in the United States.

_____ The United States of the future will be even more ethnically and culturally diverse than it is today.

_____ The United States is attempting to become a really multicultural society.

A Closer Look

1. According to the writer, what action or actions of the government promote multiculturalism?

       a. requiring bilingual education in public schools
       b. making discrimination illegal
       c. encouraging the employment of minorities

2. Current figures suggest that the population of the so-called other races in the United States will more than double by 2025.   T F

3. The great majority of Americans approves of the fact that the country is becoming more culturally diverse.   T F

4. What specific topic or topics will this article cover?
       a. why people disagree with a policy of multiculturalism in the United States
       b. what problems can be caused by cultural diversity
       c. how the problems of cultural diversity might be solved
       d. multiculturalism in other countries of the world
       e. the causes of ethnic and cultural diversity in the United States

Vocabulary in Context

Here are some words from section 1 that you may not have known. You either guessed their meaning from context or from your knowledge of word families, or you omitted the word and were still able to understand the sentence. Now check and learn the meanings of the words. Use your dictionary to help you.

to hire (line 17)   to disrupt/disruption (line 39)
to represent (line 26)   to promote (line 49)
projections (line 29)

2. ORIGINS OF U.S. CULTURAL DIVERSITY

Main Idea Check

Choose the sentence that best expresses the main idea of each paragraph.

1. Paragraph 7
       a. Between 1921 and 1965, U.S. policy kept the numbers of immigrants fairly low and favored immigration from Europe.
       b. Between 1921 and 1965, the United States placed obstacles in the way of potential immigrants from non-European countries.
       c. The number of refugees admitted to the United States raised the total number of immigrants in any given year.

2. Paragraph 8
   a. In the early 1960s, people in the United States realized that African-American citizens were being excluded from power by discrimination.
   b. The United States reconsidered its immigration laws in the 1960s.
   c. The realization in the 1960s that minorities inside the United States suffered discrimination also caused the discriminatory immigration laws to be changed.

3. Paragraph 9
   a. The law of 1965 changed U.S. immigration very significantly in the next twenty-five years.
   b. As a result of the 1965 law, Asian immigration to the United States increased approximately 900 percent in the next twenty-five years.
   c. The 1965 law caused the number of European immigrants to fall drastically in the next twenty-five years.

A Closer Look

1. Between 1921 and 1965, U.S. immigration laws were biased in favor of non-Europeans.   T F

2. Complete the cause-effect diagram for paragraph 8 from the list below. Write only the correct letter in each box.

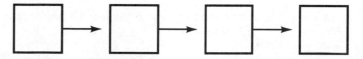

   a. In 1965, Congress changed the Immigration and Nationality Act.
   b. People began to take another look at the laws controlling the immigration policy of the time.
   c. U.S. society became aware of the discrimination that African Americans suffered.
   d. Politicians and the general public began to believe that the rights of all minorities needed to be protected by the law.

3. What effect or effects did the 1965 immigration law have?
   a. The numbers of Asian, Latin American, and Caribbean immigrants increased.
   b. The number of European immigrants fell significantly.
   c. The overall number of immigrants declined.

4. The influence of the 1965 Immigration Act was limited to the number of immigrants admitted to the United States every year.   T F

Vocabulary in Context

Here are some words from section 2 that you may not have known. You either guessed their meaning from context or from your knowledge of word families, or you omitted the word and were still able to understand the sentence. Now check and learn the meanings of the words. Use your dictionary to help you.

to reflect (line 55)	entirely (line 65)
to restrict (line 61)	discrimination (lines 68, 74)
to be the case (line 62)	to discriminate (against X) (line 78)

3. U.S. IMMIGRATION: PERCEPTIONS AND ATTITUDES

Main Idea Check

Here are the main ideas for paragraphs 10–13. Write the correct paragraph number beside its main idea.

_____ It is a common belief that immigrants damage the U.S. economy.

_____ A common criticism of immigrants is that they are unwilling to learn English and really become a part of U.S. society.

_____ According to research studies, the presence of immigrants generally benefits the U.S. economy.

_____ In U.S. history, each new wave of immigrants has been met with some hostility.

For paragraphs 14–16, choose the sentence that best expresses the main idea of the paragraph.

1. Paragraph 14
   a. Immigrants have a tendency to settle in their own ethnic neighborhoods.
   b. The ethnic enclaves of the late nineteenth and early twentieth centuries helped European immigrants establish themselves in the United States.
   c. There is evidence that ethnic neighborhoods play a positive, not a negative, role in helping immigrants become members of U.S. society.

2. Paragraph 15
   a. Not learning the language of a community could be interpreted as a clear sign that you do not wish to become a member of that community.
   b. Most first-generation immigrants learn some English but continue to feel more comfortable in their native language.
   c. It is reasonable to believe that recent immigrant communities will shift to using English in more or less the same way as earlier immigrants did.

3. Paragraph 16
   a. Today's immigrants, like their European predecessors, are assimilating successfully into U.S. society.
   b. European immigrants are now fully integrated into American society and have brought part of their culture into that society.
   c. Today's new immigrants have many similarities to the earlier immigrants who came from Europe in the nineteenth and early twentieth centuries.

A Closer Look

1. The anti-immigrant feeling that exists today among some Americans is a new phenomenon in U.S. history.   T F

2. Some people believe that immigration has negative consequences for the U.S. economy.   T F

3. Immigrants may be willing to work for lower wages than American workers.   T F

4. Empirical research has found the following economic effect or effects of immigration:
   a. Many American skilled workers lose their jobs.
   b. Immigrants pay more in taxes than they receive in government benefits.
   c. Immigrants increase the demand for the products of the U.S. economy.

5. For what reason or reasons do some Americans disapprove of bilingual education?
   a. They think it discourages immigrants from learning English.
   b. They think it does not help immigrants to assimilate into U.S. society.
   c. They think it costs too much money.

6. There is evidence that ethnic neighborhoods help immigrants in the transition to life in the United States.   T F

7. If the English of an adult first-generation immigrant remains poor, this is clear evidence that his or her family will not become integrated into U.S. society.   T F

8. In the process of assimilation into U.S. society, European immigrants lost all of their native culture.   T F

What Do You Think?

Can you suggest any reasons why different generations of immigrants had different degrees of success in learning English? And what could account for different degrees of success among first-generation immigrants?

Vocabulary in Context

Here are some words from section 3 that you may not have known. You either guessed their meaning from context or from your knowledge of word families, or you omitted the word and were still able to understand the sentence. Now check and learn the meanings of the words. Use your dictionary to help you.

recurrent (line 105)   resident (line 156)
charge (lines 108, 112)   to reject (line 165)
allegation (line 109)   monolingual (line 175)
to dismiss (line 112)   in similar fashion (line 187)
bilingual (line 134)   to enrich (line 191)

4. THE CHALLENGE

Main Idea Check

Here are the main ideas for this section of the article. Write the correct paragraph number beside its main idea.

_____ Immigration can cause hostile feelings and may lead to tension and even violence in American communities.

_____ We risk causing bitterness and resentment among poor Americans if we do nothing for them but at the same time allow large numbers of highly skilled immigrants into the country.

_____ The 1965–1990 immigration policy needed revision because it was biased and did not meet the needs of the country.

_____ Although some fears about immigration are unjustified, there are real problems associated with it.

_____ Immigrants tend to settle in a few areas and can cause some economic hardship for those areas.

A Closer Look

1. It can be clearly demonstrated that immigration causes no problems
   for U.S. society.   T   F

2. According to the writer, what weakness or weaknesses did immigration policy have between 1965 and 1990?
   a. It admitted too many Europeans.
   b. It made it difficult to admit people who would help the U.S economy right away.

    c. It may have admitted too many poorly educated and poorly trained people.

3. The poor American underclass is a potential source of anti-immigrant feelings.   T F

4. According to the writer, what development or developments could cause resentment against immigrants in those communities where they settle?
    a. an increase in taxes to cover increased public services
    b. a decline in public services
    c. the successful assimilation of the immigrants into the communities

5. Tension and violence between immigrants and Americans is something new for U.S. society.   T F

What Do You Think?

Look back at this section of the article, and review the situations that could cause anger, bitterness, and resentment toward immigrants among Americans. Can you identify what the situations have in common? Do you have any other ideas about what might cause a reaction against immigration here or in your country?

Vocabulary in Context

Here are some words from section 4 that you may not have known. You either guessed their meaning from context or from your knowledge of word families, or you omitted the word and were still able to understand the sentence. Now check and learn the meanings of the words. Use your dictionary to help you.

preceding/(to precede)   desperate (line 219)
  (line 194)   desperation (line 220)
to demonstrate (line 194)   unrest (line 224)
to exacerbate (line 199)   to settle (line 226)
consensus (line 203)   to arouse (line 236)
to import (line 216)

5. RESPONDING TO THE CHALLENGE

Main Idea Check

Here are the main ideas for this section of the article. Write the correct paragraph number beside its main idea.

_____ A new, fair, and flexible immigration policy is needed.

_____ Education and training programs are needed so that members of the underclass can advance socially and economically.

_____ Working to increase cultural understanding and tolerance in U.S. society will help the assimilation of immigrants.

_____ U.S. politicians need to admit that immigration can cause problems.

_____ Adequate financial support should be given to the areas that receive immigrants.

_____ The Immigration Act of 1990 attempted to establish a better immigration policy for the United States.

A Closer Look

1. Complete the cause-effect diagram for paragraph 23 from the list below. Write only the correct letter in each box.

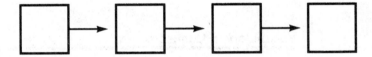

   a. We reduce the possibility of ethnic tension and violence.
   b. We provide effective programs to educate and train the underclass.
   c. There are fewer reasons to feel resentful of immigrants' success.
   d. Members of the underclass become a real part of U.S. society.

2. What step or steps would help today's U.S. society make a smooth transition to a more multicultural society of the future?
   a. The government needs to develop a better immigration policy.
   b. The different ethnic groups in the United States need to get to know each other better.
   c. The government needs to recognize the problems caused by immigration and do something about them.
   d. Immigrants need to give up their cultural habits and adapt to U.S. culture as quickly as possible.

3. The new immigration policy uses occupational background as one basis for admitting immigrants.   T F

4. The writer appears to believe that both native U.S. society and immigrant society will influence and change each other in time.   T F

What Do You Think?

1. According to the writer, the experience of living in the United States changes immigrants. Do you agree? Do you feel you have changed as a result of living here? If so, in what ways have you changed?

     Think about other people you know from your country. Do you know anyone who has changed a lot and some who have changed only a little? If you do, how do you explain the different reactions to living in the United States?

2. The writer's third recommendation for helping U.S. society is that immigrants and Americans must learn more about each other's cultural ways. However, the writer does not suggest any practical ways in which this learning could occur. What could be done to increase intercultural understanding in the United States?

Vocabulary in Context

Here are some words from section 5 that you may not have known. You either guessed their meaning from context or from your knowledge of word families, or you omitted the word and were still able to understand the sentence. Now check and learn the meanings of the words. Use your dictionary to help you.

brief (line 242)   to ease (line 259)
to acknowledge (line   to have grounds for (line 263)
   246)   flexible (line 273)
burden (line 259)

Unit Three

Aspects of Language

Text Study 1.
Reading Textbooks:
Technical Words and Definitions

When you read a textbook, you are likely to meet the definitions of new technical terms and concepts that you will need to identify and understand. In this Text Study, you will be able to practice reading for these purposes.

EXAMPLES

Read the following examples. Look for the technical terms that you might be expected to learn and use if you were taking an academic class in the subject. Look also for the definitions.

1. **Demand** can be defined as the different quantities of a product or service that would be purchased at different prices during a given period of time. [Economics]

2. A *population* refers to the whole group of people, objects, or events that show the common characteristic, or characteristics, in which the researcher is interested. A *sample* is a group of individual members that are chosen by the researcher from that population. [Statistics]

3. Matter is defined as anything that occupies space and has weight. [Physics]

4. The study of the speech sounds used in human languages is called phonetics. [Linguistics]

125

5. Movements of people within one country (internal migration) are determined largely by economic factors. [Geography]

6. Establishing national rates of fertility and mortality, i.e., the number of births and deaths per year in a country, is an essential step in predicting future population growth. [Geography]

7. Some birth defects in unborn children are identifiable through amniocentesis, a procedure by which some fluid is taken from the amniotic sac surrounding the baby and then analyzed. Others may be detected with sonograms, a picture of the developing baby produced by sound waves. [Nursing]

EXPLANATION

METHODS OF DEFINING

As you can see, there are a number of ways to define terms and concepts. Some writers make the terms and their definitions more obvious than other writers do by using clearer definition markers. These markers are:

Verbs	Writers connect the concept to the definition with verbs like *to define, to be, to refer to, to be called* (examples 1, 2, 3, and 4).
Parentheses	Writers include the technical term in parentheses (example 5).
i.e. + Explanation	The explanation of the technical terms follows the term and is introduced by *i.e.*, which means "that is" (example 6).
Appositive	The definition immediately follows the technical term and is separated from the rest of the sentence by commas (example 7).
Special print	The writers use **boldface** or *italics* to draw attention to an important concept or term (examples 1 and 2).

TECHNICAL TERMS

Notice that some of the technical terms are words that are only used in this technical sense—*phonetics* in example 3 and *amniocentesis* and *sonogram* in example 7. These technical terms may be quite easy for you to identify because they are so new and different.

Other technical terms are words that are also used in normal, nontechnical English. You may already know the nontechnical meaning of these words. However, the problem for you is that there is usually an important difference in meaning between the technical use and the nontechnical use of the word. Sometimes the technical meaning is merely much more precise and specific (examples 1, 2, and 6) than the "everyday" meaning. However, sometimes it is very different from the everyday meaning you may be familiar with (example 3).

READING STRATEGIES

1. Expect definitions and technical terms in your academic reading.

2. Use the definition markers to help you identify definitions and technical terms.

3. Look for examples to help you understand the definitions.

4. If there are other technical words in the definition, these refer to concepts that the writer has already introduced. Refresh your knowledge of these concepts if you need to.

EXERCISE

Read the following short paragraphs. Identify the technical names for the concepts being defined. Also identify the definitions. *Note:* There may be more than one concept in the paragraph.

1. We can define frustration as the unpleasant feelings that result when a desired goal is not achieved. The feelings may include disappointment, anger, and confusion.

2. Prejudice is a judgment that people make before they have all the facts and which they refuse to change in spite of evidence that their judgment is false. Discrimination, on the other hand, is behavior directed in favor of or, more usually, against a person or group and often based on prejudice.

3. Many diseases are endemic—in other words, a balance exists between humans and a disease-causing bacteria or virus that is widespread in the community but does not cause a high death rate. An epidemic is a sudden occurrence of a disease affecting large numbers of people in a community. If an epidemic spreads throughout the world, it is called a pandemic.

4. In experiments conducted in the behavioral sciences, researchers may report that their results are "statistically significant." In statistics, significance is a statement of how likely it is that a result obtained in a research project has occurred by chance and not as the result of some other factor. (In well-designed research, this will be the factor the researcher is interested in testing.)

5. Although they may have lived many years in an English-speaking community, some speakers of English as a second language never succeed in learning the grammar of English. They continue to use sentence patterns that are not typical of native speakers. Researchers have begun to examine the circumstances under which this grammatical fossilization may occur.

Text Study 2.
Reading Textbooks: Identifying and Understanding Classification

In addition to defining and exemplifying concepts, textbook writers also divide more general concepts into a number of different types. This is a process called *classification*. If you are able to identify when writers are using classification to organize their ideas, you will be a better reader. This section will give you a chance to study classification and to practice identifying it in English texts.

EXAMPLES

Look at the following examples. Ask yourself these questions:

What is being divided into types?

How many types are there, and what are they?

What words (markers) show me that the writer is using classification to organize the writing?

1. If we consider how English consonants are produced, we will be able to identify six main categories: stops, fricatives, affricates, nasals, liquids, and glides.

2. Nutritionists have determined that there are two main types of fats in food: saturated fats and unsaturated fats. Within unsaturated fats, we can distinguish between monounsaturated fats and polyunsaturated fats.

EXPLANATION

In both examples, the writer is examining a more general concept (English consonants in example 1; nutritional fats in example 2) by dividing it into types. In example 2, the writer further divides one type of fat into two subtypes.

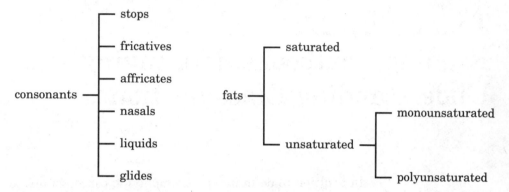

In example 1, we also see the basis (or criterion) for the classification—the ways in which English consonants are produced. This is also part of a complete classification. If you don't see the criterion immediately (for example, as in example 2), you should try to find it elsewhere in the text.

Writers very often use the following verbs and nouns to introduce classification. These words are markers of classification; they will be a clear sign that you can expect the following text to be organized as a classification.

Verbs

to classify	to (sub)divide
to categorize	to distinguish

Nouns

class	kind
category	way
type	method
sort	group

READING STRATEGIES

1. Look for markers of classification.

2. Look for (1) the general concept, (2) the types or classes, and (3) the criterion for classification.

3. Also be ready to use your strategies for processing technical words and definitions.

EXERCISE _____

In the following paragraphs, look for the writer's classification. Draw diagrams of each classification like the ones on page 130. Also identify a definition for each technical concept.

1. In an examination of the effect of motivation on second language learning, Gardner and Lambert (1972) distinguish between instrumental and integrative motivation. Instrumental motivation occurs when learners want to acquire a second language for functional reasons, for example, to pass an examination, to improve their chances of getting a good job, or to study other subjects through that second language. Integrative motivation, on the other hand, occurs in learners who are interested in the culture of the group speaking the second language and who wish to have more social contact with that group or even to become a member of it.

2. In phonetics, we may describe how speech sounds are produced by the speaker. If we study speech from this perspective, we are studying articulatory phonetics. On the other hand, speech also creates waves of pressure that move through the air. If we focus on this aspect of speech, our area of interest is called acoustic phonetics.

3. Perception, the complex process by which we make sense of incoming sensory information, seems at least to have two necessary components, selective attention and organization. Selective attention refers to our ability to focus our attention on a limited aspect of the massive amount of information our senses are experiencing at a given moment. Organization refers to our ability to integrate the individual pieces of sensory information into an entire picture, or gestalt, that has meaning for us.

4. Status is usually defined by sociologists as the position of an individual in relation to the other members of a group. Statuses are of two types. We are given ascribed status regardless of our individual abilities and wishes by virtue of being born into a given sex, into a given racial and ethnic group, and, in certain societies, into a certain class. Achieved status, on the other hand, is

a social position that an individual reaches through choice, ability, and competition.

5. Psychologists studying motivation and its effects on achievement have identified two types of motivation. Intrinsic motivation refers to the desire to perform a task successfully for its own sake. For example, answer these questions about the English class you are attending at the moment. Are you working hard in this class because the work is challenging? Do you enjoy the feeling that you're learning something new? If you had the time, would you take more classes like this? If you answer "Yes" to these questions, then you are intrinsically motivated.

Extrinsic motivation, on the other hand, is the result of incentives outside yourself, the possible rewards you will receive for doing something or the possible sanctions you will experience if you fail to do it. Are you working hard in this class to get a good grade or to be admitted to university classes? Are you going to study for an academic degree so that you can get a good job later? If your answer to these questions is "Yes," then you are extrinsically motivated.

Gardner, R. and Lambert, W. 1972. *Attitudes and motivation in second language learning.* Rowley, Mass.: Newbury House.

Background Reading and Vocabulary Development

READING PASSAGE 3.1

Imagine that this passage is in the textbook of an academic class you are taking for credit. Read the passage as many times as you need to. However, during your first reading, you should:

1. Use the strategies you have learned for dealing with unknown vocabulary.

2. Stop reading at the end of each sentence that contains boldface words, and complete the Comprehension Building Task in the left margin.

3. Use the strategies you have learned for identifying main ideas. After each paragraph, stop and choose its main idea from the sentences in the Main Idea Check.

4. Identify and note important concepts and technical vocabulary that a professor might expect you to learn. Look for definitions and/or examples of these concepts.

Variation in Language

In what part of an introduction are you likely to find the most help about the topic of the passage? Pay attention to that part.

5

The English language, a phrase heard very frequently, gives the impression that English is one uniform system of communication used by all its native speakers. Nothing could be further from the truth. The English spoken in the British Isles is recognizably different from that spoken in North America; within the British Isles, the English of Scotland is not the same as

1

133

the English spoken in England; within the United States, the English spoken in New York can be very different from the version of English spoken in Atlanta, Georgia, or Austin, Texas. The English language, like all human languages, varies in grammar, vocabulary, and pronunciation according to a number of social and cultural factors, including the region where a person grows. *Sociolinguistics*, the scientific study of that variation, seeks to observe, record, describe, explain, and ultimately predict its occurrence.

It is possible to distinguish two main types of variation. The first of these, which can be called *between-group variation*, includes the sort of *geographical* or *regional varieties* mentioned in the preceding paragraph. A between-group variety refers to that version of a language that marks a person as belonging to a specific social group, e.g., as a native of New York City. Between-group varieties also include varieties associated with social class, with gender or sex, and with ethnic group. Other varieties, which have been less extensively studied, are those associated with age and occupation.

Most people take it for granted that regional varieties, or dialects, exist in all languages. What might be surprising to some readers is that there are also distinctions between the English used by men and women. Research, however, has confirmed that such differences do exist. Researchers have found, for example, that in both British English and American English, men tend to use the nonstandard and informal pronunciation [-in] of the *-ing* ending more often than women do. **Men also tend to use nonstandard grammatical forms (e.g., *I didn't see nothing* instead of *I didn't see anything*) more often than women.**

The second main type of linguistic variation can be labeled *variation within the individual*. This variation occurs within the English of one individual and is associated with factors that may change as the social situation changes. These factors include the different roles an individual might play (e.g., as a teacher, as a parent or child) and the relationships with the person or persons to whom the individual is speaking, (e.g., a close friend, a colleague, a subordinate, or a stranger). The individual's English will also vary with the topic of the interaction (e.g., a topic related to a job or a topic related to the individual's personal life) and with the physical setting where the interaction occurs (e.g., at a professional meeting, in a classroom, in a restaurant). Variation within the individual is also referred to as *style-switching*; in it, the speaker moves between levels of English that are perceived to be more formal or more informal.

This sentence signals a classification. What is being classified? How many types? Quickly look forward in the text. Identify and mark where the writer introduces each type. Then come back, and continue reading this paragraph.

Do the examples show regional variation or gender variation in language? Use your answer when you are deciding on the main idea of this paragraph.

If this is the second main type, what is the first? Check back to refresh your memory or confirm your answer.

10
15
20
25
30
35
40
45

2
3
4

What is this second   50   **This second type of linguistic variation** becomes very clear   5
type of variation?   in forms of address, the names or titles used by an individual when
Check back to refresh   he or she speaks to another. Theoretically, for example, you could
your memory.   address a professor called Mary Williams, who is also a close fam-
                              ily friend and not significantly older than you, in one of two ways:
                        55   *Dr. Williams* or *Mary.* Your choice of address form, however, is
                              clearly determined by the factor or factors mentioned in the pre-
                              vious paragraph that are relevant for the situation you find your-
                              self in. If you speak to Mary Williams in a class you are taking
                              from her, your role is that of a student. The appropriate form to
                        60   select is *Dr. Williams.* If you are talking over vacation plans with
                              her in your home, the setting, the topic, and your role have
                              changed. Clearly in this situation, the appropriate form of address
                              is *Mary.*

Main Idea Check

Here are the main ideas for this passage. Write the correct paragraph number
beside its main idea.

_____ Research has demonstrated that men and women differ in the way they speak
English.

_____ Linguistic variation within the individual is exemplified in the different forms of
address one person can use in speaking with another.

_____ The language of each individual can vary depending on a number of factors in
the specific situation.

_____ All languages vary, and sociolinguistics is the scientific study of that variation.

_____ Language can vary from one group of people to another depending on factors
such as the regional background, sex, and social class of the members.

After you finish reading the passage for the first time, answer the questions in A
Closer Look. You may find that you need to read parts of the passage again. This
is normal. Remember that this is a reading exercise, not a memory test.

A Closer Look

1. If the English spoken by one group of people differs from that of another
group, what factor or factors might be associated with the differences?
a. where the members of each group were born and raised
b. the sex of each group

  c. the ethnic background of each group
  d. whether the people in each group are working class or middle class

2. Men's English tends to be more formal and more grammatically
   correct than women's English.   T   F

3. People tend to adjust their language for different listeners.   T   F

4. What factor or factors could cause the same speaker to switch styles?
   a. a change in where the conversation takes place
   b. a change in what the conversation is about
   c. a change in the listener or listeners
   d. a change in the speaker's role

What Do You Think?

Concrete examples help you master and remember definitions and concepts. However, this passage is a little short on helpful examples, so try to think of some of your own.

   Do you know any vocabulary differences between British English and U.S. English? What about differences between regional varieties in your own language? Try to remember some concrete examples in pronunciation, grammar, or vocabulary. What about differences between the way men and women speak in your language? Are there words that men use but that women don't use?

   Now think about how you speak your own language. Imagine how you speak with your close friends. Now imagine speaking with your parents in exactly the same way. How would your parents react? What might your parents' reaction show?

Vocabulary in Context

Here are some words from the passage that you may not have known. You either guessed their meaning from context or from your knowledge of word families, or you omitted the word and were still able to understand the sentence. Now check and learn the meanings of the words. Use your dictionary to help you.

frequently (line 1)	subordinate (line 42)
phrase (line 1)	related (line 43)
region (line 12)	setting (line 45)
to mention (line 17)	style (line 47)
colleague (line 42)	appropriate (line 59)

READING PASSAGE 3.2 _____

Imagine that this passage is in the textbook of an academic class you are taking for credit. Read the passage as many times as you need to. However, during your first reading, you should:

1. Use the strategies you have learned for dealing with unknown vocabulary.

2. Stop reading at the end of each sentence that contains boldface words, and complete the Comprehension Building Task in the left margin.

3. Use the strategies you have learned for identifying main ideas. After each paragraph, stop and choose its main idea from the sentences in the Main Idea Check.

4. Identify and note important concepts and technical vocabulary that a professor might expect you to learn. Look for definitions and/or examples of these concepts.

The Scientific Study of Language

The goal of linguistics, the scientific study of language, is to   1
describe linguistic competence, the unconscious knowledge a native speaker of a language must have in order to speak it comprehensibly and understand others when they speak it.

Quickly look forward   5
through the text. Mark
where the writer intro-
duces these three
areas. Then come
back, and continue
reading this para-   10
graph.

To assist them in their investigation of language, lin-   2
guists have traditionally divided this complex phenomenon
into at least three major areas of study. The first of these, phonology, is concerned with the sounds of language. Phonologists analyze the sounds and the sound patterns of a given language and then attempt to describe the components of a native speaker's phonological competence. This knowledge would include, for example, a list of all the consonants and vowels of English and how to produce them. It would also include information about how to combine certain sounds into sequences and about how to modify certain

15   sounds in certain circumstances.

The following piece of conversation will help illustrate what   3
is involved in phonological competence:

Steve: You look worried, Mary.
Mary: We've got our first economics test tomorrow.
20   Steve: Well, I could help you study for it. I'm free all afternoon.

Look back at the example when you are trying to understand these details of Mary's pronunciation.

In addition to being able to pronounce all the single conso-   4
nants and vowels of her answer, **Mary is able to produce se-**
quences of three consonants—for instance, [rst] at the end of
the word *first.* **In the words** *test tomorrow,* **she knows she**
25   **can omit either the final [t] in** *test* **or the initial [t] in** *tomor-*
row **so that the two words sound like [testomorrow]. She also**
knows that she should weaken the first and last vowels of
tomorrow **(but not the vowel in the second syllable) so that**
the word sounds like [tiMAWRi]. As a native speaker of En-
30   glish, Steve will still understand her without difficulty; however,
students who are just beginning to learn English as a second language will have problems.

Do you expect the writer to continue to deal with phonology here or to move to another aspect of language?

Phonological competence allows you to understand and   5
produce sounds in sequence. As a description of linguistic
35   **competence, however, it is clearly not sufficient.** Consider this
version of Mary's response to Steve's opening remark:

> got first tomorrow our ve test we economics

In spite of the random word order, your competence in English will
probably enable you to work out what this sentence means—pro-
40   vided you have both sufficient time and a written version of it.
Imagine, however, listening to a person who was producing utterances like this at a normal rate of speech. You would find the
conversation totally incomprehensible.

What is shown by our inability to process utterances like the   6
45   one above? Clearly we also know how to put words together into
meaningful sequences. **This knowledge,** often referred to as
grammatical competence, includes a knowledge of syntax—what
grammatical category each word belongs to (e.g., noun, verb, adjec-

What knowledge? Check back for the meaning of this phrase.

THE BORN LOSER   Art Sansom

© 1983 Newspaper Enterprise Association, Inc.

The driver's linguistic competence does not seem to be functioning properly. In which
component or components does the problem lie? (Reprinted by permission.)

tive, etc.) and the rules for combining words into phrases and
50 phrases into sentences. It also includes a knowledge of morphology—the rules for adding elements to words to change their meaning in some significant way.

The third traditional area of investigation for linguistic research is semantic competence, our knowledge of word, phrase, and
55 sentence meanings. Our example conversation would be impossible to understand if we did not know what type of actions or states, people, and concepts the words in it refer to. Steve knows, for example, that the meaning of *we* and *our* includes *I* (i.e., Mary) and *mine* (Mary's) and that *tomorrow* means "the next day," not "some

Again, to help you understand the significance of these "peculiar" responses, you need to look back at Steve's "normal" responses in the original example.

60 day in the past." His semantic knowledge allows him to continue the conversation meaningfully. Without such knowledge, Steve might respond to Mary's news about the coming test in ways that we would find very peculiar, for example:

Well, have you got the results yet?
or
65 **So what has this test got to do with you?**

7

Main Idea Check

Here are the main ideas for this passage. Write the correct paragraph number beside its main idea.

_____ To produce meaningful utterances, we need more than phonological competence.

_____ Our grammatical competence allows us to process and produce utterances in which words are combined into sequences.

_____ This paragraph gives examples of the type of abilities included in phonological competence.

_____ Semantic competence is our knowledge of word, phrase, and sentence meanings.

_____ Linguistics seeks to describe the unconscious knowledge that allows native speakers to use their language.

_____ In phonology, we attempt to describe the knowledge that enables native speakers to produce and understand the sounds of their language.

After you finish reading the passage for the first time, answer the questions in A Closer Look. You may find that you need to read parts of the passage again. This is normal. Remember that this is a reading exercise, not a memory test.

A Closer Look

1. What ability or abilities does the phonological competence of English speakers consist of?
   a. knowledge of how to pronounce English sounds
   b. knowledge of the meanings of English words
   c. knowledge of how to combine words into correct sequences for sentences
   d. knowledge of how to change the pronunciation of certain English sounds

2. What is the writer's purpose in including the example in paragraph 4?
   a. to illustrate what is meant by random word order
   b. to show that understanding English depends on more than just phonological competence
   c. to demonstrate that English can be incomprehensible

3. Grammatical competence simply means knowing the grammatical category of the words of a language.   T   F

4. Under what circumstances would Steve give peculiar answers similar to the examples in paragraph 6?
   a. if his semantic competence in English were inadequate
   b. if his grammatical competence were inadequate
   c. if his phonological competence were inadequate

5. This passage introduces you to the concept of linguistic competence and the different types of knowledge included in linguistic competence. Fill in the following classification with the correct technical vocabulary from the passage.

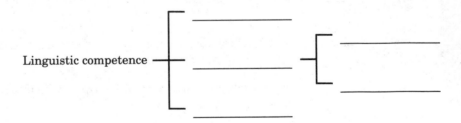

What Do You Think?

Again imagine that this is one of the first readings in your academic class on language. Since it is a short introductory reading, it may not have made everything clear to you. Mark with a question mark (?) parts of the text that are unclear. Then make a list of questions you need to have answered—either by looking for them in your later reading or by asking the professor teaching the class.

Vocabulary in Context

Here are some words from the passage that you may not have known. You either guessed their meaning from context or from your knowledge of word families, or you omitted the word and were still able to understand the sentence. Now check and learn the meanings of the words. Use your dictionary to help you.

phenomenon (line 6)   total(ly) (line 43)
to combine (line 13)   utterance (line 44)
initial (line 25)   peculiar (line 63)

VOCABULARY PRACTICE

Same or Different?

Writers sometimes express the same ideas with very different grammar and vocabulary. This exercise will help you identify such occurrences.

Read the first sentence in each example carefully. Then read each of the two following sentences to decide whether they are the same or different in meaning to the first sentence. Choose *S* when the sentence expresses the same idea as the first sentence. Choose *D* when it expresses a different idea.

1. I don't see the relevance of linguistic comprehension to the topic under discussion.

   a. I don't understand what linguistic comprehension refers to.   S   D

   b. It's not clear to me what understanding language has to do with
      what we are talking about.   S   D

2. To what extent is competence in the English language required for this position?

   a. Why is a knowledge of English needed for this job?   S   D

   b. How much English do you need to know for this job?   S   D

3. The company's version of the story is that the employee was dismissed from his position for incompetence.

   a. According to the company, the worker lost his job because he
      lacked the skills necessary to do it properly.   S   D

   b. The company claimed that his inability to do the job was the
      reason for the employee's dismissal.   S   D

4. Researchers are investigating the role played by memory in the acquisition of a second language.

    a. Scientific research has established that memory plays an important function in second language learning.   S D

    b. Research is trying to establish the contribution of memory to learning a second language.   S D

5. The development of early child language has been the focus of extensive scientific investigation in the last twenty-five years.

    a. In the past twenty-five years, a great deal of research has been conducted into how young children acquire language.   S D

    b. In the past twenty-five years, researchers have extended their research into language to include the phenomenon of child language development.   S D

6. Initially I felt that a restaurant would not be an appropriate setting for our meeting.

    a. I finally concluded that it would be inappropriate to hold our meeting at a restaurant.   S D

    b. At first, I thought that a restaurant would not be the proper place for our meeting.   S D

7. In his recent speeches, the president has referred to the role played by immigration in U.S. history.

    a. In his recent speeches, the president has mentioned the historical significance of immigration for the United States.   S D

    b. The president's recent speeches have been about the importance of immigration in U.S. history.   S D

8. The early utterances of young children are often incomprehensible to all except those people involved in looking after them.

    a. It is often the case that only the people taking care of young children can understand their early speech.   S D

    b. It is often possible to observe the language of young children while you are looking after them.   S D

Making Connections

Each example in this exercise has a lead sentence and two sentences (*a* and *b*) that might or might not logically follow the lead sentence. Read the lead sentence, and ask yourself what kind of idea you could expect in the next sentence. Then read sentence *a*. Decide whether it can follow the lead sentence and make good sense. Choose *Y* for "Yes" or *N* for "No." Do the same for sentence *b*. *Remember:*

1. Look for the ideas that make a logical connection between each pair of sentences.

2. This is also a vocabulary learning exercise. If you have problems with any new words, check their meanings as you work.

1. There is a widespread impression that educational standards in the United States have dropped in the last twenty-five years.

    a. An extensive body of research shows that levels of educational achievement have remained fairly uniform during this time.   Y N

    b. According to polls, people believe that it is easier to get grades of A or B in school than it used to be.   Y N

2. My initial impression of the town was that you could find an apartment there quite easily, provided you arrived a month or so before the beginning of the semester.

    a. This was confirmed by a number of students I met.   Y N

    b. There seemed to be a large and varied selection of appropriate housing available.   Y N

3. For some time, researchers have been investigating the role of physical exercise in maintaining good health.

    a. This version is clearly very important and relevant to the general public.   Y N

    b. Specific findings vary from study to study, but there is extensive agreement that regular exercise is associated with better health.   Y N

4. If we define linguistic competence as the native speaker's ability to comprehend and produce an infinite number of correct utterances in English, what exactly does this ability consist of?

    a. Scientific investigations of English are not always directly rele-
       vant to the task of teaching English.   Y N

    b. Clearly one component is phonological knowledge, i.e., know-
       ing the sounds of English, their possible sequences, and the
       ways to modify them without damaging communication.   Y N

5. The physical setting of an interaction is one of the factors that may influence
the stylistic level of language used in a given situation.

    a. For example, people are likely to use more formal English in
       public than they do in private.   Y N

    b. The more formal the surroundings, the more formal a person's
       speech tends to be.   Y N

Background Reading and Vocabulary Development

Imagine that this passage is in the textbook of an academic class you are taking for credit. Read the passage as many times as you need to. However, during your first reading, you should:

1. Use the strategies you have learned for dealing with unknown vocabulary.

2. Stop reading at the end of each sentence that contains boldface words, and complete the Comprehension Building Task in the left margin.

3. Use the strategies you have learned for identifying main ideas. After each paragraph, stop and choose its main idea from the sentences in the Main Idea Check.

4. Identify and note important concepts and technical vocabulary that a professor might expect you to learn. Look for definitions and/or examples of these concepts.

Sociolinguistic Rules

Modern linguistic researchers have focused most of their attention on investigations of linguistic competence—in other words, on semantics, on grammar, and on phonology. In so doing, they have unintentionally reinforced the widespread but erroneous belief that knowing the grammar, vocabulary, and pronunciation of a

What knowledge?
Check back for the
meaning of this
phrase.

second language will make you an effective communicator in that
language. Although you need **this knowledge** in order to produce
correct utterances in a second language, sociolinguists argue that
it is by no means sufficient for successful communication. Its cru-
10 cial shortcoming is that it does not enable you to produce utterances that are socially appropriate.

To see what sociolinguists mean, consider the following con-   2
versation and its outcome. The conversation is hypothetical, but
the type of situation has been documented and discussed in the
15 research literature (e.g., Rubin 1983; Thomas 1983).

> U.S. Host (to foreign student): Would you like some more dessert? Do
>   have some!
> Student (trying to appear polite): No, thank you very much.

> The host changes the topic of conversation and doesn't mention des-
> 20 sert again. The student, who really did want some more dessert, re-
> mains hungry and might even feel that the host has not been
> attentive or polite enough.

Look for an explana-
tion of this breakdown
as you continue read-
ing.

Clearly the speech of each participant is linguistically correct.
Equally clearly, however, there has been a breakdown of
25 **communication in this situation.** The student has communicated
to the host an inaccurate impression of his wishes: he does, in fact,
want some dessert. The host, however, has interpreted his refusal
as a genuine refusal. On the other hand, the host, attempting to be
attentive and polite, might somehow be giving the opposite impres-
30 sion to the student. Neither participant in the conversation real-
izes, however, that there has been a misunderstanding.

Look for the repeated
idea in this sentence.
It should help confirm
for you the main pur-
pose of paragraph 2.

For sociolinguists, such misunderstandings offer evi-   3
dence that there are rules for socially appropriate speech
(sociolinguistic rules) just as there are rules for linguistically
35 **correct speech.** These rules are acquired and applied, usually un-
consciously, by members of a given culture. In our example, the
host is following a sociolinguistic rule that states

> Offers of more food are made once, twice at most. More is impolite.

The student, on the other hand, applies a different rule from his
40 own culture:

> Never accept the first, or even the second, offer of more food. To be
> polite, wait until the third or fourth offer (which is sure to be made).

What do you expect to
read in this para-
graph?

There is a growing amount of empirical data to support   4
both the claim that sociolinguistic rules exist and that they
45 **may differ from culture to culture.** Christopher (1982) reports
the relative reluctance of Japanese culture (compared with Ameri-

can culture) to directly refuse to do something someone is asking you to do. Apte (1974) reports that South Asians, unlike Americans and Europeans, do not thank shopkeepers, close friends, or family members. Others studies have suggested that different cultures differ in how and how often they apologize (Cohen and Olshtain 1981; Cohen and Olshtain 1983; Olshtain, 1983).

It is clear then that there are different standards for what is socially appropriate linguistic behavior in given circumstances. While actions such as thanking, apologizing, accepting, and refusing are probably universal, the rules for when and how to perform such actions may differ greatly from culture to culture. Does it follow, however, that a second language learner needs to master these standards, or rules?

To answer **this question,** let us return to the example of the foreign student and U.S. host. Both follow the rules of politeness of their own society; both are unaware that there are other ways to show politeness and other standards that may be applied in assessing politeness. What is especially significant is that the student is slightly offended and is already beginning to judge the host negatively. Reactions like this are relatively common in situations where there is intercultural miscommunication. One typical response is to jump to a negative conclusion and to attribute a negative quality—in this case, lack of politeness—to the person whose language was understood linguistically but misinterpreted sociolinguistically.

Learners of a second language, therefore, need to be aware that the rules for polite interaction are not all universal. They need to be able to identify situations where the rules of the cultures involved are different; to reduce the risk of being misunderstood and even of giving offense, they must also be ready to modify their speech to conform to the sociolinguistic conventions of the culture they are in. **Accomplishing these two tasks is not simple;** but failure to do so will lead to misunderstandings that may have serious consequences for the people involved.

As you read this paragraph, identify the repeated ideas. Use them to confirm your understanding of paragraphs 3–4. Also identify a new idea. This will be the topic for the next section of the article.

What question? Check back for the meaning of this phrase.

What are these two tasks? Check back to identify them precisely.

References

Apte, M. L. 1974. "Thank you" and South Asian languages: a comparative sociolinguistic study. *International Journal of the Sociology of Language*, 3:67–89.

Christopher, R. C. 1982. *The Japanese mind: The Goliath explained.* New York: Simon and Schuster.

Cohen, A. D., and Olshtain, E. 1981. Developing a measure of sociolinguistic competence: The case of apology. *Language Learning* 31(3): 113–134.

Cohen, A. D., and Olshtain, E. 1983. Apology: A speech act set. In N. Wolfson and E. Judd (Eds.) *Sociolinguistics and language acquisition*. Rowley, MA: Newbury House.

Olshtain, E. 1983. Sociocultural competence and language transfer: The case of apology. In S. Gass and L. Selinker (Eds.) *Language transfer in language learning*. Rowley, MA: Newbury House.

Rubin, J. 1983. How to tell when someone is saying "no" revisited. In N. Wolfson and E. Judd (Eds.) *Sociolinguistics and language acquisition*. Rowley, MA: Newbury House.

Thomas, J. 1983. Cross-cultural pragmatic failure. *Applied Linguistics* 4(2):91–109.

Main Idea Check

Here are the main ideas for this passage. Write the correct paragraph number beside its main idea.

_____ Do differences in sociolinguistic rules mean that second language learners need to learn new rules for appropriate speech in their second language?

_____ According to sociolinguists, just having good linguistic competence in a second language is not enough for a second language learner.

_____ Empirical research has demonstrated the existence of rules for socially appropriate speech and of cultural differences in these rules.

_____ This paragraph offers an example of a situation in which people fail to communicate effectively although their speech is without linguistic errors.

_____ To avoid the potentially serious consequences of intercultural miscommunication, second language learners need to be prepared to identify and use the sociolinguistic rules of the new culture.

_____ Because they are unaware of differences in sociolinguistic rules, people will often form an unjustifiably negative opinion about a person from another culture.

_____ Scientists conclude that there are rules for socially and culturally appropriate speech because miscommunication occurs between people whose speech is correct phonologically, grammatically, and semantically.

After you finish reading the passage for the first time, answer the questions in A Closer Look. You may find that you need to read parts of the passage again. This is normal. Remember that this is a reading exercise, not a memory test.

A Closer Look

1. According to all language experts, all you need to communicate well in a second language is to know the pronunciation, the grammar, and the vocabulary of that language. T F

2. What comment or comments about the situation in paragraph 2 are justified?
   a. The student did not want any more dessert.
   b. The student was using the sociolinguistic rules of his own culture.
   c. The host was following international rules for politeness.
   d. The student did not totally comprehend the meaning of his host's question.

3. It is possible that some cultures do not express thanks as often as Americans do. T F

4. According to the passage, what outcome or outcomes can we expect when linguistically competent speakers of English as a second language ignore sociolinguistic rules when they talk with native speakers of English?
   a. Native speakers of English may consider them rude or worse.
   b. The ESL speakers may unintentionally offend native speakers with whom they interact.
   c. Native speakers to whom they are talking will ignore their sociolinguistic errors.
   d. The ESL speakers may get the wrong impression of native speakers and judge them negatively.

5. After you have finished reading this passage, explain what the difference is between linguistically incorrect speech and socially inappropriate speech. Use examples to illustrate your explanation.

What Do You Think?

1. Have you ever been in a situation where you feel there was a misunderstanding between you and a native speaker of English? Did the misunderstanding occur because of linguistic or sociolinguistic problems?

2. Have you ever experienced a situation where you got a negative impression of a native speaker of English from the way he or she talked? Was your reaction justified? Does this passage offer you any new explanation for your reaction? Have you observed any frequent speech behavior here that seems appropriate but would definitely be inappropriate back home? What is it?

Vocabulary in Context

Here are some words from the passage that you may not have known. You either guessed their meaning from context or from your knowledge of word families, or you omitted the word and were still able to understand the sentence. Now check and learn the meanings of the words. Use your dictionary to help you.

shortcoming (line 10)	to offend (line 65)
participant (line 23)	offense (line 76)
breakdown (line 24)	convention (line 77)
universal (lines 56 and 73)	

READING PASSAGE 3.4

Imagine that this passage is in the textbook of an academic class you are taking for credit. Read the passage as many times as you need to. However, during your first reading, you should:

1. Use the strategies you have learned for dealing with unknown vocabulary.

2. Stop reading at the end of each sentence that contains boldface words, and complete the Comprehension Building Task in the left margin.

3. Use the strategies you have learned for identifying main ideas. After each paragraph, stop and choose its main idea from the sentences in the Main Idea Check.

4. Identify and note important concepts and technical vocabulary that a professor might expect you to learn. Look for definitions and/or examples of these concepts.

Child Language Acquisition: Phonology

When language first emerges in young children (usually between eighteen and twenty-four months), their pronunciation often bears little resemblance to that of mature users of the language. For example, they are by no means able immediately to produce the full range of English sounds. As a result, with the word [da], for example, a child could be saying *car, down, truck, ball, star,* or possibly something else. Despite the difficulties caused by imperfect pronunciation, however, family members are usually able to interpret the child's utterances accurately.

Use the repeated ideas in this sentence to help you decide the main idea of paragraph 1.

If children's pronunciation is so imperfect, how can we account for the fact that it is comprehensible to those adults regularly exposed to it? One commonsense possibility is that family members somehow adjust to the child's speech. This answer, although general and rather vague, is valuable because it suggests another question that can be empirically investigated: What characteristics in the child's pronunciation might help adults adjust to it?

When researchers examine the early utterances of children, they find that their pronunciation is not random. Although their utterances are rather poor imitations of English words, they reveal clear regularities in pronunciation. Table 1 shows the English consonants in a speech sample taken from the same child at the age of twenty-four and thirty months.

Look at Table 1. Make sure you are looking at the correct column. Then find examples to illustrate the writer's generalizations.

Even at the earlier stage (twenty-four months), there are distinct patterns in the child's pronunciation. **He clearly prefers certain categories of consonant sounds:** The data contains many examples of consonants produced near the front of the mouth, for example, [d], [b], [m], and [n], but no sounds produced farther back in the mouth like [g] and [k]. He favors [m], [b], and [d], sounds that are voiced, (i.e., the vocal cords are vibrating dur-

Table 1. Michael's pronunciation at twenty-four and thirty months.[1]

Word	At Twenty-four Months	At Thirty Months
door	do	dow
toast	do	dof
Dan	dan	dan
toe	do	do
car	da	daw
bed	be	bet
cheese	dee	deef
cat	da	dat
big	bee	bik
star	da	daw
spoon	boon	boon
pig	bee	bik
goat	doa	doat
clothes	do	dof
Beth	be	bep
mouth	mou	mouf

Quickly look at this table for evidence of (1) poor imitation and (2) regularities.

ing these sounds). Voiceless sounds like [k], [t], and [p] are avoided. He can produce stops, consonants that completely stop the flow of air coming through the mouth, for example, [d] and [b], but not fricatives, consonants that only restrict the flow of air and produce a hissing noise, for example, [f], [s], and [z].

35

Again, look back at Table 1. Make sure you are looking at the correct columns. Then find examples to illustrate the writer's generalizations.

The data also shows regular patterns of substitution, in which certain sounds are replaced consistently by other sounds. **For example, the child is clearly substituting [w] for [r], and [b] for [p]. The consonant [d] replaces a wide range of consonant sounds ([t], [s], [z], [sh], [k], and [g]). Consonant clusters, sequences of two consonant sounds, are replaced by single consonant sounds at the beginning of words.**

5

40

Once again, look back at Table 1. Make sure you are looking at the correct column. Then find examples to illustrate the writer's generalizations.

The child's developing capacity to pronounce English sounds becomes evident when you compare the forms produced at twenty-four months with the later versions of the same words. **He is now able to produce some final as well as initial consonants; he can produce voiceless stops like [t] and [k], but only at the ends of words; his first fricative [f] has emerged at the end of words and is being used as a substitute for [s] and [z] in this position.**

6

45

50

Find the repeated ideas in this sentence. What paragraph or paragraphs do these repeated ideas summarize?

From the regular patterns and the original forms in the data, it is evident that the child is not merely imitating adults; he is constructing his own system for pronouncing English sounds. For some researchers, the child's ability to do this is evidence that confirms their basic view of language acquisition: Humans possess an innate ability to learn language. In other words, they are genetically programmed to listen to language and construct a simple system of pronunciation; this system becomes progressively more complex and more accurate until, by the age of five or six, children are speaking just like the people around them.

7

55

60

Note
1. Data from K. J. Pakenham, Personal files, 1991.

Main Idea Check

Here are the main ideas for this passage. Write the correct paragraph number beside its main idea.

_____ Empirical data show that children's early pronunciation of English is systematic, not random.

_____ Children will regularly replace certain English sounds with certain other sounds.

_____ Although the pronunciation of very young children is very different from that of adult English, it is quite easily understood by family members.

_____ As children grow, they become able to produce sounds that they were not able to say earlier.

_____ The fact that children develop their own systematic version of English pronunciation is evidence for some researchers that humans are innately programmed to learn language.

_____ We need to analyze children's pronunciation if we want to explain how adults can understand their imperfect pronunciation.

_____ In the early stages of their English, children regularly use certain classes of English sounds and avoid others.

After you finish reading the passage for the first time, answer the questions in A Closer Look. You may find that you need to read parts of the passage again. This is normal. Remember that this is a reading exercise, not a memory test.

A Closer Look

1. Scan the text for information. Then write definitions and examples for the following technical concepts:

   stops   voiced sounds
   fricatives   patterns of substitution
   voiceless sounds   consonant clusters

2. What generalization or generalizations can you use to describe this child's pronunciation of English at the age of twenty-four months?
   a. He can correctly pronounce all consonants at the beginning of words.
   b. He can pronounce [b], [d], and [m] at the beginning of words.
   c. He can correctly produce English [d] wherever it occurs.
   d. He prefers voiced sounds to voiceless sounds.
   e. The consonants he can pronounce are unrelated and have nothing in common.

3. What has this child learned about pronunciation between the ages of twenty-four and thirty months?
   a. how to produce consonant clusters
   b. how to produce his first fricative sound
   c. how to produce more consonants at the end of words

4. Children seem to learn pronunciation by creating their own simplified system of pronunciation and then gradually making it more sophisticated.   T   F

5. From this passage, you could conclude that in children's very early English, a word like [bee] could have a number of different meanings.   T F

What Do You Think?

At the age of twenty-four months, the child in this passage pronounces *star* and *car* in the same way—as [da]. Does this mean that the child doesn't hear and understand the difference between *star* and *car*? How could you find out if he knows the difference or not?

Vocabulary in Context

Here are some words from the passage that you may not have known. You either guessed their meaning from context or from your knowledge of word families, or you omitted the word and were still able to understand the sentence. Now check and learn the meanings of the words. Use your dictionary to help you.

to emerge (line 1)   to reveal (line 20)
by no means (line 4)   to avoid (line 31)
despite (line 7)   hissing (line 35)
to account for (line 11)   evident (line 44)
to be exposed to (line 12) innate (line 56)

READING PASSAGE 3.5

Imagine that this passage is in the textbook of an academic class you are taking for credit. Read the passage as many times as you need to. However, during your first reading, you should:

1. Use the strategies you have learned for dealing with unknown vocabulary.

2. Stop reading at the end of each sentence that contains boldface words, and complete the Comprehension Building Task in the left margin.

3. Use the strategies you have learned for identifying main ideas. After each paragraph, stop and choose its main idea from the sentences in the Main Idea Check.

4. Identify and note important concepts and technical vocabulary that a professor might expect you to learn. Look for definitions and/or examples of these concepts.

Second Language Learning

Again, use your expe-rience with introduc-tions to identify the specific ideas that will be addressed in this article.

The question of how people learn a second language is one that has received a great deal of scientific attention—especially over the last twenty-five years or so. Research has offered evidence that has been used to support a number of conflicting claims about second language (SL) learning. However, there is one fundamental observation that is less open to dispute than others. If success in adult second language learning is measured by how close the learner comes to the level of a native speaker, it is possible and quite common for adults to achieve a high degree of success in learning SL grammar and vocabulary. Strangely enough, the same degree of success does not seem to be attainable in SL phonology; adult SL speakers who sound like native speakers are extremely rare, perhaps even nonexistent.

Check back for the meaning of this phe-nomenon. Does this help you identify the probable topic of this article?

Evidence for the existence of **this phenomenon** is offered in a number of research studies. Scovel (1978) asked native speakers of Standard American English to distinguish between native and nonnative English speech and writing. His subjects were able to identify nonnative speakers 97 percent of the time. In the task of identifying nonnative writers, however, they only attained an accuracy level of 47 percent. In other words, they performed no better than a person completing the task by random guessing. Other studies (Asher and Garcia 1969; Oyama 1976) found that Cuban and Italian immigrants who arrived in the United States before the age of ten were less likely to speak English with a foreign accent. Fathman (1975) found that among children learning English in Germany, those in the six to ten age range had better pronunciation, while the eleven- to fifteen-year-olds had better grammar.

Use the repeated ideas to refresh your mem-ory of the previous paragraph(s). Use the new ideas to help you with this new para-graph.

How have scientists attempted to account for the re-markable inability of adult second language learners to ac-quire a nativelike pronunciation in the second language? One likely explanation is to be found in the so-called critical period theory. Proponents of this theory argue that the acquisition of native-speaker pronunciation in any language is biologically possible only until about the age of twelve. This is the age at which cerebral

35 lateralization is completed. Cerebral lateralization is the process by which the two hemispheres of the brain increasingly specialize in different functions. At the end of this process, for example, control of most language functions is permanently located in the left hemisphere while the right hemisphere is apparently responsible,

40 among other things, for visual and spatial perception. When lateralization is complete, according to the theory, it closes the critical period of life during which humans will acquire native speaker pronunciation in a language.

Check back to refresh your comprehension of this theory.

Much of the evidence to support **the critical period theory**   4

45 comes from observations of patients suffering from aphasia, a loss of language abilities associated with brain damage from injury or disease. A vast amount of evidence has accumulated over the last one hundred years that language is localized in the brain's left hemisphere. Seventy percent of adult patients with some injury to

50 the left hemisphere suffer some language disability. However, patients with injuries to the right hemisphere remain able to speak and understand language perfectly. Their problems are with such activities as recognizing faces and patterns or finding their way from one place to another.

What is this cerebral lateralization? Check back to refresh your memory.

Evidence for the effects of **cerebral lateralization** on language learning also comes mainly from research with patients suffering from aphasia after a hemispherectomy, surgery to remove one hemisphere of the brain. Lenneberg (1967), in his own research and in the relevant medical literature, found that 97 percent of

60 children undergoing this operation before the age of ten recovered their language abilities after some temporary aphasia. They also continued to learn their first language. In those rare cases where the same type of surgery was performed on adults, however, all the patients were left with complete and permanent aphasia. From

65 this research, it seems that in children the brain has a degree of flexibility that allows the right hemisphere to take over the functions of the left when necessary. After lateralization, this flexibility disappears; one result is that adults who lose language through brain injuries are unable to regain it. Another result, ac-

70 cording to Lenneberg, Scovel (1988), and others, is that the less flexible brain limits later phonological development in uninjured adults; they cannot acquire native speaker pronunciation in a second language.

The critical period theory has certain, though limited, impli-   6

75 cations for second language learners. It suggests strongly that learners who wish to acquire a native speaker accent need to start

Pay attention to this word when you are working on the main idea of this paragraph.

80 on the task before their teen years. **However,** it must be emphasized that the theory does not justify a halt in attempts to teach and learn SL pronunciation. There is too much counterevidence for such a conclusion to be valid; there are too many cases of adults who acquire adequate or good pronunciation in a second language through instruction and practice. While they will never be mistaken for native speakers, their efforts are rewarded by speech that is perfectly comprehensible.

References

Asher, J., and Garcia, R. 1969. The optimal age to learn a foreign language. *Modern Language Journal*, 38:334–341.

Fathman, A. 1975. The relationship between age and second language productive ability. *Language Learning*, 25:245–253.

Lenneberg, E. 1967. *Biological foundations of language*. New York: Wiley.

Oyama, S. 1976. A sensitive period for the acquisition of a nonnative phonological system. *Journal of Psycholinguistic Research*, 5:261–283.

Scovel, T. 1978. The recognition of foreign accents in English and its implications for psycholinguistic theories of language acquisition. *Proceedings of the Fifth International Association of Applied Linguistics* (389–401). Montreal: Laval University Press.

Scovel, T. 1988. *A time to speak*. New York: Newbury House.

Main Idea Check

Here are the main ideas for this passage. Write the correct paragraph number beside its main idea.

_____ Evidence from aphasia patients confirms that the left hemisphere of the brain controls language in most people.

_____ Although a native speaker's pronunciation in a second language may be unattainable, this does not suggest that adults should stop trying to improve their second language pronunciation.

_____ Although adults can achieve a high level of competence in the grammar and vocabulary of a second language, they are generally not so successful in mastering its pronunciation.

_____ Evidence from child and adult brain surgery patients shows that lateralization causes the brain to lose some of its earlier capacity to acquire language.

_____ Research studies have supported the claim that adults can rarely acquire native speaker's pronunciation in a second language.

_____ The critical period theory argues that the ability to acquire native speaker pronunciation in a language disappears around the age of twelve, when, after lateralization, language functions permanently settle in the left hemisphere of the brain.

After you finish reading the passage for the first time, answer the questions in A Closer Look. You may find that you need to read parts of the passage again. This is normal. Remember that this is a reading exercise, not a memory test.

A Closer Look

1. Adults learning a second language can come closer to native speaker performance in pronunciation than they can in grammar and vocabulary.   T   F

2. From the research, we can expect that people who learn ESL as children will have better pronunciation than people who learn ESL as adults.   T   F

3. The critical period theory argues that adults have difficulty learning a second language because they do not practice enough.   T   F

4. Each of the following two diagrams represents two research findings and the conclusion that can be drawn from them (paragraphs 4 and 5). Choose the correct idea from the list below, and write its letter in the appropriate box.

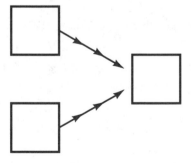 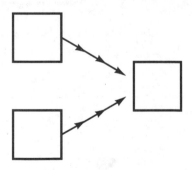

a. Language is processed in the left hemisphere of the brain.
b. Language disabilities result after injuries to the left side of the brain.
c. Injuries to the right side of the brain cause problems with visual perception, not with language.

a. Most children with left hemispherectomies fully regained their ability to learn and use language.
b. Lateralization causes the brain to lose its earlier flexibility to acquire and process language also in the right hemisphere.
c. Adults with left hemispherectomies suffer total and permanent loss of language.

5. What conclusion(s) can be drawn from research on patients, both children and adults, suffering from aphasia?
   a. Language is usually processed in the left hemisphere of the brain.
   b. The uninjured side of the brain can take over the language functions of the injured side in children but not in adults.
   c. Lateralization limits the brain's ability to acquire language.

6. Look for definitions of the following technical concepts: *cerebral lateralization*, *aphasia*, and *hemispherectomy*.

What Do You Think?

1. From your own experience of learning English, what do you think of the ideas in this article? Do they make sense? Do you agree or disagree?

2. This article offers one explanation why adult ESL pronunciation is rarely like that of a native speaker of English. However, it does not explain why there are different foreign accents in ESL. How would you explain this phenomenon?

Vocabulary in Context

Here are some words from the passage that you may not have known. You either guessed their meaning from context or from your knowledge of word families, or you omitted the word and were still able to understand the sentence. Now check and learn the meanings of the words. Use your dictionary to help you.

attainable (line 11)	to undergo (line 60)
rare (lines 13 and 62)	temporary (line 61)
to attain (line 19)	permanent (line 64)
remarkable (line 28)	implication (line 74)
theory (line 31)	to justify (line 78)
localize (line 48)	

VOCABULARY PRACTICE

Same or Different?

Writers sometimes express the same ideas with very different grammar and vocabulary. This exercise will help you identify such occurrences.

Read the first sentence in each example carefully. Then read each of the two following sentences to decide whether they are the same or different in meaning to the first sentence. Choose *S* when the sentence expresses the same idea as the first sentence. Choose *D* when it expresses a different idea.

1. The lecture hall has a seating capacity of 250.

   a. There are seats for 250 students in the lecture hall.   S D

   b. Two hundred and fifty students are sitting in the lecture hall.   S D

2. In most social groups, conformity to that group's behavioral conventions is required of all members.

   a. If you are a member of a social group, you are expected to follow the rules of behavior of that group.   S D

   b. Membership in most social groups involves a requirement that individuals adjust their behavior to conform to the group's accepted standards.   S D

3. Over the last ten years, an accumulation of evidence from a wide range of research studies has confirmed the validity of Dr. Green's conclusions.

   a. Over the past ten years, a wide variety of research studies have questioned the validity of Dr. Green's findings.   S D

   b. Evidence provided by a wide variety of research investigations conducted over the past ten years has demonstrated that Dr. Green's findings are valid.   S D

4. The obvious capacity of adults to acquire a second language is not in dispute.

   a. There is general agreement that adults are clearly able to learn a second language.   S D

   b. Everyone agrees that acquiring a second language is an accomplishment for an adult.   S D

5. Accuracy in recording data is a fundamental element in empirical research.

   a. When you are involved in empirical research, it is essential that you make no errors when you write down what you observe.   S D

   b. In research, keeping an accurate record of your observations is of critical importance.   S D

6. Applying the rules for apologies of your own culture in interactions with speakers of other languages has the potential to cause serious misunderstandings.

    a. Serious misunderstandings may occur if you follow your own cultural conventions for apologizing when you speak with speakers of another language.   S D

    b. You might make a serious mistake if you use your own cultural rules when you want to say you are sorry in another language.   S D

7. Accounting for the wide range of individual achievement in learning a second language has so far been an impossible task for researchers.

    a. Researchers have developed a wide range of theories to account for why learning a second language is impossible for some people.   S D

    b. Up to now, researchers have been unable to explain why different people attain vastly different levels of proficiency in a second language.   S D

8. An examination of the early utterances of English-speaking children will reveal consistent substitutions of certain categories of sounds (e.g., stops) for others (e.g., fricatives and affricates).

    a. If we analyze the early speech of children, we find that children regularly replace certain types of English sounds, i.e., affricates and fricatives, with other types of sounds, namely stops.   S D

    b. According to observations of early child language, English-speaking children produce a wide range of sounds, including stops, fricatives, and affricates.   S D

9. The achievement of native speaker proficiency in the pronunciation of English is an extremely rare occurrence among adult learners of English as a second language.

    a. It is very unusual for adult learners of English as a second language to imitate the pronunciation of native speakers of English.   S D

    b. A native speaker's pronunciation in English is seldom attainable by adults who acquire English as a second language.   S D

10. In adults, language loss caused by injury to the brain is normally permanent.

   a. Adults who lose their language as a result of brain damage
      usually do not regain it.   S D

   b. Adults who lose language due to brain injury rarely recover
      it.   S D

Making Connections

Each example in the exercise has a lead sentence and two sentences (a and b)
that might or might not logically follow the lead sentence. Read the lead sentence, and ask yourself what kind of idea you could expect in the next sentence.
Then read sentence a. Decide whether it can follow the lead sentence and make
good sense. Choose Y for "Yes" or N for "No." Do the same for sentence b.
Remember:

1. Look for the ideas that make a logical connection between each pair of sentences.

2. This is also a vocabulary learning exercise. If you have problems with any
   new words, check their meanings as you work.

1. The accident left the driver with some permanent disability in his right leg.

   a. After some time, he regained full use of his injured leg.   Y N

   b. He suffered a 30 percent loss of flexibility and range of move-
      ment in his right knee.   Y N

2. The proponents of the government's new economic program argue that raising the gasoline tax is crucial to the success of the program.

   a. Without such an increase, the government's capacity to finance
      other critical parts of the program would be severely reduced.   Y N

   b. However, many experts dispute the government's assessment
      that raising the gasoline tax is the best way to generate needed
      funds.   Y N

3. It is a widespread assumption that the rules and conventions for polite linguistic interaction are universal.

   a. Data from recent empirical research in apologizing, however,
      are inconsistent with this popular notion.   Y N

   b. This view holds, for example, that there are rules that apply to
      all cultures and specify the appropriate occasions and forms
      for expressing thanks.   Y N

4. The report of a group of independent experts who investigated the oil spill disputes the oil company's own assessment of the impact of the spill on the environment.

   a. It identifies, for example, a number of critical shortcomings in the company's methods of collecting water samples from the affected area.   Y N

   b. Although they identify a number of minor inaccuracies in the company's report, the experts agree with the conclusion that the damage is neither extensive nor permanent.   Y N

5. Most researchers believe that the ability to acquire language is innate in humans.

   a. Such a view is supported by a vast amount of empirical data from studies in child language acquisition.   Y N

   b. Without such an assumption, it would be difficult to account for the universal success of normal children to acquire language merely through interaction with adults and others.   Y N

6. One fundamental weakness of this particular theory of second language learning is that it is too general and too vague to be tested.

   a. However, this is only a minor shortcoming.   Y N

   b. As a result, it makes conflicting predictions about how second language learners will behave in given circumstances. .   Y N

7. Consumer-protection groups believe that all new cars should undergo a series of lengthy and rigorous tests conducted by independent experts.

   a. If the tests show that a car does not conform to the established safety standards, it cannot be marketed until appropriate modifications have been made.   Y N

   b. The automobile industry's counterargument is that such a vast testing program would guarantee only more expensive, not safer or better, cars.   Y N

8. After we examine this theory of second language learning, a number of its critical defects emerge.

   a. The first of these is that it accounts for a vast amount of data provided by empirical research in second language learning.   Y N

   b. First, it makes two erroneous assumptions about second language learners.   Y N

Synonyms and Paraphrases

Review the meanings of the words to the left of each paragraph below. Find out how to use these words by studying examples from the Vocabulary Study and from the reading passages of this unit. Then read each paragraph for its details. Replace the words in boldface with the correct new words. Sometimes you will need to change the grammar of the sentence so that the new word or expression fits into it correctly.

temporary
despite
vast
proponent
conflict
emerge
dispute
halt
document

1. The developing countries of the world are **appearing** as a **huge** new market for the products of Western tobacco companies. **Although** there is evidence that **makes clear** the dangers of smoking, tobacco use continues to increase in these countries. In Western countries, some people have begun to argue that laws should be passed to **stop** or at least restrict the export of tobacco products to other countries. The **supporters** of such laws do not **disagree** that they would damage the economies of areas where tobacco is produced or processed. They point out, however, that such damage would **not last forever.** They also point out that a policy of permitting tobacco exports **is inconsistent with** a policy that spends billions of dollars on medical assistance to developing countries.

apply
universally
attain
by no means
innate
construct
acquire
rare
error
relatively
possess
reveal
account for
capacity
crucial
imitate

2. The **mistakes** children make when they are **learning** their native language provide evidence that is **very important** to our attempts **to explain** the process of first language acquisition. For example, English-speaking children around three or four may say "I sawed Santa Claus" or "We readed a book." Such new verb forms are **not at all** (1) **infrequent** (2) in children's English; in fact, they are **quite** common. They show that young children are not content to merely **copy** the speech that they hear around them. The mistakes **show** that children **have** (1) **the ability** (2) to **develop** and **use** their own grammar rules for the language they are learning. Without this **natural, genetically transmitted** ability, it would be impossible for children to **reach** that level of mastery of the language that children **throughout the world** achieve by around the age of five.

Using New Vocabulary

Review the meanings of the following verbs. To learn how to use them in sentences, study the examples in the Vocabulary Study and the sentences of Reading Passages 3.3 to 3.5 where they occur. Words marked with an asterisk (*) are Vocabulary in Context words.

to regain	to conform
to account for*	to substitute

                    to dispute   to accomplish
                    to apply   to assess

Now finish each of the following sentences in a way that seems appropriate and interesting to you. You may want to use ideas connected with your readings in this unit or in earlier units.

1. After the surgery, the patient regained . . .

2. This theory cannot account for . . .

3. This new study disputes . . .

4. The new law does not apply . . .

5. Cars that don't conform . . .

6. When they are learning their first language, very young children often substitute . . .

7. We haven't been able to accomplish . . .

8. It's difficult to assess . . .

Main Reading

PREREADING THE ARTICLE: GETTING A FIRST IDEA

Before you begin reading, you should try to develop your expectations for the textbook chapter—an idea of what the chapter will be about.

Read the main title and section titles of the chapter carefully. Then read the sentences below. Choose *Y* for sentences expressing ideas that you can reasonably expect in the chapter. Answer *N* for sentences containing ideas you can't really expect.

1. The chapter will be about learning a second language. Y N

2. The chapter will discuss how children learn their first language. Y N

3. The chapter will discuss all aspects of child language acquisition. Y N

4. The chapter will describe and assess theories of language acquisition. Y N

5. The chapter will limit itself to examining the acquisition of pronunciation by children. Y N

Now remember what you know about introductions. Where in an introduction should you look first for clear, helpful information about the organization and ideas of the article?

Quickly look through the introduction. Identify where the author outlines the chapter. Then review expectations 1–5, and complete expectations 6–8.

6. The chapter will examine the language that caregivers use with children. Y N

7. The chapter will show how developmental psycholinguistics collects data for the study of language acquisition. Y N

8. The chapter will discuss the influence of school on the development of children's language. Y N

MAIN READING _____

Imagine that this passage is in the textbook of an academic class you are taking for credit. Read the passage as many times as you need to. However, during your first reading, you should:

1. Use the strategies you have learned for dealing with unknown vocabulary.

2. Stop reading at the end of each sentence that contains boldface words, and complete the Comprehension Building Task in the left margin.

3. Use the strategies you have learned for identifying main ideas. After each paragraph, stop and choose its main idea from the sentences in the Main Idea Check.

4. Identify and note important concepts and technical vocabulary that a professor might expect you to learn. Look for definitions and/or examples of these concepts.

After you finish reading each section for the first time, answer the questions in A Closer Look. You may find that you need to read parts of the passage again. This is normal. Remember that this is a reading exercise, not a memory test.

Language Acquisition: The Early Years

1. Introduction

When you read this introduction, remember to look for information about the content and organization of the chapter.

By the time children have reached the age of about five, they have accomplished something we all take for granted: They have learned how to speak their native language. In the years that follow, of course, they will continue to learn vocabulary; they will also acquire a few additional grammar patterns and new styles of speaking for new situations. Many, but by no means all, will learn to read and write—if they are given favorable opportunities to do so. **However,** what remains true for all children is the enormous achievement of those first five years of life. They have acquired perfect pronunciation of their language, a goal most adults learning a second language fail to achieve. They have acquired most of the grammatical knowledge they need to speak and understand their language. The systems of grammar and sounds that they have learned, apparently with ease, are so complex that highly trained linguists still have difficulty giving an adequate description of them.

Pay attention to this word when you think about the main idea of this paragraph.

1

5

10

15

*What achievement?
Check back for the
meaning of this
phrase.*

20

25

30

*Check back for other
characteristics. How
many can you see?
What are they?*

35

40

45

*Remember specific in-
formation about a text
often comes at the end
of an introduction.
Read carefully.*

*Now quickly check
through the chapter,
and look at the titles
of its sections. Can
you confirm the expec-
tations you formed
while you were read-
ing the introduction?*

50

55

The achievement is even more remarkable because it takes   2
place with little or no formal teaching. Parents generally do not
correct their children's utterances even when these utterances contain pronunciation and grammatical errors; they do not offer explanations of grammatical and pronunciation rules; in fact, most parents have no conscious knowledge of the vast majority of the rules
governing their own language. Parents and others, known in the
research as caregivers, simply allow and encourage infants and
young children to take part in conversations. They speak to them
and wait for responses; they interpret the responses and react naturally to what the child has said or to what they think the child
has said. This linguistic interaction between children and their
caregivers and perhaps later, their peers, is the only language to
which children are exposed. In a sense, it is a language "course,"
but it is one that bears little or no resemblance to traditional language courses in schools.

Another characteristic of first language acquisition is its   3
universal 100 percent success rate. All normal children brought
up in a normal linguistic environment will acquire the language of
that environment. Language acquisition will take place regardless
of whether the caregivers are educated, prosperous citizens of a
so-called advanced society or are uneducated, even illiterate, impoverished members of a so-called developing society. It will occur
regardless of the differences in individual children's intellectual abilities; during these first five years or so, a future dishwasher will be
as successful in language learning as a future Nobel Prize winner
in physics. Deaf children will also successfully acquire their own
first language—provided that the language of their environment is
accessible to them. If the caregivers know and use sign language,
the deaf child will acquire a native knowledge of that sign language and will use it as naturally as a hearing child uses English.

How do children acquire their native language? This is a   4
question that has fascinated people for centuries. However, it is
only in the last forty years that the question has been a subject of
rigorous scientific investigation. In this chapter, we will first examine the goals and methods of developmental psycholinguistics,
the scientific study of language acquisition. In the next section, we
will examine some data—what English-speaking children and
their caregivers actually do and say during the first three or four
years of the language acquisition process. **Finally, in the last section, we will attempt to assess the adequacy of theories that
have attempted to account for child language acquisition.**

As you read this section, identify goals and methods and distinguish between them.

What goal? Check back for the meaning of this phrase.

2. Goals and Methods

Like all sciences, the study of language acquisition seeks to describe and then explain a natural phenomenon, in this case, how children go about the task of learning their native language. In order to advance toward **this goal**, language acquisition researchers, as do other scientists, construct hypotheses on the basis of theories. These hypotheses are then empirically tested against data obtained from experiments and observation. If hypotheses are not confirmed by experimental or observational data, then they are revised or discarded, and theories are modified.

In developmental psycholinguistics, as in all sciences, observing the phenomenon in natural or experimental settings and recording data are basic steps in the process of investigation. In recording the data, a high degree of accuracy is essential, of course. In addition, however, scientific researchers must obtain representative data, in this case an adequate sample of the language of young children. In other words, the sample must be large enough for scientists to feel confident that they are observing what children in general do as they learn their first language and not merely what, for example, two or three American middle-class children of well-educated parents do. Failing to ensure **accuracy and representativeness in our observations** will automatically call into question the validity of the entire scientific investigation.

Are these new or repeated ideas? Do they help you with the main idea of the paragraph?

Because of the complexity of their subject, language acquisition researchers frequently adopt a narrow approach to their task. They typically focus on a narrow range of linguistic phenomena within one of **the main components of language.** In phonology, for example, they may examine the development of a small number of sounds in children's emerging English; in syntax, they may investigate the way a small number of children first begin to ask questions and how their formulation of questions changes over time; in morphology, they may conduct experiments that measure a child's ability to produce certain word-endings (e.g., plural *-s* or past tense *-ed*) at a given moment in his or her development; in semantics, they may look at how a child's comprehension of certain words develops.

Quickly look forward to identify where the writer mentions these "components." Then come back to this sentence, and continue reading the paragraph.

3. The Data

Any comprehensive treatment of child language acquisition would involve looking at data on a child's *phonological, grammatical,* and *semantic* development as well as at the

Check this paragraph for information about what to expect in the following pages. Then quickly look forward to confirm your predictions.

60 65 70 75 80 85 90 95

5 6 7 8

speech of caregivers. However, this brief introduction to the field will limit itself to examining data on children's acquisition of English grammar and on caregiver speech. This is justifiable because the learning strategies visible in children's emerging grammar also play an important role in their phonological and semantic development. It is likely that they are also universal strategies of first language acquisition.

Children's English and the Development of Grammar

The grammar of children's English first starts to become evident when they are able to produce utterances consisting of two words. Consider the examples in Table 1. For clarity, the examples are in normal English spelling. This gives a false impression of their phonological competence. It should be remembered that the children's pronunciation is still developing. For example, "Katie crying" is pronounced [deedee dying] and "Michael sleep" is pronounced [mabil deep].

Quickly look forward in the text. Identify and mark where the writer introduces these characteristics. Then come back to this sentence, and continue reading.

From these examples, which are similar to the two-word utterances documented by other researchers, a number of the typical characteristics of child grammar are evident. First, the utterances are clearly and significantly different from what the children could have heard. The children are therefore producing new utterances. It is in this sense that we can begin to use the term *creative* in order to describe child language.

Simplicity is another characteristic of child language. The utterances in Table 1 are all simpler in a number of ways than the equivalent utterances in adult English. For one thing, they are shorter. **They all consist of a noun combined with another type of word: noun + adjective (1–3), noun subject + verb (4–8), possessive noun + possessed noun (9), adjective + noun (10), and verb + noun (11).**

Look at Table 1, and find examples to support the writer's claims.

The children have simplified the grammar of English also by omitting or avoiding certain elements of the equivalent utterances in mature English. Consider the type of words represented in Table 1. They are nouns, verbs, and adjectives—words that refer to persons, animals, objects, actions, quantities, and qualities. **There is a clear absence of words in other grammatical categories, like *a* or *the*, *to* or *in*, *he*, *she*, or *I*, words that are part of the grammatical system of English.** It is inconceivable that these high frequency words do not occur in the caretaker language to which the children would be exposed. Yet they are conspicuously absent from the English of these children.

Again, look at Table 1 to identify evidence for the writer's claims.

9

10

11

12

Study this table for a minute or so. Identify differences between the children's English and the adult equivalent.

Table 1. Utterances of two children at twenty-four months. (Pakenham, 1991)

Child's English	Adult Equivalent
1. Dada wet	Daddy is wet.
2. Dada dry	Daddy is dry.
3. Mama pretty	Mommy is pretty.
4. Mama help	Mommy, help me.
5. Katie do	Let me (Katie) do it.
6. Katie dying	Katie is crying
7. Michael night-night	I (Michael) want to go to bed.
8. Michael sleep	Michael is sleeping.
9. Michael book	(That is) Michael's book.
10. more juice	(Give me) More Juice.
11. bye-bye car	Are we going/I want to go for a drive in the car.

What is this property? Be sure to look for it as you continue reading the paragraph.

    A third important property of child language only be- 13 **comes evident when we consider what children do *not* say.** To express the same ideas as those contained in Table 1, for exam-
140 ple, neither of the children were ever heard to say

    *help Mama
    *do Katie
    *night-night Michael
    *sleep Michael
145   *book Michael
    *juice more
    *car bye-bye

The total absence of such examples, in which the word order is reversed, draws our attention to the consistent word order used by
150 children at this stage. Their correct use of adult word order suggests that they have learned two fundamental facts about English grammar: Word order is crucial for communication in English, and the basic pattern is a sequence of subject and verb.
    Children's developing competence becomes even clearer when 14
155 children leave the two-word utterance stage. They begin to add more words (or parts of words) and to combine utterances they have produced at an earlier stage. Consider the examples listed in Table 2. **In these utterances, the speakers are obviously producing grammatically more complex and sophisticated pat-**
160 **terns of English than they were producing initially.**

Here the writer expects you to find examples of the increasing complexity of the children's language. Compare Tables 1 and 2.

Table 2. Utterances of two children at thirty months. (Pakenham, 1991)

Child's English	Adult Equivalent
1. bye-bye white car	Let's go for a drive in the white car.
2. Dada work white car	Is Daddy going to work in the white car?
3. Katie crying	Katie is crying.
4. Michael no night-night	I (Michael) don't want to go to bed

Look for examples of this phenomenon in the conversation below.

The errors that children produce in their utterances can also   15
show that they are able to construct and use grammatical rules
without direct teaching. The following example (Cazden, 1972:92)
shows **a child extending the rule for regular past-tense verbs**
165 **to an irregular verb:**

> Child: My teacher holded the baby rabbits and we patted them.
> Adult: Did you say your teacher held the baby rabbits?
> Child: Yes.
> Adult: What did you say she did?
> 170 Child: She holded the baby rabbits and we patted them.
> Adult: Did you say she held them tightly?
> Child: No, she holded them loosely.

These and many other similar utterances documented in the literature show the phenomenon of overgeneralization, where a child
175 clearly applies a rule he or she has constructed to a case where it is
not applicable. Significantly, the child also persists in the overgeneralization despite feedback from the adult that contains the
correct form.

Caregiver Language

A large number of researchers have investigated the type of   16
180 language used by caregivers, especially mothers, in their interactions with infants and young children. **The empirical evidence
provided by this research has clearly established that child-
directed language (CDS), the language used by caregivers
with their children, has properties that make it significantly
185 different from the type of language they use with adults.**

Quickly identify and mark where the writer introduces these differences. Then come back, and continue reading the next paragraph.

In textbooks and research writing, writers often make some general claims and then support them by citing the findings of specific research studies.

Caregivers simplify their speech in a number of ways.   17
They pronounce sounds more clearly. Malsheen (1980) found that
caregivers made their pronunciation of vowels and consonants temporarily more precise and distinct when they were talking with
190 children in the one-word stage of language learning. For infants
and for linguistically more advanced children, however, the pro-

What feature of children's English is the basis for this humorous situation? (Glenn Bernhardt. Reprinted by permission.)

"No, Jimmy, it's not 'I sawed a chair'— it's 'I have seen a chair' or 'I saw a chair'."

1. *First identify and count each general claim.*
2. *Then identify the research findings that support each claim.*
3. *Use the specific research examples to help you understand the claims.*

nunciation was similar to that used with adults. Caregivers also repeat words they might not normally repeat. Newport (1975), for example, found that caregivers tended to repeat important nouns [195] rather than replace them with pronouns. They speak about topics directly related to the physical setting of the interaction. Many studies (e.g., Cross, 1977; Snow, 1972) have documented the tendency of the caregiver to focus on the "here and now" in conversations with young children and to label relevant objects (Tomasello [200] & Farrar, 1986) while they are performing some task such as dressing or washing the child. Caregivers also avoid words and grammatical forms perceived to be beyond the child's capacity to comprehend. Some studies (e.g., Anglin, 1977; Mervis & Mervis, 1982) have shown that caregivers may select more appropriate vocabu- [205] lary, based on their assessment of their child's linguistic level. Sachs (1983) suggests that caretakers may avoid the use of the past tense in their speech until they feel that the child is ready for it.

In other respects, however, CDS is similar to natural speech [18] directed toward adults. In responding to children's utterances, [210] caregivers do not directly correct any phonological or grammatical errors in children's speech. The only natural corrections seem to occur when a child has mislabeled an object or concept such as in the following example:

Child: (pointing to sun) Moon!
215   Adult: Well, no. That's the sun. But it looks a bit like the moon,
doesn't it?

Research has also found that caregivers may expand chil- 19
dren's utterances as often as 30 percent of the time. Such expansion is not a normal feature of speech directed towards adults; nor,
220   significantly, does it seem to help children acquire language (Cazden, 1972). However, what follows it in CDS is clearly typical of
adult-adult interaction. With or without expansion, caregivers almost invariably treat the child's utterance as one component of a
genuine conversation and respond naturally to its perceived mean-

*Look for the writer's
two claims here about
caregiver reaction.
Then look for evidence
in the example to sup-
port them.*

225   ing. **The following example illustrates these two common
types of caregiver reaction.**

Child: Water, Dada. [wawa dada]
Adult: Oh, you want some water, do you? OK, I'll get you some.

*Remember that this
section will assess the
adequacy of these the-
ories. Be ready to
identify where the
writer is explaining
the theories and where
the writer is assessing
their strengths or
weaknesses.*

4. Theories of Language Acquisition

For the purpose of this introduction, we will distinguish two 20
230   main types of formal theories that attempt to account for language
acquisition. The first and earlier of these types is the behaviorist
theory, often referred to as the imitation-reinforcement theory. It
claims that children imitate what they hear; when they say something that is correct, they receive a reward from the caregiver (e.g.,
235   they are understood and praised and perhaps the caregiver does
what they want). This reward reinforces the connection in the
child's mind between his or her utterance and the situation for
which it was appropriate and increases the likelihood that the
child will use this correct example of language again. Conversely,
240   when children say something incorrect, they receive a correction
and no reward. The lack of reward makes it less likely that the
child will use the incorrect example of language again.

*Will this paragraph
deal with the
strengths or weak-
nesses of the theory?
Test your hypothesis
as you continue to
read the paragraph.*

**It seems clear that imitation and reinforcement are fac- 21
tors to some extent in language acquisition.** Imitation explains
245   why children brought up in an English-speaking environment
learn to speak English and not some other language as their native
language, why Japanese children acquire Japanese, and so on. It
also explains why, for example, an English-speaking child from
Britain will speak with a British accent while a child from the
250   United States will have an American accent. Reinforcement also
plays a role, but probably a more limited one than behaviorist researchers once thought. It is fairly well established, for example,

that children will attempt to change an utterance—to the extent that they can change it—if the caregiver clearly does not understand their original utterance.

255

Quickly look forward through the text. Identify and mark where the writer introduces each flaw in the theory. Then come back, and continue reading this paragraph.

There are, however, a number of major flaws in the imitation-reinforcement theory, shortcomings that are serious enough to destroy its claim to be an adequate account of how a first language is acquired. First, countless examples of early child language, including those presented previously in this chapter and below, show that children are not good imitators; their early language, especially in its pronunciation and grammar, is very different from the adult version. **They are, however, wonderful creators of novel language forms, forms they have never heard in their linguistic environment.** Imitation as a language acquisition strategy cannot adequately account for children's novel utterances. 22

260

Look back and look forward in the text for evidence to support this claim.

265

Second, the creativity and originality evident in the forms of child language is not random. In fact, as we have pointed out earlier, it is systematic and governed by rules. However, there is nothing in the imitation-reinforcement theory that can account for the **rule-governed creativity** that is to be found in the utterances produced by young children. 23

270

This is not an easy concept. Do what a good English reader would do: check back in an earlier section for concrete examples of rule-governed creativity.

275

Third, empirical research has not confirmed the assumption that reinforcement plays the central role in language acquisition that behaviorist theories claim. From the observation of child-caregiver interaction, it is clear that caregivers rarely attempt to correct children's pronunciation and grammar. When such corrections do occur, **as in the following example,** (Braine, 1971:161) they are usually an informal experiment, an attempt by the caregiver to observe the child's reactions. As deliberate language-teaching lessons using the techniques of correction and imitation, these attempts invariably end in failure and, perhaps, frustration. 24

Examine the example closely. How is the writer justified in referring to this conversation as a language lesson that fails?

280

Child: Want other one spoon, Daddy.
285   Father: You mean you want "the other spoon."
Child: Yes, I want other one spoon, please, Daddy.
Father: Can you say "The other spoon"?
Child: Other . . . one . . . spoon.
Father: Say "other."
290   Child: Other.
Father: "Spoon."
Child: Spoon.
Father: "Other . . . spoon"
Child: Other . . . spoon. Now give me other one spoon?

What theory? If necessary, check back to refresh your memory.

295

The theory, because it stresses the role of reinforcement, also 25 has a problem accounting for the fact that children's grammar and phonology continue to develop. Even though children's English is far from perfect, caregivers understand it and react positively to it. According to the theory, **successful outcomes like these** should reinforce children's use of incorrect English and cause them to stop trying to perfect their pronunciation and grammar. Yet the halt in linguistic development predicted by the theory does not occur. Instead, children go on changing their language and, as they do, their English increasingly resembles the English of their environment.

How are these outcomes successful? Check back for the meaning of this phrase.

In this brief introduction, we will not attempt to distinguish between the four or more competing theories that are better equipped to account for language acquisition. **We will refer to them as creative construction theories.**

Since these theories are better, look for their strengths as you read the following paragraphs.

Each of these theories argues that the ability to acquire language is innate and biologically programmed in human beings. This innateness assumption, as it is called, explains why language, under normal circumstances, emerges at more or less the same time in all children. **It also explains why all children, despite vast differences in their living and learning conditions, attain a fairly uniform level of ability in their spoken language during those first five years of life.**

Notice that the paragraph both describes and assesses an aspect of the theory. The same pattern of organization may occur again.

Creative construction theories also believe that children themselves contribute greatly to the language acquisition process. They look for patterns in the language they hear; then they formulate rules that they subsequently apply to produce utterances. The assumption that children make such a contribution accounts for much of the language acquisition data left unexplained by the imitation-reinforcement theory. It explains children's creativity: their use of forms that they have never heard in mature English. It also explains the errors of overgeneralization that occur: for example, the use of the -*ed* ending for the past tense of irregular English verbs, which we have already seen.

Creative construction theories, therefore, are generally much more adequate accounts of language acquisition than the imitation-reinforcement theory. **However,** there are many crucial questions still to be answered before a fully adequate theory of language acquisition can be developed. Some of the questions concern what the child contributes to the acquisition process. For example, what does the innate capacity of the human mind to learn language consist of? Is it a capacity that is specifically and exclusively designed to process language? Or is it part of the same process of

Pay attention to this word when you think about the main idea of this paragraph.

300

305

310

315

320

325

330

335

26

27

28

29

340 cognitive development that allows us to remember, think, understand concepts, and solve problems? Other questions focus on the contribution of the environment. For example, are there any normal caregiver behaviors that can help or hinder language acquisition?

30 At present, language acquisition research is offering conflicting answers to such questions. At the same time, as more research 345 is conducted all over the world, evidence is accumulating that the language produced by children has a great deal of individual variation, more than many researchers previously assumed. Thus, in addition to the other unanswered questions, research now has to account for the differences that appear to exist between individual 350 children. It is clear, therefore, that despite the progress we have made until now, much of the process of first language acquisition remains a mystery to us.

References

Anglin, J. 1977. *Word, object, and conceptual development*. New York: Norton.

Braine, M. D. S. 1971. The acquisition of language in infant and child. In C. E. Reed (Ed.), *The learning of language*. New York: Appleton-Century-Crofts.

Cazden, C. 1972. *Child language and education*. New York: Holt, Rinehart and Winston.

Cross, T. G. 1977. Mothers' speech adjustments: The contributions of selected child listener variables. In C. Ferguson and C. Snow (Eds.), *Talking to children: Language input and acquisition*. Cambridge: Cambridge University Press.

Malsheen, B. 1980. Two hypotheses for phonetic clarification in the speech of mothers to children. In G. Yeni-Komshian, J. S. Kavanagh, and C. A. Ferguson (Eds.), *Child phonology: vol. 2. Perception*. New York: Academic Press.

Mervis, C. B., and Mervis, C. A. 1982. Leopards are kitty-cats: Object labelling by mothers for their thirteen-month-olds. *Child Development*, 53, 258–266.

Newport, E. L. 1975. *Motherese: The speech of mothers to young children*. Technical Report No. 52. San Diego: Center for Human Information Processing, University of California.

Pakenham, K. J. 1991. Personal data collection.

Sachs, J. 1983. Talking about then and there: The emergence of displaced reference in parent-child discourse. In K. Nelson (Ed.), *Children's language*. New York: Gardner Press.

Snow, C. 1972. Mothers' speech to children learning language. *Child Development*, 43, 549–565.

Tomasello, M., and Farrar, M. J. 1986. Joint attention and early language. *Child Development*, 57, 1454–1463.

WORKING WITH THE MAIN READING

1. INTRODUCTION

Main Idea Check

Here are the main ideas for the introduction. Write the correct paragraph number beside its main idea.

_____ Access to the language used in their environment will ensure that all normal children, regardless of differences in such factors as intellect or social and economic background, will successfully learn the language of that environment.

_____ Children's acquisition of their native language during their first five years of life is an impressive achievement.

_____ This chapter will examine psycholinguistic research into how children acquire their native language.

_____ The fact that first language acquisition occurs without the help of formal teaching makes it an even more impressive achievement.

A Closer Look

1. Children have learned the sounds of their native language by about the age of five. T F

2. Acquiring the spoken language means that people will also learn how to produce and understand the written version of that language. T F

3. What fact or facts does the writer report about the linguistic interaction between children and their caregivers?
   a. Parents do not need to correct their children's language because it contains no errors.
   b. Parents ignore grammar and pronunciation errors in their children's language.
   c. Parents involve children in natural communication.

4. In the United States, a deaf child is born to deaf parents who communicate with American Sign Language. What language will the child learn as his or her native language?
   a. American Sign Language

            b. English
            c. No language

     5. Find a definition for *developmental psycholinguistics*.

Vocabulary in Context

Here are some words from this section that you may not have known. You either guessed their meaning from context or from your knowledge of word families, or you omitted the word and were still able to understand the sentence. Now check and learn the meanings of the words. Use your dictionary to help you.

favorable (line 7)	deaf (line 43)
apparently (line 14)	to fascinate (line 49)
peers (line 29)	rigorous (line 51)
intellectual (line 40)	

2. GOALS AND METHODS

Main Idea Check

Here are the main ideas for this section of the chapter. Write the correct paragraph number beside its main idea.

_____ Ensuring that the data are accurate and representative is essential in child language acquisition research.

_____ Because of the complexity of language and human behavior, research projects in developmental psycholinguistics usually concentrate on one small aspect of language acquisition.

_____ Developmental psycholinguistics seeks to account for language acquisition through a process of developing hypotheses and theories and subjecting them to empirical testing.

A Closer Look

1. The following diagram represents the process described in paragraph 5. Choose from the list below the correct step in the process. Write only the correct letter in each box.

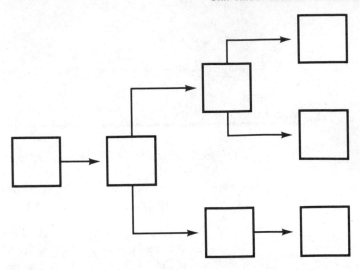

a. The hypothesis is not rejected; the researcher continues to develop the theory without modifications.
b. The hypothesis is revised or discarded.
c. The researcher constructs a hypothesis based on a theory.
d. The data supports the hypothesis.
e. The theory is modified.
f. The researcher tests the hypothesis against experimental or observational data.
g. The data does not support the hypothesis.

2. It is valid to make conclusions about language acquisition in general from research studying the language development of individual American middle-class children.   T   F

3. A typical research project in language acquisition will examine the development of pronunciation, grammar, and meaning in large numbers of children.   T   F

Vocabulary in Context

Here are some words from section 2 that you may not have known. You either guessed their meaning from context or from your knowledge of word families, or you omitted the word and were still able to understand the sentence. Now check and learn the meanings of the words. Use your dictionary to help you.

to obtain (line 65)   to ensure (line 78)
to discard (line 67)   approach (line 82)
confident (line 75)   formulation (line 88)

3. THE DATA (Children's English and the Development of Grammar)

Main Idea Check

Here are the main ideas for this section of the chapter. Write the correct paragraph number beside its main idea.

_____ Children's English shows that they realize early that word order is important.

_____ Children's English is simpler than adult English because they omit grammatical words and concentrate on content words.

_____ Children's developing grammar is first visible when they start producing two-word utterances.

_____ Children's errors of overgeneralization show that they develop and apply grammatical rules.

_____ Children's English is simpler because their utterances are shorter than the adult equivalents.

_____ This chapter will be restricted to an examination of caregiver speech and grammatical aspects of child language.

_____ As children's utterances become longer, the development of their grammar becomes more obvious.

_____ The data show that children produce original utterances that they could not have heard before.

A Closer Look

1. This new section considers data from all aspects of child language acquisition.   T F

2. The children producing the utterances in Table 1 have no trouble pronouncing them correctly.   T F

3. According to the writer, the grammatical characteristics of the child language data in Table 1 are generally representative of children's English.   T F

4. What qualities of the grammar of children's English does the writer mention and exemplify?

a. its originality
b. its increasing complexity as children grow older
c. its close similarity to adult grammar
d. its relative simplicity
e. its random omission of words
f. the emergence of patterns of word order at an early stage
g. its tendency to overgeneralize
h. its early use of words that are the most frequently used in mature English

5. Construct a definition for the phenomenon of *overgeneralization*.

6. What is the significance of overgeneralization in children's English?
   a. It shows that children have the capacity to create grammatical rules.
   b. It shows that children learn grammar by imitating and memorizing what they hear.
   c It shows that children need grammar classes in order to learn their native language.

Vocabulary in Context

Here are some words from this section that you may not have known. You either guessed their meaning from context or from your knowledge of word families, or you omitted the word and were still able to understand the sentence. Now check and learn the meanings of the words. Use your dictionary to help you.

sense (line 117)	property (line 137)
equivalent (line 121)	to reverse (line 149)
inconceivable (line 133)	applicable (line 176)
yet (line 135)	feedback (line 177)

3. THE DATA (Caregiver Language)

Main Idea Check

Here are the main ideas for this section of the chapter. Write the correct paragraph number beside its main idea.

_____ Caregivers seem only to correct vocabulary mistakes in children's English, not mistakes in grammar or pronunciation.

_____ The language caregivers use in interactions with young children is different from the language they use with adults.

_____ Caregivers always react to children's speech as a natural attempt to communicate.

_____ CDS is simpler than normal adult speech in a number of ways.

A Closer Look

1. Caregivers try to simplify their own speech when addressing young children.   T F

2. The pronunciation of CDS is always clearer and more precise than the pronunciation of speech directed toward adults.   T F

3. What characteristics of CDS does the writer mention?
   a. the use of pronouns to avoid repeating nouns
   b. a focus on elements of the situation in which the interaction is taking place
   c. the expansion of children's utterances
   d. frequent attempts to correct children's pronunciation and grammar
   e. a tendency to choose words and grammar felt to be appropriate for the child's linguistic level
   f. attempts by the caregiver to teach grammar to the child
   g. the integration by the caregiver of children's utterances into natural conversations

4. CDS bears no resemblance to the speech adults use with other adults.   T F

Vocabulary in Context

Here are some words from this section that you may not have known. You either guessed their meaning from context or from your knowledge of word families, or you omitted the word and were still able to understand the sentence. Now check and learn the meanings of the words. Use your dictionary to help you.

beyond (someone's capacity (line 202)   invariably (line 223)

4. THEORIES OF LANGUAGE ACQUISITION

Main Idea Check

Here are the main ideas for this section of the chapter. Write the correct paragraph number beside its main idea. The section has been divided into two parts. Can you identify the basis for the division?

1. Paragraphs 20–25

_____ The imitation-reinforcement theory makes the false prediction that children will stop developing their grammar and pronunciation before they reach adult standards.

_____ Because children are clearly not good imitators, the theory's reliance on imitation is one of its weaknesses.

_____ One theory of language acquisition believes that the processes of imitation and reinforcement are crucial for learning your first language.

_____ The imitation-reinforcement theory cannot account for the fact that children's language shows originality and regularity.

_____ Imitation and reinforcement play some role in language acquisition.

_____ Reinforcement, in the form of correction, is too rare an occurrence to be a major factor in child language acquisition.

2. Paragraphs 26–30

_____ There still remains a great deal to be understood about the process of language acquisition.

_____ Although they are more adequate than the imitation-reinforcement theory, creative construction theories still leave many important questions unanswered.

_____ By arguing that children are born with the ability to formulate linguistic rules, creative construction theories can explain both the originality and the regularities in children's language.

_____ Creative construction theories are better able to account for language acquisition phenomena than the imitation-reinforcement theory is.

_____ By assuming that the ability to acquire language is innate in humans, creative construction theories can account for universal features of language acquisition.

A Closer Look

1. The diagram below is intended to describe the process of language acquisition as it is viewed by proponents of reinforcement-imitation theories. Complete the diagram with the appropriate ideas from the following list. Write only the correct letter in each box.
   a. The caregiver corrects the child or does not reward the child.
   b. The child produces an utterance by imitating adult language.
   c. The utterance is incorrect.

d. The reward increases the likelihood that the child will produce similar correct utterances.

e. The child is rewarded when the caregiver understands and perhaps praises the child or does what the child wants.

f. The utterance is correct.

g. The lack of reward reduces the probability that the child will use the incorrect utterance again.

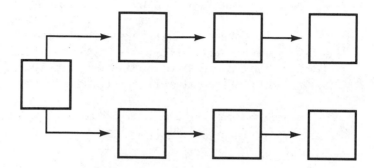

2. According to the writer, imitation and reinforcement play some role in child language acquisition.　　　　　　　　　　　　　　　T　F

3. What weakness or weaknesses of the imitation-reinforcement theory does the writer mention?
   a. It cannot explain why a child's utterances have their own original organization.
   b. It cannot explain the random quality of child language.
   c. It places too much emphasis on reinforcement and imitation.
   d. It makes at least one false prediction about language acquisition.
   e. It cannot explain why children acquire the accent used in the area where they are brought up.

4. Find two phenomena in child language that creative construction theories can account for better than other theories.

5. According to the writer, what issue or issues does language acquisition research need to address in the future?
   a. overgeneralization in child language
   b. the nature of our innate ability to acquire language
   c. individual variation in child language
   d. the impact of caregiver language on language acquisition
   e. the emergence of language in all children at approximately the same age

What Do You Think?

You are now an expert in early child language development. Imagine that the parents of a three-year-old child come to you. They are very concerned about the speech of their child. Here are some of the things they are worried about:

> Our daughter still can't pronounce many words correctly. For example, she says ["dand"] instead of *stand* and ["tar"] instead of *star;* ["wiver"] instead of *river.*
>
> She makes many mistakes in grammar—things like *foots* for *feet, going* for *is going* or *are going,* and *my belly hurt go away now.*
>
> We are worried because she doesn't seem to speak as well as other kids of her age. We try to correct her sometimes but we find we don't always have the time for that. Also neither of us were very good in grammar class in school. What should we do?

Talk this problem over with your colleagues in your group, and decide what advice you would give these parents.

Vocabulary in Context

Here are some words from section 4 that you may not have known. You either guessed their meaning from context or from your knowledge of word families, or you omitted the word and were still able to understand the sentence. Now check and learn the meanings of the words. Use your dictionary to help you.

reward (line 234)	flaw(s) (line 256)
to praise (line 235)	subsequent(ly) (line 321)
conversely (line 239)	to hinder (line 341)
to the extent that (line 253)	mystery (line 352)

Unit Four

Looking after Planet Earth

Text Study.
Recognizing Text Organization:
Problem and Solution

Read this example. The ideas in it will be familiar to you because, as well as being general knowledge today, they were discussed in Unit 1.

> The cheapest and most effective solution to the problem of heart disease is for people to start taking more responsibility for maintaining their own health. They can do this by developing healthier eating habits, by taking more exercise, by reducing stress in their lives and by avoiding activities, e.g., smoking, that clearly increase the risk of a heart attack.

In these two sentences, the writer clearly introduces a problem (*heart disease*), describes a general solution to the problem (*people taking more responsibility for staying healthy*), and describes four specific components of this general solution.

Writers often use the same type of *problem-solution* organization for longer texts—for paragraphs, for groups of paragraphs, for sections in an article, or for an entire article. If you can identify the problem-solution method of organization when you meet it, you will be able to read more efficiently and more effectively.

EXPLANATION: MARKERS OF PROBLEM-SOLUTION ORGANIZATION

Often you will know if something is a problem just by using your common sense. However, writers may also use vocabulary that will make it more obvious to you that you are reading about a problem or about a solution to the problem. We call this vocabulary *problem-solution markers*.

The following list is not complete. We could expand it by adding a large number of negative or positive adjectives. However, the list contains the most common problem-solution markers. Read through it, and make sure you know all the words and expressions.

Describing Problems

problem	puzzle	burden
difficulty	mystery	complication
crisis	risk	concern
challenge	danger	issue
obstacle	threat	dispute
dilemma		

Describing Solutions

to solve	to relieve	to overcome
to resolve	to ease	to address
to respond	to benefit	to tackle
to remedy	to settle	to deal with
to improve		

READING STRATEGIES

1. Scan for (A) problem markers and (B) solution markers.

2. Use A to identify passages containing problems.

3. Use B to identify passages containing solutions.

4. Look for causes of problems.

5. Look for the logical connection between the problem's cause(s) and the suggested solution(s).

EXERCISE

Practice the five strategies while you read these short texts. Identify the problem and solution markers. Then identify the problems and their solutions.

1. Culture shock has been described as a problem afflicting people who find themselves living in a culture not their own. Its effects can range from mild feelings of homesickness to severe depression and disorientation that can leave a person incapable of coping with even the minor demands of life. The two basic remedies for culture shock are interest in the new culture and time. Provided that we are interested in adjusting to a new culture, time gives us the

opportunity to make contacts in it. From our contacts, we gain knowledge of the culture and make friends with people in it. From our friends and newly acquired knowledge, we gain an understanding and appreciation of the culture. At some stage in this process, the symptoms of culture shock disappear.

2. According to some experts, the irresponsible behavior of insurance companies was a major contributor to the rapidly rising costs of U.S. health care in the 1980s and early 1990s, costs that threatened business and public alike. To increase their profits, insurance companies increasingly refused to pay for all preexisting medical conditions and denied insurance to people with a higher risk of developing disease. These people, however, were often still able to obtain treatment from hospitals, who cover their losses by increasing costs for insured patients.

   For these experts, therefore, one component of a comprehensive response to rising health-care costs was for the U.S. government to force insurance companies to provide health-insurance coverage to all who need it and for all conditions, preexisting and new. An alternative was for the government to follow the example of Sweden, Canada, and other countries and adopt a system of national health insurance funded by a federal health tax.

3. The number of unmarried teenage girls who become pregnant and have babies has reached crisis level in contemporary American society. These young, unmarried mothers fail to complete school. With few marketable skills, they cannot find employment that will allow them to support themselves and their children. They become dependent on government welfare, often permanently.

   In an attempt to address the problems associated with teenage pregnancy and motherhood, some progressive school districts have established special schools. The schools provide regular health clinics for the expectant mothers and for the children. They also offer free day care for the children, which allows the mothers to continue to attend classes until graduation. The students also work in the school's day care center, where they gain more experience in and knowledge of how to care for children. The success of such programs can be measured in their high graduation rates and in their low rates of repeat pregnancies. In one such program in New Mexico, only 9 percent of the girls become pregnant again within two years; outside such programs, the rate is a depressing 80 percent.

Sometimes a writer's problem-solution organization will extend across a larger number of paragraphs. For practice in reading texts like this, go back and re-read paragraphs 18–21 in the Main Reading in Unit 2. After you read each paragraph, scan forward through paragraphs 23–27, and identify where the same problem is again discussed. You will find four pairs of matched paragraphs. Identify problems and solutions for each pair of paragraphs.

Background Reading and Vocabulary Development

READING PASSAGE 4.1

The Aral Sea: An Environmental Crisis*

In what part of an introduction are you likely to find the most help about the topic of the passage? Pay special attention to that part.

For many decades, environmental scientists have been warning us that immense damage can be caused to the ecology of a given region by pressure for economic development and by apparently reasonable, but in reality short-sighted, responses to this pressure. The damage will not only negate any economic progress the region might have experienced but also has the potential to make the region unlivable. The story of the Aral Sea, described in an article in *Environment* magazine by V. M. Kotlyakov, a Soviet geographer, is a clear example of **the damage that poorly planned human economic activity can have on the environment.** 1

As you read the article, identify the environmental damage and the poorly planned human economic activity *that may cause it.*

The Aral Sea is located in a semi-arid region of south-central Asia, close to the former Soviet republics of Karakalpakia, Kazakhstan, Uzbekistan, Turkmenia, and Tajikistan (see Figure 1). As recently as the 1950s, the sea covered an area of sixty-six thousand square kilometers, with a mean depth of sixteen meters. Its waters were fresh, with a mean salinity (salt content) of 1 percent to 1.1 percent. Two large rivers, the Amu Darya and the Syr 2

*Adapted from V. M. Kotlyakov, "The Aral Sea Basin: A Critical Environmental Zone." *Environment* 33.1 (1991), pp. 4–38. Reprinted with permission of the Helen Dwight Reid Educational Foundation. Published by Heldref Publications, 1319 Eighteenth St., N.W., Washington, D.C. 20036–1802. Copyright © 1991.

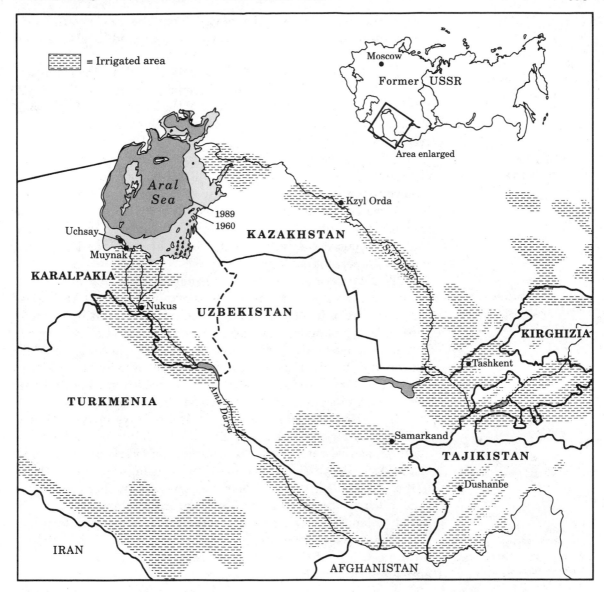

Figure 1. This map of the Aral Sea basin shows some of the changes between 1960 and 1989 brought about by the decision to divert huge quantities of water from the region's rivers for irrigation purposes. Especially noteworthy are the changes in the coastline of the sea. (*Source: National Geographic*, Feb. 1990.)

This is a "before" description of the Aral Sea. As you read the article, look for the "after" description, and identify the changes.

Darya, flow into the sea. **The water from the two rivers, plus the annual rainfall, maintained the volume and level of water in the sea.**

By 1990, however, the Aral Sea had shrunk to about 55 percent of its original area and had become two separate lakes; its total water volume had dropped to less than one-third of its 1950s volume. The salt content of the sea, on the other hand, had increased by almost 300 percent.

Draw simple cause-effect diagrams as you read.

The root cause of these massive changes in the physical character of the Aral Sea was the decision, made in the late 1950s, to develop agriculture by using water from the Amu Darya and the Syr Darya rivers for irrigation. Since the early 1960s, the area of irrigated agricultural land has expanded rapidly, an expansion that has reduced the flow of water into the Aral Sea to approximately 13 percent of its pre-1960 total.

Continue using simple cause-effect diagrams to help you understand the details.

The consequences of this reduction in water flow have been catastrophic for the area surrounding the Aral Sea. Whole species of fish have died out, and commercial fishing, which used to be a productive economic activity, has practically stopped. Without the moderating influence of the vast expanse of the original sea, the climate of the territory within one hundred to two hundred kilometers of the sea has become more extreme. Rainfall has decreased, while summers have become shorter and warmer. As a result, there are no longer enough frost-free days in the year for growing cotton, once the main crop of the Amu Darya delta. In addition, as the water level has dropped, the forests on either side of the Amu Darya river have dried up, causing the loss of about half of the region's bird and mammal species. Another problem is that salt from the exposed sea bed is spread by storms on the surrounding land, increasing its salt content and reducing its fertility.

Use the continued ideas in this sentence to clarify the general idea of Paragraph 5.

The impact of recent attempts at economic development on the ecology of the region, however, is not restricted to the consequences of the falling water levels in the Aral Sea and its two main rivers. Inefficient methods of irrigation allow much of the water to evaporate, causing crop-damaging salts to accumulate in the soil. Then farmers use more water to wash these salts out of the soil; the salts enter into the rivers where they ultimately increase the salinization of areas downstream and the Aral Sea itself. Other agricultural practices in the irrigated land include the extensive use of artificial fertilizers and chemical pesticides to support production of the two main crops, rice and cotton. As a result, the water that ultimately drains back into the Amu Darya and the

20

25

30

35

40

45

50

55

60

3

4

5

6

Syr Darya from the fields also carries high concentrations of phosphates and nitrates, as well as chemical pesticides.

The accumulation of these toxic chemicals in the rivers is now   7
contaminating local supplies of drinking water. As a result, in the
65   years since 1975, people living in the area have begun to suffer
increasingly from a number of serious health problems. As is often
the case with environmentally linked illness, infants and children
are the most vulnerable. In the city of Karalpakia, for example, the
1989 mortality rate for children was among the highest in the
70   world.

In 1990, a conference of international scientists met to con-   8
sider "the Aral crisis." The scientists concluded that the Aral region was already an ecological disaster area and that massive
changes in agricultural policy and practices were urgently needed
Check back for the   75   to reverse the process of environmental destruction. If **such mea-**
meaning of such mea-   **sures** were not taken without delay, the Aral basin would become
sures.   a wasteland, incapable of supporting the human settlements and
activities it once supported.

The case of the Aral Sea and its basin is not unique; it is   9
A technical term!   80   merely one example of the process of **anthropogenic desertifica-**
Look for a defini-   **tion,** the conversion of agricultural land to desert by environmen-
tion.   tally destructive human activities. This is a global problem. Indeed
the United Nations Environment Program estimates that about 60
percent of all agricultural land in drier regions may be affected to
85   some degree by desertification. Salinization, for example, threatens
20 percent of all irrigated land in the United States. The Aral
crisis, therefore, offers a clear warning of the dangers of poorly
planned economic development. It also offers an opportunity to
gather information needed in the search for solutions and alterna-
90   tive models of economic development.

Main Idea Check

Here are the main ideas for this passage. Write the correct paragraph number
beside its main idea.

_____ The basic cause of the deterioration in the Aral Sea was the use of irrigation to
expand agriculture.

_____ In 1990, a scientific conference decided that the Aral Sea region was an ecological disaster area in need of urgent action to prevent its complete destruction.

_____ This paragraph gives details of how the Aral Sea changed between 1950 and 1990.

_____ The story of the Aral Sea is one example of the global problem of desertification through human activities.

_____ The Aral Sea illustrates the massive ecological damage that can be caused by the careless economic development of a region.

_____ As a result of the chemical contamination of drinking water, there has been an increase in human health problems.

_____ This paragraph gives physical details of the Aral Sea in 1950.

_____ The reduced flow of water into the Aral Sea has had disastrous consequences both for the sea and its basin.

_____ Short-sighted agricultural practices have increased levels of salt, pesticides, and other damaging substances in the environment.

A Closer Look

1. The following diagram represents the process of environmental degradation in the region surrounding the Aral Sea. Reread the relevant paragraphs, and check your own cause-effect diagrams. Then complete the diagram with sentences from the list that follows. Write only the correct letter in each box.
   a. Commercial fishing is ruined.
   b. The region's human population, especially the young, suffer severe and widespread health problems.
   c. The volume of water flowing into the Aral Sea from its two main rivers is considerably reduced.
   d. The area experiences less rainfall and more frost.
   e. Entire species of fish in the sea die out.
   f. Agriculture uses large amounts of water from the Aral Sea's two main rivers for irrigation purposes.
   g. Toxic chemicals drain into the region's rivers.
   h. Traditional cotton growing is no longer possible.
   i. Because irrigation methods are inefficient, a large proportion of the water evaporates and leaves salt in the soil of the agricultural fields.
   j. The coastal forests surrounding the Aral Sea dry up.
   k. The region's drinking water is contaminated by toxic chemicals.

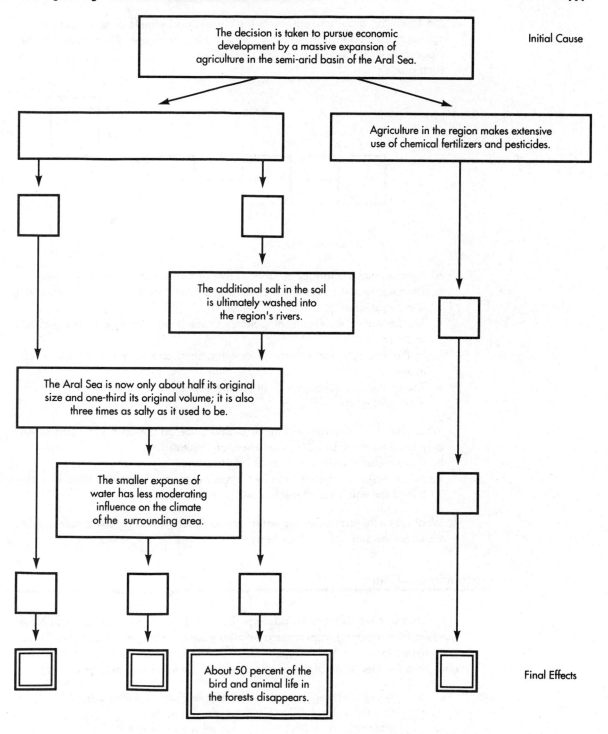

The decision is taken to pursue economic development by a massive expansion of agriculture in the semi-arid basin of the Aral Sea.

Initial Cause

Agriculture in the region makes extensive use of chemical fertilizers and pesticides.

The additional salt in the soil is ultimately washed into the region's rivers.

The Aral Sea is now only about half its original size and one-third its original volume; it is also three times as salty as it used to be.

The smaller expanse of water has less moderating influence on the climate of the surrounding area.

About 50 percent of the bird and animal life in the forests disappears.

Final Effects

2. The following diagram represents the causes and effects of ecological damage as described in paragraph 1. Reread the paragraph. Then complete the diagram with sentences from the list below. Write only the correct letter in each box.

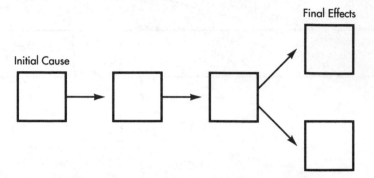

a. Humans may no longer be able to live or make a living in the region.
b. The people and government of the region feel that economic development is a major priority.
c. The economic development policies cause great damage to the region's ecology.
d. In the pressure for economic development, short-sighted decisions are taken.
e. The ecological damage will offset the economic advances that the region may have made.

3. What change or changes did the Aral Sea undergo between 1960 and 1990?
a. It became much smaller, shallower, and saltier.
b. It expanded rapidly because of irrigation.
c. No changes. The water from two large rivers and the annual rainfall maintained the volume and level of water in the sea.

4. What technical term does the writer use to describe the general process illustrated by the story of the Aral Sea?

Vocabulary in Context

Here are some words from the passage that you may not have known. You either guessed their meaning from context or from your knowledge of word families, or you omitted the word and were still able to understand the sentence. Now check and learn the meanings of the words. Use your dictionary to help you.

to negate (line 5)	inefficient/efficient (line 52)
shrunk/to shrink (line 22)	artificial (line 58)
practically (line 37)	mortality rate (line 69)
moderating/to moderate (line 38)	basin (line 79)

READING PASSAGE 4.2 _____

As you read the article, look for a connection between the three ideas in the title of the article.

Ecology, Overpopulation, and Development

Approximately ten thousand years ago, when the first permanent human settlements emerged after about 2 million years of hunter-gatherer society, the total population of the earth was only about 5 million people. It was the beginning of the nineteenth century before the population had increased to 1 billion. During this time, the human species had a negligible influence on the ecology of the planet as a whole.   1

This article has a two-paragraph introduction. Check in a likely place for helpful information about the topic of the article.

By the beginning of the twentieth century, however, the population stood at 2 billion. By 1950 it was 2.5 billion.[1] Then, in the next thirty years, it more than doubled to 5.2 billion. According to United Nations' projections, although the rate of population growth will fall in the future, the total population will continue to increase significantly and will reach 8.5 billion by 2025. The greatest proportion of this growth (95 percent) will be in less developed countries. Today, as a direct result of this population growth, the impact of human activities on the world's ecology is already substantial; in the future, it may be catastrophic.   2

Scan ahead to identify where you find information about these three levels of threat. Then come back, and continue reading.

Studies have shown that runaway population growth represents a massive threat to the environment on the local, national, and global levels. In areas of Nepal, for example, the pressure of overpopulation and poverty has forced farmers into the hills, where they cut down the vegetation to provide fuel for themselves, food for their animals, and land to raise crops. In a short time, the fertile topsoil is eroded by rain because it is now without the protection offered by the natural vegetation. The hillside fields become unproductive, incapable of supporting the people who have settled there.   3

Draw simple cause-effect diagrams while you read. They will help you understand and remember details.

Continue to draw simple cause-effect diagrams while you read.

Elsewhere 55 percent of the world's tropical forests have already disappeared.[2] **To provide employment and earn money from exports, Indonesia, Malaysia, and Thailand are cutting down their hardwood forests faster than they can replace these valuable national resources.** Central and South American countries, in a desperate attempt to relieve poverty and create economic growth, have permitted the destruction of vast areas of trop-   4

1. Figures from U.N. Population Division, *World Population Prospects 1990* (New York: United Nations, 1991).
2. E. O. Wilson, Threats to biodiversity, *Scientific American*, September 1989, p. 108.

Poor rural families like this one in Guatemala survive by clearing a plot of land in the tropical forests. They grow crops on the plot for a few years and then abandon it when the soil is eroded or loses its fertility. The population of this area of Guatemala has increased 2000 percent since 1950. (Kenneth Garrett)

35   ical rain forest for agricultural use. Ironically, because the destruc-
      tion of the forest has interrupted the natural cycle by which the
      soil receives nutrients from plant and animal life of the forest,
      much of the cleared land loses its fertility. After only a few years,
      it is no longer capable of supporting the farmers who have settled
40   on it.

          The destruction of tropical forests has consequences that cross   5
      national borders and are felt globally. First, the burning of the
      forests releases large amounts of carbon dioxide into the atmo-
      sphere and may contribute to a dangerous warming of the global
45   climate in the next fifty years. Second, as the forest vanishes, so
      too does its diverse plant and animal life. The human race is thus
      losing, along with the tropical forests, a vast amount of natural
      material with potential benefit to the world and a vast source of
      scientific knowledge.

50

Scan ahead to identify where another solution is described. Then come back, and continue to read.

55

60

Distinguish between repeated ideas and new ideas in this sentence. As you read the paragraph, look for an explanation of the new ideas.

75

80

85

Check back for this apparently simple solution.

Clearly, if action is not taken soon, the ecological damage   6
caused by overpopulation and unwise development threatens to
run out of control. **A partial solution to the crisis may lie in the
family-planning programs that have been operating in a
number of developing countries for some time.** In Indonesia,
for example, the family-planning program established a large
number of village centers that distribute free contraceptives and
information about family planning. The program has had considerable success. Since 1972, the fertility rate has fallen by almost 40
percent, and the number of couples practicing birth control has increased fiftyfold.[3] A reduction in the birthrate has also been experienced by other countries with family-planning programs, including
South Korea, Thailand, Mexico, and Tunisia.

Birth-control programs are a necessary component of an effec-   7
tive response to the potentially disastrous collision between the
needs of a growing population and the environment. They are not,
however, a sufficient response for at least one good reason. Since a
large proportion of the population of developing countries consists
of children below normal reproductive age, the world's population
is certain to increase when these children reach adulthood and begin having children. Even if birth control were accessible and acceptable to everyone and even if these people limited their family
size to two, both highly unlikely events in the near future, an increase of the world's population to around double its present total
is inevitable in the next thirty years.

**According to most experts, the second essential compo-   8
nent of a solution to the overpopulation-environment problem is social and economic development.** The history of the industrial world clearly shows that birthrates begin to fall when a
society offers the majority of its people an acceptably high standard
of living. Prosperity, better educational and career opportunities,
especially for women, adequate health care, and relative financial
security for people in their old age are probably all factors that
have contributed to the drop in the birthrate of industrial nations.
For this reason, most experts believe that the birthrates of the less
developed nations will decline as their populations experience the
benefits of economic development.

**The situation today, however, is more complex than this   9
apparently simple solution would suggest.** The first complication is that one essential component of the solution is also a cause

3. N. Keyfitz, The growing human population, *Scientific American*, September 1989,
   p. 124.

90   of the problem. Birthrates will not fall without economic development; however, most of the danger to the world's ecological systems comes directly from the attempts of nations to pursue economic development. A second complication is that developing nations
are now pursuing the same policies as those that brought pros-
95   perity to the industrial nations. In other words, they are continuing the tradition of exploiting the natural resources of the world
with little thought for the future. We need to remind ourselves, for
example, that Europeans, in the course of their history, have destroyed almost 80 percent of the forests that originally covered
100   their continent and 75 percent of the forests covering North America. Today North Americans and Europeans are asking the people
of developing nations to cease doing what they themselves have
been doing for centuries.

If one accepts that all countries have the right to pursue the   10
105   goal of economic development, **two conclusions are unavoidable.** First, the traditional development policies pursued by developing countries must be fundamentally revised. The policies now
in force will both exhaust those countries' own ecological resources
and cause serious, perhaps irreversible, damage to the world's ecol-
110   ogy. They are, in a word, unsustainable. Second, since unsustainable economic development is also a clear characteristic of the industrial world, it is the obligation of the leading industrial nations
to modify many of their own policies and practices so that they
support, not undermine, the global goal of sustainable develop-
115   ment.

Scan ahead to identify where the writer intro-duces each conclusion. Then come back, and continue reading.

Main Idea Check

Here are the main ideas for this passage. Write the correct paragraph number beside its main idea.

_____   The number of children already in the world's population means that birth control alone cannot be a solution to the problem of overpopulation.

_____   The disappearance of tropical forests, a result of countries' attempts at economic development, is causing great damage to the natural resources and the ecology of those countries.

_____   Policies for sustainable economic development must replace the traditional poli-cies of both developing and developed countries.

_____   Family-planning programs, which have proved successful in some developing countries, could contribute to the solution of the overpopulation problem.

_____ The destruction of the world's tropical forests will have negative consequences for the entire globe.

_____ However, economic development, which is the answer to the problem of overpopulation, is also traditionally the cause of massive damage to the environment.

_____ Up until ten thousand years ago, humans did not have a significant effect on the ecology of the earth.

_____ Locally, people respond to the pressures of overpopulation in ways that destroy the ecology of the areas they live in.

_____ Birthrates will only begin to fall when the less developed countries achieve an acceptably high standard of living for their populations through economic development.

_____ Because of the massive increase in population in the twentieth century, damage to the ecology from human activities is considerable and may become much worse.

A Closer Look

1. The following diagram represents the process of environmental degradation occurring specifically in Nepal. Reread the relevant section(s) of the passage. Then complete the diagram with sentences from the list below. Write only the correct letter in each box.

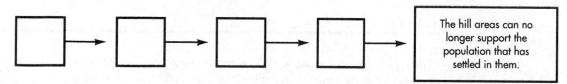

The hill areas can no longer support the population that has settled in them.

    a. The fertile topsoil is eroded by rain.
    b. The country is poor, and some areas are massively overpopulated.
    c. The soil's natural protection from erosion is removed.
    d. To support their families, farmers move into the hills, where they cut down the natural vegetation.

2. The following diagram represents the general process of environmental degradation described in this passage. Reread the relevant section(s) of the passage. Then complete the diagram with sentences from the list below. Write only the correct letter in each box.

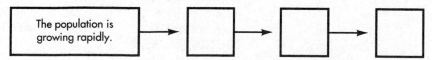

The population is growing rapidly.

    a. Countries traditionally follow policies that lead to unsustainable development.

    b. There is massive real and potential damage to the environment.

    c. Economic development is seen as the natural way to meet the needs of an expanding population.

3. What reason or reasons does the writer give for the claim that birth-control programs are only a partial solution to the overpopulation problem?

    a. It is unrealistic to imagine that birth control will be acceptable at present to all societies and cultures.

    b. It is unrealistic to expect that we can quickly make birth control freely available everywhere it is needed.

    c. The large proportion of children in the world's population guarantees a massive population increase in the future.

    d. Developing nations are becoming more prosperous, and as their people become wealthier, they can afford to have larger families.

4. What factor or factors does the writer see as contributing to a decline in a nation's birthrate?

    a. increasing prosperity

    b. poverty

    c. adequate health care

    d. financial security for the elderly

    e. economic development

5. Scan for an explanation of *unsustainable development*. Then write your own brief definition of this idea.

What Do You Think?

The writer does not make it clear exactly why economic and social development and a higher standard of living might bring about lower birthrates. In your opinion, how could this happen?

Vocabulary in Context

Here are some words from the passage that you may not have known. You either guessed their meaning from context or from your knowledge of word families, or you omitted the word and were still able to understand the sentence. Now check and learn the meanings of the words. Use your dictionary to help you.

runaway (line 18)	to release (line 43)
vegetation (line 22)	security (line 82)
tropical (line 28)	to undermine (line 114)
ironically (line 35)	

VOCABULARY PRACTICE

Same or Different?

Writers sometimes express the same ideas with very different grammar and vocabulary. This exercise will help you identify such occurrences.

Read the first sentence in each example carefully. Then read each of the two following sentences to decide whether they are the same or different in meaning to the first sentence. Choose *S* when the sentence expresses the same idea as the first sentence. Choose *D* when it expresses a different idea.

1. Lack of easy access to modern contraceptive methods is one of the problems facing family-planning programs in developing countries.

   a. One of the problems that has to be solved by programs to reduce the birthrate in developing countries is that modern methods of birth control are not readily available to people.   S D

   b. The work of family-planning programs in developing countries is made difficult by, among other things, the unavailability of modern methods of birth control.   S D

2. By 1990, commercial fishing in the Aral Sea had practically ceased because whole species of fish had died out.

   a. In the period up to 1990, entire varieties of fish vanished from the Aral Sea; this brought commercial fishing to an almost complete halt.   S D

   b. Up to 1990, there was a substantial expansion in commercial fishing in the Aral Sea because of the disappearance of certain types of fish.   S D

3. As a result of the 45 percent reduction in area of the Aral Sea, the climate of the region has undergone substantial changes.

   a. The climatic changes that have occurred in the region because the Aral Sea has become 45 percent smaller have been negligible.   S D

   b. Weather patterns in the region have changed significantly as a direct result of the Aral Sea's shrinking to 55 percent of its former area.   S D

4. We must relieve the pressure caused by poverty and inadequate health care before people in developing countries will be willing to listen to contraceptive advice.

    a. People in developing countries will listen to advice on birth control only after we begin to successfully address the problems of poverty and poor health care.   S D

    b. In developing countries, contraceptive advice must be made available to people living in poverty and without adequate health care.   S D

5. In the 1980s and early 1990s, the massive amounts of interest that poorer countries were paying on loans from Western countries and banks undermined their attempts at economic development.

    a. In the 1980s and early 1990s, the goal of economic development was difficult to achieve for poorer countries because of the immense burden of the debt they owed to Western nations and banks.   S D

    b. In the 1980s and early 1990s, the huge amounts of money borrowed by developing countries from Western nations and banks contributed significantly to their rapid economic development.   S D

6. In some developing countries, the efforts of birth-control programs were badly undermined by their misperception of what the root cause of overpopulation was.

    a. In some developing countries, family-planning programs had negligible success because they failed to correctly identify the fundamental reason why people have large families.   S D

    b. In some developing countries, an understanding of the basic cause of overpopulation allowed birth-control programs to be successful in their efforts.   S D

Making Connections

Each example in the exercise has a lead sentence and two sentences (*a* and *b*) that might or might not logically follow the lead sentence. Read the lead sentence, and ask yourself what kind of idea you could expect in the next sentence. Then read sentence *a*. Decide whether it can follow the lead sentence and make good sense. Choose *Y* for "Yes" or *N* for "No." Do the same for sentence *b*. *Remember:*

1. Look for the ideas that make a logical connection between each pair of sentences.

2. This is also a vocabulary learning exercise. If you have problems with any new words, check their meanings as you work.

1. Birth-control programs in some developing countries have had a substantial impact on fertility rates.

   a. In many of these countries, people have ceased using modern contraceptive methods.   Y N

   b. In other countries, however, a failure to address the problem of poverty, one of the root causes of overpopulation, has negated any possible benefits of such programs.   Y N

2. The extensive use of surface irrigation and chemicals to improve crop production often proves to be a short-sighted practice.

   a. Often the ecological damage caused by these practices negates any benefits they might bring.   Y N

   b. Surface irrigation, by allowing a substantial percentage of the water to evaporate, can cause an accumulation of crop-damaging salts in the soil.   Y N

3. Often measures taken to encourage economic development in a country have unforeseen consequences that ultimately negate any benefits that might have emerged.

   a. For example, cutting down tropical rain forests to provide farmland disrupts the process by which nutrients are recycled into the soil, which then loses its fertility.   Y N

   b. For example, irrigation can make arid and semi-arid regions fertile and capable of producing substantial quantities of crops.   Y N

4. Thirty years after the decision to expand agriculture in the Aral basin by making extensive use of irrigation, clear evidence began to emerge that the economic growth that was planned for the Aral basin was ultimately unsustainable.

   a. By 1990, the use of water from its two main rivers for irrigation had disrupted the region's ecology so badly that crop harvests were declining instead of increasing.   Y N

   b. By 1990, it was clear that the Aral Sea was an almost inexhaustible source of water.   Y N

5. In 1990, scientists concluded that massive changes in agricultural policies and practices were urgently needed to reverse the process of environmental destruction in the Aral basin.

a. Without such measures, the water supply would soon be exhausted, and the economy would disintegrate.   Y   N

b. The policies and practices in operation since 1960 had clearly undermined the region's ability to sustain its traditional human economic activities.   Y   N

Background Reading and Vocabulary Development

READING PASSAGE 4.3 _____

Scan the passage, and find where it begins to discuss the Mayas. Assume that everything before this is the introduction.

As you have seen, this article has a four-paragraph introduction. Scan for the clearest, most specific information about the article.

Sustainable Development from a Historical Perspective: The Mayan Civilization*

1   **In most discussions of environmental issues, it is generally assumed that environmental problems have only affected contemporary societies.** In some cases this may be true. For example, the damage to the ecology and to human health from the use of toxic pesticides is clearly a phenomenon of the last forty years. Acid rain and air pollution are, to a great extent, the result of the burning of fossil fuel, which has characterized economic development in the past century or so. However, an examination of history reveals that the negative impact of human activities on the environment goes back much farther than the last one hundred years.

2   One of the most environmentally significant events in history was the development of agriculture approximately ten thousand years ago. Agriculture involved a massive disruption of natural ecosystems: As humans cleared areas to provide fields for crops and domesticated animals, the native vegetation disappeared and the recycling of natural nutrients to the soil was disturbed. Humans

*Adapted from C. Ponting, "Historical Perspectives on Sustainable Development." *Environment* 32.9 (1990), pp 4–33. Reprinted with permission of the Helen Dwight Reid Educational Foundation. Published by Heldref Publications, 1319 Eighteenth St., N.W., Washington, D.C. 20036–1802. Copyright © 1990.

209

were required to intervene to sustain the new system, usually by
providing water and fertilizing material.

*Draw a simple cause-
effect diagram to help
you understand how
this happened.*

20   **Agriculture also brought about a major social develop-**   3
ment that caused additional strain on natural ecosystems. It
led to the first settled societies, where the extra food produced by
efficient farmers could be used to support growing numbers of non-
producers—rulers, priests, soldiers, and bureaucrats. Settled soci-
25 eties created environmental pressure in the areas they occupied
because of the deforestation required to provide space for fields, construction materials for houses, and fuel for cooking and heating.

     Historically, the spread of agriculture and the rise of settled   4
societies placed immense strain on those ecosystems that were par-
30 ticularly susceptible to disruption. Such was the situation in Mesopotamia, where the first civilizations and the most extensive
modifications to the natural environment occurred; in the Mediterranean basin; and in the lowland jungles of Central America,
where the Mayan civilization briefly flourished.

*[The original article deals with the first two of these historical ex-
amples, then moves to the third.]*

35   Over many centuries, the Mayan culture developed in the   5
tropical jungle of what is now parts of Mexico, Honduras, Belize,
and Guatemala (see Figure 1). By the seventh century, the Mayas
had built a number of cities with magnificent temples, palaces, and
public buildings and large permanent populations. The cities ap-
40 pear to have been in competition with one another, and war among
them was frequent. It is estimated that the largest of these cities,
Tikal, had a permanent population of between thirty thousand and
fifty thousand and that the total Mayan population could have
been 5 million.

*Now read on to iden-
tify the features of this
system.*

45   **To support such a population, the Mayas also devel-**   6
oped a complex agricultural system. They cleared the tropical
forest from the hillsides and made extensive use of terracing to
control the inevitable soil erosion on the new farmland. In addition, in the swampy lowland, they constructed extensive systems of
50 drainage ditches and used the material from the ditches to form
raised fields protected from flooding, where cotton and food crops
could be grown.

     This vast system of intensive agriculture was the basis for all   7
the achievements of the Mayan civilization. However, when too
55 much was demanded of it, the system could not withstand the

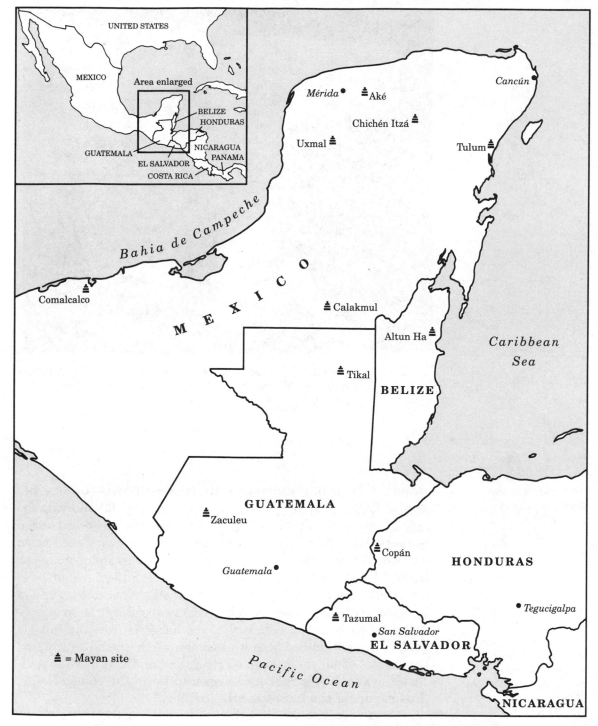

Figure 1. The Mayan civilization. (*Source: National Geographic*, Nov. 1990)

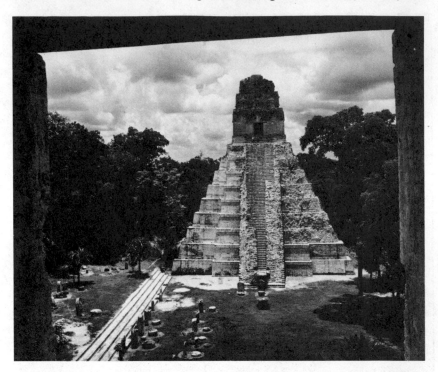

The Temple of the Grand Jaguar in Tikal is one of the magnificent buildings constructed by the Mayas at the height of their civilization in the ninth century A.D. (Photo Researchers)

Now read on to identify the steps in this process. Draw a diagram as you read.

strain. In the end, it collapsed. **The process seems to have begun after the year 600,** at a time when the population increased rapidly to meet the rulers' growing demands for construction workers and soldiers. To satisfy the need of the growing population
60 for food, fuel, and land, the Mayas cut down more and more of the tropical forests on hillsides. Although the soil in the forest areas is fertile, much of it was, and still is, extremely vulnerable to erosion by wind and rain. Probably soil erosion caused by the extensive deforestation began to reduce the crop harvests from the hillside

Use the repeated ideas in the first sentence of the next paragraph to clarify the main idea of this paragraph.

65 fields. The soil that had been washed down from the hills increased the amount of silt in the lowland rivers and drainage ditches. **As a result, water levels rose and began to flood the raised fields, thus reducing the harvests still further.**
        As a result of the deterioration of the artificial environ-
70 **ment created by the Mayas, food production dropped dan-**

8

Continue your cause-effect diagram from the previous paragraph

gerously low. The consequences were disastrous. The first signs of the decline can been seen in human skeletons from the years leading up to 800. They show increased mortality among infants and mothers and increasing levels of nutritional deficiency. After this, conflicts among the Mayan cities over the declining resources of the region probably intensified. Wars among them became more common and widespread. The wars, together with the loss of food production, brought about very high death rates and a catastrophic fall in population, which ended the Mayan civilization. Within a few decades, the cities and fields were abandoned. Today the region supports a population consisting of only a few tens of thousands.

Develop a definition of unsustainable development as you read on.

What happened to the Mayas is one example of the **unsustainable development** that destroyed many of the world's earliest settled societies. By using the natural resources available, by finding ways to exploit these more fully, by creating artificial environments, the Mayas were able to build a complex society capable of great cultural and intellectual achievements. For a considerable time, their society continued to develop and flourish. Ultimately, however, the demands of their ever-expanding society outgrew the ability of the modified environment to support it. Actions which at first must have looked like solutions to environmental limitations proved to have disastrous long-term effects. Ultimately, the Mayas destroyed the environment on which they relied for food, the environment that was the basis for their survival as a civilization.

9

Main Idea Check

Here are the main ideas for this passage. Write the correct paragraph number beside its main idea.

_____ The loss of food production caused increased fighting for the available resources; this destroyed the Mayan civilization.

_____ The Mayas' expanding system of agriculture collapsed when the ecology of the region could no longer sustain it.

_____ The settled societies that agriculture made possible also placed considerable strain on the environment.

_____ Clearing fields for agricultural use, which began ten thousand years ago, had a very disruptive effect on the environment.

_____ The expansion of the Mayan civilization was unsustainable; it ultimately destroyed the environment that supported it.

_____ To grow the crops needed to support their large population, the Mayas built a sophisticated system of drainage, raised fields, and terracing.

_____ Mesopotamia, the Mediterranean basin, and the Central American basin were areas where the ecology was disrupted by early human activities.

_____ Humans have been damaging the environment for much longer than the last century.

_____ The Mayas built a large, city-based civilization in the tropical forests of Central America.

A Closer Look

1. The following diagram represents the relationship that has historically existed between agriculture and environmental damage. Reread the relevant paragraphs, and then complete the diagram with ideas from the list below. Write only the correct letter in each box.

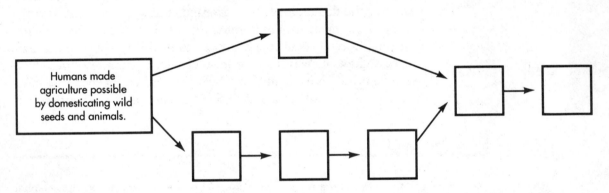

a. The natural ecosystems in sensitive areas came under immense strain.
b. Agriculture allowed people to produce food very efficiently.
c. Efficient food production enabled the development of larger, settled communities.
d. Agriculture demanded open fields for crops and domesticated animals.
e. Humans cleared land, by cutting down the natural vegetation in an area.
f. There was an increased demand for fuel, construction materials, and agricultural land.

2. The following diagram represents the process that ended with the collapse of the Mayan civilization. Scan to identify the relevant paragraphs of the passage and reread them. Then complete the diagram with ideas from the list on page 216. Write only the correct letter in each box.

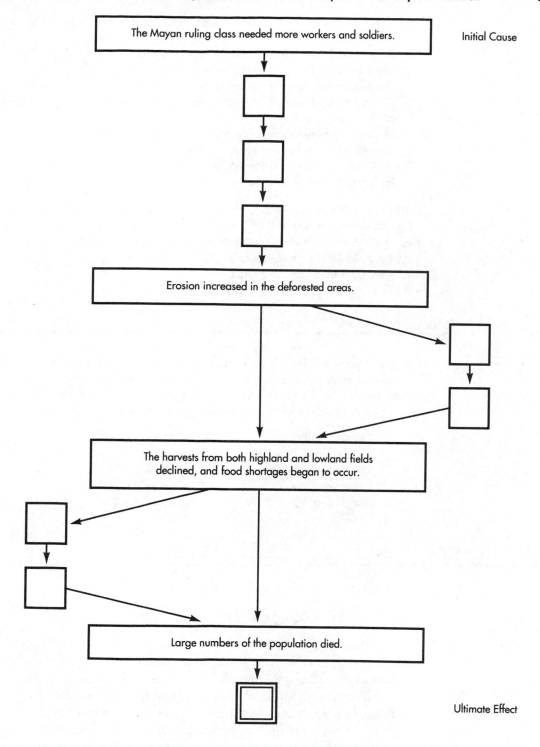

Initial Cause

The Mayan ruling class needed more workers and soldiers.

Erosion increased in the deforested areas.

The harvests from both highland and lowland fields declined, and food shortages began to occur.

Large numbers of the population died.

Ultimate Effect

    a. The population increased to meet the demand for more soldiers and workers.

    b. Silt accumulated in the lowland rivers and drainage ditches.

    c. Wars became more widespread and common.

    d. The Mayas cut down more and more of the forest.

    e. Competition intensified between Mayan cities for the declining resources of the region.

    f. The Mayan civilization collapsed.

    g. There was an increased need for food, fuel, and land.

    h. Drainage ditches overflowed, and the agricultural fields of the lowland began to suffer from flooding.

3. What modification or modifications did the Mayas make to the natural ecology of the region where they lived?

    a. They constructed drainage systems for naturally wet areas.

    b. They planted large numbers of trees.

    c. They built fields on the sides of hills.

    d. They converted forest to farmland.

Vocabulary in Context

Here are some words from the passage that you may not have known. You either guessed their meaning from context or from your knowledge of word families, or you omitted the word and were still able to understand the sentence. Now check and learn the meanings of the words. Use your dictionary to help you.

toxic (line 5)	to withstand (line 55)
magnificent (line 38)	silt (line 66)
terracing (line 47)	skeleton (line 72)
swampy (line 49)	to outgrow (line 89)
ditch (line 50)	long-term (line 92)

READING PASSAGE 4.4

Quickly scan for an explanation of biological diversity *and how it is threatened. Also scan for solutions. Then come back, and start to read.*

Biological Diversity under Attack

5

    To date, biologists have described fewer than 1 million of the earth's natural species.[1] There is no certainty about how many species exist, although scientific estimates range from a conservative 3 million[2] to 30 million.[3] However, despite disagreement about the total number of species, there is general consensus among scientists that at least half of the world's species live in the rain forests of the earth's tropical regions. To appreciate the immense biodiver-

1

sity in these forests, consider the following figures: There are approximately thirty-two native species of trees in the United Kingdom today.[4] However, in each of two small plots of rain forest in Peru (roughly one-millionth the area of the United Kingdom), a U.S. researcher identified approximately three hundred tree species.[5]

For some years, however, the moist forests of the earth's tropical regions have been the scene of massive destruction as humans cut down or burn the trees to provide hardwood or land for agriculture and settlement. By 1990, for example, the total deforestation in Brazil's Amazon region amounted to 41.5 million hectares, the equivalent of an area as large as Sweden.[6] Elsewhere in the 1980s, Malaysia destroyed an estimated 2.7 million hectares of its tropical forests at an annual rate of 1.3 percent.[7] During the same decade, Indonesia lost 10 million hectares of rain forest,[8] an area larger than Portugal or the state of Indiana. **Today the tropical rain forests of Southeast Asia and South America continue to retreat at a rate in excess of ninety thousand square kilometers a year.**[9]

For tropical species, such massive deforestation means equally massive habitat destruction, which in turn is causing the extinction of species on a scale unprecedented in human history. A 1989 study, which assumed a conservative total of 2 million species living exclusively in the tropical rain forests, estimated that between four thousand and six thousand species a year are currently being driven to extinction.[10] Even these conservative estimates, the study points out, represent a rate of extinction approximately ten thousand times greater than the extinction rate that existed prior to the appearance of humans on the earth. Other studies suggest that the extinction rate could rise to between seven thousand and twenty-seven thousand species a year.[11]

For a number of reasons, the threatened species of the rain forests are an immense and irreplaceable resource. First, because of their genetic diversity, they are a source of genetic material that can be utilized to support or replace domesticated varieties that become susceptible to pests or disease. For example, the wild American oil palm has a natural resistance to spear rot, a disease that is destroying the domesticated African oil palm. Researchers are using genes from the American plant to develop resistance to the disease in its African cousin.[12]

Second, tropical species are a potentially vast source of tree and plant species that could be domesticated for human use. Twenty-four crop species have been domesticated in the Amazon region alone, and countless numbers remain. *Caryocar villosum* is

Use the repeated idea in the first sentence of the next paragraph to clarify or refresh the main idea of this paragraph.

Quickly scan forward for and mark how the writer supports this claim. Then come back, and resume reading here.

a tree that produces fruit valued highly by Amazonian peoples. The *Copaifera* tree species produce substances that can substitute for diesel fuel.[13]

55   As a potential source of medicinal drugs, tropical species are   6
irreplaceable. Wilson[14] cites the example of *Catharanthus roseus,* a small plant native to Madagascar. It produces two substances, vinblastine and vincristine, which are extremely effective in the treatment of two forms of cancer. The income from these two substances exceeds $100 million a year. None of the five other species of *Ca-*
60   *tharanthus* has been carefully studied. One of the five is close to extinction because its habitat is threatened by deforestation.

     What can be done to preserve the biological diversity of the   7
tropical rain forests, with its wealth of scientific information and its unrealized potential as a source of material benefits? The pros-
65   pects are poor that the extinctions can be completely halted.[15] **However, many experts are cautiously optimistic that today's rate of extinction can be slowed if we address both the immediate and the root causes of the crisis.**[16]

     Establishing forest reserves—areas where all economic ex-   8
70   ploitation of the forest is forbidden—will protect tropical species by preserving their habitats. Conservation measures such as these are necessary in the fight against deforestation, the immediate cause of biodiversity loss; by themselves, however, they are insufficient responses to the problem.

75   A second essential step is to address the root cause of the   9
problem—the economic pressures that cause people to destroy the forests for short-term gain. Accomplishing this, however, will be a major challenge for the international community because it will involve tackling the complex and related problems of poverty, over-
80   population, and unsustainable development.

     At the same time, we need to accelerate the pace of scientific   10
research into the species of the tropical rain forests. Such research is our only means of identifying areas that should be given priority in conservation decisions. It will also provide necessary informa-
85   tion about the value of as yet unstudied species. This information will help reduce human ignorance about our dependence on the natural world and will clearly be needed if we are eventually to convince people that the biological resources of the rain forests are worth preserving.

Scan forward to iden-
tify and mark how to
address each of these
causes. Then come
back, and resume
reading here.

Notes

1. O. T. Solbrig, "The origin and function of biodiversity," *Environment* 33.5 (May 1991), p. 16.

2. Op. cit. 1, p. 16.
3. Figure proposed by T. L. Erwin and cited by E. O. Wilson, "Threats to biodiversity," *Scientific American*, September 1989, p. 108.
4. Figure from C. Hart, *British Trees in Colour* (London: Michael Joseph Ltd., 1973).
5. Op. cit. 3, p. 110.
6. World Resources Institute, *World Resources 1992–1993* (New York: Oxford University Press, 1993).
7. Op. cit. 6, p. 287.
8. Op. cit. 6, p. 287.
9. Op. cit. 6, pp. 286–287.
10. Op. cit. 3, p. 112.
11. Op. cit. 6, p. 128.
12. Cited from original source by N. J. H. Smith, J. T. Williams, and D. L. Plucknett, "Conserving the Tropical Cornucopia," *Environment* 33.6 (July/August 1991), p. 8.
13. Op. cit. 12, p. 9.
14. Op. cit. 3, pp. 115–116.
15. M. W. Holdgate, "The Environment of Tomorrow," *Environment* 33.6 (July/August 1991), p. 18.
16. J. A. McNeely, K. R. Miller, W. V. Reid, R. A. Mittermeier, and T. B. Werner, "Strategies for Conserving Biodiversity," *Environment* 32.3 (April 1990), pp. 16–40.

Main Idea Check

Here are the main ideas for this passage. Write the correct paragraph number beside its main idea.

_____ This paragraph gives an example of a tropical plant that is of great medicinal value to humans and another plant of potential value that is threatened by extinction.

_____ Economic development is necessary if the loss of the world's biodiversity is to be halted.

_____ The rapid loss of tropical species can be slowed if we address all its causes.

_____ To preserve tropical biodiversity, we also need to speed up research into the species that have not yet been studied.

_____ Tropical forests are rapidly being destroyed by humans.

_____ The wild species of the tropical forests are an underused and very valuable source of crop plants for humans.

_____ The destruction of tropical forests is causing the rapid extinction of the natural species that are native there.

_____ Conservation is a necessary component of a solution to the biodiversity crisis.

_____ The loss of species diversity is immensely significant because it also means a permanent loss of genetic resources.

_____ More than half of all the world's natural species have their home in the earth's tropical forests.

A Closer Look

1. For what reason or reasons are the tropical forests being destroyed?
   a. to make land available for agriculture
   b. to provide places for people to live
   c. in response to the demand for hardwood

2. How fast are tropical species now becoming extinct?
   a. at a rate similar to the rate that existed before the appearance of humans on the earth
   b. at a pace much faster than the rate that existed before the emergence of humans
   c. at a rate of exactly six thousand species per year

3. In what way or ways does the writer justify the claim that wild species in tropical forests are extremely valuable resources for humans?
   a. by illustrating their potential as domesticated species
   b. by illustrating their potential as suppliers of genetic material
   c. by illustrating their potential medicinal value
   d. by illustrating their potential role in maintaining the ecological balance of the forests

4. Identify the examples in the passage that support your answer or answers to question 4.

5. What factor or factors does the writer mention as contributing to the biodiversity crisis?
   a. sustainable economic development
   b. poverty
   c. overpopulation
   d. lack of appreciation of the value of biological resources

What Do You Think?

Conservation is one obvious answer to the problem of the loss of the earth's biological diversity. However, the writer also believes that economic development is essential. Can you explain why the writer might believe this?

Vocabulary in Context

Here are some words from the passage that you may not have known. You either guessed their meaning from context or from your knowledge of word families, or you omitted the word and were still able to understand the sentence. Now check and learn the meanings of the words. Use your dictionary to help you.

deforestation (lines 16, 26, 61)
scale (line 28)
exclusively (line 30)
currently (lines 31)

unrealized (line 64)
optimistic (line 66)
reserve (line 69)
pace (line 81)
worth (line 89)

READING PASSAGE 4.5

In this article, Edith Brown Weiss, an authority on international law, uses the legal concept of a trust to suggest one way to approach the issue of conservation. A trust is something of value that we inherit and that provides us with income in the form of interest. However, we may not spend the capital of the trust.

In Fairness to Future Generations*

Scan this introduction for clear information about the topic of the article.

1   **Recently we, the living generation, have begun to question the centuries-old assumption that conditions will be better for the next generation than they have been for us.** We now recognize that, for the first time in human history, humans
5 have the power to alter earth irreversibly, on a global scale, and in many different ways. Desertification, the increasing rate of species extinction, and the disposal of hazardous wastes in vulnerable areas are just a few of the many global environmental changes that will affect the well-being of future generations. For the first
10 time then, humans must concern themselves with the condition of the planet that is passed to future generations.

2   From the perspective of later generations, if we deplete re-

*Adapted from Edith Brown Weiss, "In Fairness to Future Generations." *Environment* 32.3 (1990), pp. 7–31. Reprinted with permission of the Helen Dwight Reid Educational Foundation. Published by Heldref Publications, 1319 Eighteenth St., N.W., Washington, D.C. 20036–1802. Copyright © 1990.

*As you read this para-
graph, look for details
on how this inter-
ference occurs. Draw
simple cause-effect di-
agrams.*

sources and degrade the quality of the environment, **we are interfering with their ability to share in the benefits of the planet.**
15 If we deplete resources—for example, fossil fuels—by consuming
them faster than they can be replenished, we are depriving future
generations of the opportunity to use such fuels. We are also im-
posing on future generations the scientific, economic, and social
burden of adapting society to life without those resources. When
20 our exploitation of the environment causes the extinction of species, as does the clear-cutting of tropical forests, we are narrowing
the range of genes that future generations will have for the development of new food crops and medicines. When we gain short-term
economic benefits by carelessly disposing of wastes in the air, land,
25 and water, we are passing on massive costs to future generations.
It is they who will need to clean up the disposal sites or abandon
them altogether at the same time as they deal with the health
problems associated with pollution.

*As you read this para-
graph, look for an ex-
planation of this
theory.*

As a response to this situation, a new theory of inter- 3
30 **generational equity is proposed for international law.** The
theory argues that the earth is a natural legacy that each generation receives in trust from its ancestors and holds in trust for its
descendants. The trust imposes on each generation the obligation
to conserve the environment and natural resources for future gen-
35 erations. The trust also gives each generation the right to use and
benefit equally from the natural legacy of its ancestors. Each generation, therefore, has the right to receive the planet in no worse
condition than that experienced by previous generations, to inherit
similar diversity in natural resources, and to have fair access to
40 the benefits that come from using the planet's resources.

To be enforceable, theoretical planetary rights and obliga- 4
tions must become part of international, national, and local law.
An initial step in **this process** would be to formulate an international declaration of intergenerational rights and obligations that

*As you read, diagram
the process that is de-
scribed in this para-
graph.*

45 could be signed by a large number of countries. Such a declaration
would then help the negotiation of more specific international
agreements or treaties that participating governments would have
to comply with.

New policies within our institutions will also be necessary if 5
50 we are to meet our responsibilities to future generations. This will
be difficult because most of our institutions—international, national, and local, public and private—are designed to handle short-
term problems. However, it is essential that our generation develop strategies to make us accountable to future generations at

*Check back to identify
the goals of these
strategies*

55   the same time as we exercise our right to use the natural environment for our own benefit. **These strategies** should include

- the representation of future generations in decision
  making
- conservation assessments that focus on the environmental
60   impact of present actions on future generations
- the sustainable use of renewable resources
- scientific monitoring of the diversity and quality of the environment
- trust funds financed by fees for the use of natural re-
65   sources, which would compensate future generations for
  any losses or costs that are the result of today's actions
- education to develop a new awareness that, as users and
  trustees of planet earth, we are accountable to future generations for its care

Main Idea Check

Here are the main ideas for this passage. Write the correct paragraph number
beside its main idea.

_____ The signing of a declaration of intergenerational rights and obligations would be
a good first step toward protecting the planet for future generations.

_____ The present generation needs to adopt specific strategies in order to meet its
responsibilities to future generations.

_____ By our mistreatment of the environment, we are creating problems that future
generations will have to bear the costs of resolving.

_____ Because of the long-term effects of environmental changes, people are beginning to think about their responsibilities toward future generations.

_____ This paragraph describes a proposed new theory of intergenerational equity in
international law to protect the earth's resources and ecology.

A Closer Look

1. According to the writer, people have traditionally believed that life
   would be better for future generations than it was for their own
   generation.   T F

2. How can our actions affect future generations? First identify and reread the
   relevant paragraph of the passage. Then complete this cause-effect diagram
   with the sentences below. Write only the correct letter in each box.

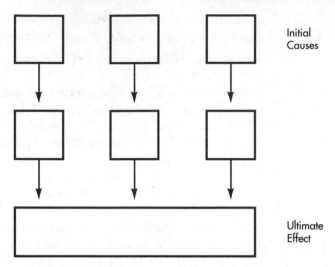

a. We limit the opportunity of future generations to develop new food crops and medicines.
b. Future generations have to pay the costs of adapting to life without fossil fuels.
c. The rights of future generations to share in the benefits of the planet are considerably limited.
d. We consume fossil fuel stocks without replenishing them.
e. Future generations must pay the economic and health costs of living in and cleaning up the environment we have polluted.
f. Our deforestation policies cause the extinction of potentially valuable natural species.
g. Because it is initially cheaper for us, we dump wastes on our land and in our air and water.

3. What obligation(s) and/or right(s) does a theory of "intergenerational equity" give the present generation?
   a. the obligation to leave the earth in no worse condition than we received it
   b. the right to benefit from the earth's resources
   c. the obligation not to deplete the earth's resources

4. The author of this article believes that current international laws are sufficient to protect the rights of future generations.   T   F

What Do You Think?

Look at the last strategy suggested by the writer as necessary for creating in the present generation a sense of responsibility toward future generations. Do you agree that programs of education are necessary? How do you support your opinion?

   If you accept that education is necessary, who needs to be educated, and in what countries? How could you carry out such a program of education? Would some groups of people be more difficult to convince than others? If so, who might these groups be, and what makes it harder to convince them?

Vocabulary in Context

Here are some words from the passage that you may not have known. You either guessed their meaning from context or from your knowledge of word families, or you omitted the word and were still able to understand the sentence. Now check and learn the meanings of the words. Use your dictionary to help you.

hazardous (line 7)	equity (line 30)
well-being (line 9)	to propose (line 30)
to replenish (line 16)	enforceable (line 41)
to deprive someone of X (line 16)	to monitor (line 62)
	fee (line 64)
to impose (line 17)	trustee (line 68)
site (line 26)	

VOCABULARY PRACTICE _____

Same or Different?

Writers sometimes express the same ideas with very different grammar and vocabulary. This exercise will help you identify such occurrences.

Read the first sentence in each example carefully. Then read each of the two following sentences to decide whether they are the same or different in meaning to the first sentence. Choose *S* when the sentence expresses the same idea as the first sentence. Choose *D* when it expresses a different idea.

1. Population growth has accelerated considerably in the twentieth century.

    a. We urgently need to consider the rapid rate of increase in the population in the twentieth century.   S   D

    b. The twentieth century has seen a substantially faster rate of population growth than earlier centuries.   S   D

2. Today natural species are dying out in greater numbers than at any time in human history.

    a. The rate of extinction among natural species is today higher than at any time in human history.   S   D

b. The high rate at which natural species are vanishing today is unprecedented in human history.   S D

3. The prospects are good that the present talks will lead to a resolution of the dispute.

    a. It is unlikely that the negotiations now under way will result in the dispute being settled.   S D

    b. At present, the likelihood of negotiations on the dispute is low.   S D

4. Some experts believe that Mayan society collapsed when the ecology of the region could no longer support it.

    a. According to some experts, the disintegration of Mayan society occurred because it made excessive demands on its environment.   S D

    b. It is believed by some experts that the Mayan civilization was able to flourish because it successfully modified its environment.   S D

5. There is an urgent need for industry to find safe ways to get rid of harmful waste materials.

    a. It is very important that industry swiftly identify procedures for safely disposing of dangerous waste.   S D

    b. Identifying methods for the safe disposal of hazardous waste must be a high priority for industry.   S D

6. The intense cold obliged us to change our plans for the next day.

    a. A change in our plans for the next day was made necessary by the extremely cold weather.   S D

    b. It was so cold that we had to alter our plans for the next day.   S D

7. The Mayas were obliged to alter their natural environment in order to sustain their economic and social system.

    a. The Mayan economic and social system collapsed because the natural environment could not sustain it.   S D

    b. The modifications the Mayas made to their natural environment caused the eventual deterioration of their economic and social system.   S D

8. Ensuring total compliance with an international treaty by all participating nations is a difficult task.

    a. It is difficult to make sure that all countries signing an international agreement completely obey the terms of that agreement.   S D

    b. Negotiating an international treaty is a difficult task.   S D

9. Before the late twentieth century, people generally did not appreciate the negative impact that human activities like agriculture and industry could have on the environment.

    a. Prior to the late twentieth century, there was little public awareness of the extent of the ecological damage that could result from human activities like industry and agriculture.   S D

    b. Before the late twentieth century, few people perceived human activities like agriculture and industry as a threat to the environment.   S D

10. Our destruction of the dense rain forests of tropical regions will deprive future generations of an immense source of scientific knowledge.

    a. By abandoning the dense tropical rain forests, we are leaving future generations a vast source of scientific knowledge.   S D

    b. Future generations will lose a vast source of scientific knowledge because we are cutting down the dense tropical rain forests.   S D

Making Connections

Each example in the exercise has a lead sentence and two sentences (*a* and *b*) that might or might not logically follow the lead sentence. Read the lead sentence, and ask yourself what kind of idea you could expect in the next sentence. Then read sentence *a*. Decide whether it can follow the lead sentence and make good sense. Choose *Y* for "Yes" or *N* for "No." Do the same for sentence *b*. *Remember:*

1. Look for the ideas that make a logical connection between each pair of sentences.

2. This is also a vocabulary learning exercise. If you have problems with any new words, check their meanings as you work.

1. The government needs to enforce our domestic antipollution laws much more strictly.

    a. Failure to do so will mean a further deterioration of our environment.   Y N

    b. At present, all companies and organizations are complying
       fully with these laws.   Y N

2. The business climate for U.S. domestic car manufacturers deteriorated in the
1980s.

    a. The major car companies flourished as consumer demand for
       new cars often exceeded the supply.   Y N

    b. They came under intense competition from foreign, especially
       Japanese, car makers.   Y N

3. From an ecological perspective, many common agricultural practices are environmentally disruptive.

    a. Water supplies may be contaminated through the heavy use of
       artificial fertilizers and pesticides to increase crop harvests.   Y N

    b. The irrigation of land in semi-arid areas depletes water re-
       sources and often causes salt to accumulate in the soil.   Y N

4. Some legal experts are suggesting that we find ways to compensate future
generations for our depletion of the earth's natural resources.

    a. We are, therefore, under no obligation to pay for what we con-
       sume.   Y N

    b. Environmentalists, however, argue that such a move might
       cause some people to abandon conservation as the primary
       means to protect the environment.   Y N

5. The negotiations between the electronic company and its workers have collapsed.

    a. Because a long strike would threaten national security, there is
       now the possibility that the government will intervene and im-
       pose a settlement on both sides.   Y N

    b. Both sides in the dispute are talking amicably and show a will-
       ingness to try to understand the other's perspective.   Y N

6. The site that the petrochemical company has selected for its new plant is close
to an ecologically sensitive area.

    a. Environmental scientists and conservationists have already ex-
       pressed their approval of the plan.   Y N

    b. In fact, according to biologists, the area provides the only re-
       maining habitat for at least three species of fish.   Y N

7. There was unprecedented flooding in this region of the country last year.

    a. At one stage, the total area under water exceeded three hundred square miles and included two large towns.   Y N

    b. The water retreated long before it had reached the levels of the 1973 flood.   Y N

8. The complex system of intensive agriculture developed by the Mayas experienced more and more difficulty satisfying the ever-increasing needs of a growing population.

    a. Evidence for a disruption of the food supply can be found in skeletons from the time that show malnutrition among adults and increased mortality among infants.   Y N

    b. It was eventually unable to withstand the strain and collapsed.   Y N

Synonyms and Paraphrases

Review the meanings of the words to the left of each paragraph below. Find out how to use these words by studying examples from the Vocabulary Study and from the reading passages of this unit. Then read each paragraph for its details. Replace the words in boldface with the correct new words. Sometimes you will need to change the grammar of the sentence so that the new word or expression fits into it correctly.

prospects
to deteriorate
treaty
to abandon
to collapse
negotiations

1. The situation in Yugoslavia **worsened** in August 1991. The **talks** between Croatia and Serbia **failed completely.** This meant that **the chances** of a peaceful settlement of their dispute had almost vanished. The United Nations, however, did not **give up** its efforts to persuade the two republics that an **agreement** between them was much more preferable than total war.

excessive
to dispose of
to conserve
strain
to collapse
hazardous
to reduce consumption

2. Environmental scientists are demanding that we **make less use** of fossil fuels, that we **stop wasting** the world's resources, especially its soil, water, and forests, and that we find safe ways to **get rid of** waste materials that are **harmful** to health. Some politicians, however, are unwilling to do the necessary things to achieve these goals. They fear the costs will be **too great** and will **impose a burden** on the economy that may cause it to **disintegrate.**

to exhaust
to become extinct
to alter
to oblige
perspective
to deplete

3. Some influential people believe that the **point of view** of future generations should be included when we discuss environmental issues today. By **completely using up** some of the world's resources today, they argue, we are **taking away from** future generations the right to enjoy and use these resources. We are also **forcing** them to find alternatives. By destroying natural habitats and causing species to **die out,** we are **reducing** the world's biological wealth. This is eliminating sources of scientific knowledge which our chil-

descendants
to deprive

dren and our children's children could use for the development of new food crops and medicines. By polluting our land, air, and water, we are **changing** the ecology of our world in ways that will impose enormous costs on future generations. For these reasons, the present generation has a moral obligation to protect the earth and conserve its resources for the following generation.

Using New Vocabulary

Review the meanings of the following verbs. Study the examples in the Vocabulary Study and in Reading Passages 4.3 to 4.5 to learn how to use them in sentences.

to appreciate	to comply
to interfere	to monitor
to compensate	to enforce

Now finish each of the following sentences in a way that seems appropriate and interesting to you. You may want to use ideas connected with your readings in this unit or in earlier units.

1. Not everyone appreciates the fact that . . .

2 Thank you. I appreciate . . .

3. By polluting the world today, we are interfering with . . .

4. If I were you, I wouldn't interfere in . . .

5. The government is going to have to compensate . . .

6. Many companies are not complying with . . .

7. Today scientists are carefully monitoring . . .

8. Sometimes governments do not enforce . . .

Main Reading

PREREADING THE ARTICLE: GETTING A FIRST IDEA

Quickly read the article title and the introduction (the first three paragraphs) to identify the topic of the article. Then answer questions 1–4. Justify your answers by referring to the text.

1. The article will describe a science-fiction movie.   Y   N

2. The article will deal with potentially dangerous climate changes.   Y   N

3. The article will describe how certain gases are increasing in the atmosphere.   Y   N

4. What words suggest that this article will have an overall problem-solution organization?

Now read the headings of sections 2–5, and look briefly at the illustrations. Then answer questions 5–7. Again, justify your answers by referring to the text.

5. In what section or sections do you expect to find a description of the problem?

6. In what section or sections do you expect to find a discussion of possible solutions?

7. Which section or sections would you read if you wanted information about what climate change might mean for the earth?

MAIN READING _____

Managing the Global Greenhouse

1. Introduction

Scan this introduction to identify clear information about the topic of the article.

"**The world is warming.** Climatic zones are shifting. Glaciers are melting. Sea level is rising. These are not hypothetical events from a science-fiction movie; these changes and others are already taking place, and we expect them to accelerate over the next years as the amounts of . . . gases accumulating in the atmosphere through human activities increase. . . . A rapid and continuous warming will not only be destructive to agriculture but also lead to the widespread death of forest trees, uncertainty in water supplies and the flooding of coastal areas." (Houghton & Woodwell, 1989).   1

Warnings like what? Check back.

For some years now, **warnings like this** have been heard from leading authorities in the scientific community. According to   2

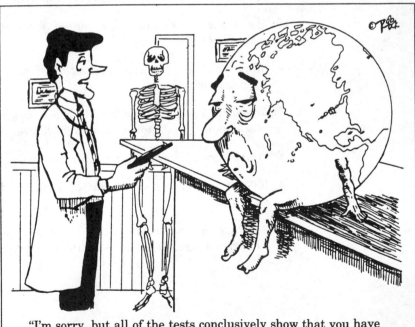

"I'm sorry, but all of the tests conclusively show that you have
a chronic case of civilization."

(© Rob Rock, 1991. Reprinted by permission.)

15

these experts, we are leaving our children a frightening legacy: An accumulation of so-called greenhouse gases in the atmosphere and the potentially disastrous climate changes that this build-up may bring about. However, the scientific community is not speaking with one voice. Other leading scientists point out that the evidence for greenhouse warming is inconclusive and argue that predictions based on it are questionable. The scientific debate has been intense. It has also fueled the political controversy about what measures, if any, need to be taken to address the possible problem of greenhouse warming.

20

Before you continue, make a list of questions you expect to find answers to. For example, "What is greenhouse warming?"

25

In the presence of scientific debate and political controversy,   3
what is a concerned public to think about greenhouse warming?
For an adequate assessment of the issue, an essential first step is
to identify what is known and what is not yet known about **the phenomenon.**

As you read each paragraph in this section, decide if it contains facts or uncertainties. Mark each paragraph appropriately.

30

2. Facts and Uncertainties

First, there is unanimous scientific agreement that gases like   4
carbon dioxide (CO_2), chlorofluorocarbons (CFCs), and methane
(CH_4) have the potential to produce a greenhouse effect. These relatively transparent gases allow sunlight to pass through and warm
the earth; however, when that heat is released by the earth in the
form of infrared radiation, it is absorbed very efficiently by these
gases and not allowed to escape out into space (see Figure 1).

35

There is also little doubt among atmospheric scientists that   5

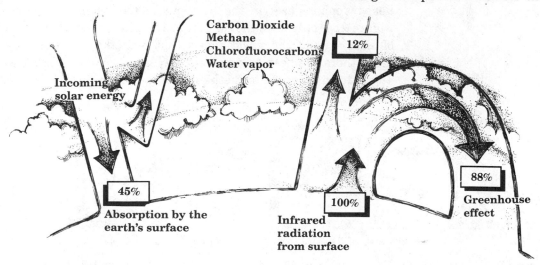

Figure 1. The greenhouse effect

an increase in the greenhouse gases will have a warming effect on
the earth's climate. Evidence for a historical connection between
these gases and climate changes has been provided by a team of
scientists from the Laboratory of Glaciology and Geophysics of the
40   Environment (Lorius et al., 1990), who have analyzed the gases
trapped in a 2,000-meter core of Antarctic ice extracted by Soviet
engineers. The ice, formed from snow that accumulated over the
last 160,000 years, contains a record of the earth's atmosphere and
climate during that time. The analysis showed that during the pe-
45   riods between or after the ice ages, the atmosphere contained 25
percent more carbon dioxide and 100 percent more methane than
during the ice ages. The analysis also revealed that Antarctic temperatures were 10° C higher during the nonglacial periods than
they were during the glacial periods.

50   Also undisputed is the fact that any potential effects of green-   6
house gases will be both long-term and global. Sulfur dioxide (SO_2)
and nitrous oxides (NO), which are the primary causes of acid rain
and photochemical smog, only remain in the atmosphere for days
or weeks; their effects are local or regional, rather than global.
55   Carbon dioxide, methane, and CFCs, however, remain in the atmosphere between ten and one hundred years and clearly do not stay
localized in the areas where they are originally released or in adjacent regions. They spread throughout the global atmosphere. Their
long life means that their effects are likely to be felt more by our
60   descendants than by the current generation.

           Another well-established fact is that the concentration of   7
heat-trapping gases in the atmosphere has been increasing (see
Figure 2). Analysis of the air trapped in glacier ice from a number
of sites around the world shows that over the last one hundred
65   years there has been a 25 percent increase in carbon dioxide and a
100 percent increase in methane. CFCs, which have only been in

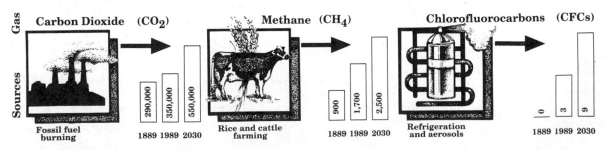

Figure 2. Increases in greenhouse gases, 1889–2030. (*Source:* T. E. Gradel and P. J. Grutzen, "The Changing Atmosphere," *Scientific American* 261.3 [1989]: 58–68.)

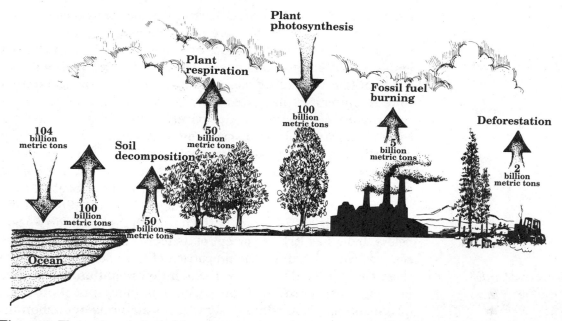

Figure 3. The carbon cycle and increases in atmospheric carbon dioxide (CO_2). Most CO_2 in the atmosphere is produced by processes occurring in nature. Other natural processes extract CO_2 from the atmosphere, maintaining a CO_2 balance that allows life as we know it to continue. The small but highly significant annual increase of 3 billion tons in atmospheric CO_2 is the result of human economic activities. (*Source:* R. A. Houghton and G. M. Woodwell, "Global Climatic Change," *Scientific American* 260.4 [1989]: 36–44.)

use for the last several decades and which, of course, were unknown one hundred years ago, are a new addition to the two traditional greenhouse gases.

As you read this para- 70
graph, draw a simple
cause-effect diagram
to help you under-
stand the details.

What has caused this very significant increase in atmospheric greenhouse gases? We know that carbon dioxide and methane are both released into the atmosphere by processes occurring in nature (see Figure 3). Methane comes from vegetation rotting in swamps and other wetlands. However, it is clear that the
75   source of their increased presence in the atmosphere is the growth of those human activities that produce the greenhouse gases—industry and agriculture. During the past century, a large number of countries have experienced some degree of industrialization, a process that has depended on the burning of coal, oil, and gas to pro-
80   duce energy. The burning of these so-called fossil fuels is known to be the main human source of carbon dioxide emissions. Industrial expansion also brought about the development of CFCs, gases widely used in refrigeration, air-conditioning, and other applications. These gases, although they are present in the atmosphere in

8

85   much smaller quantities than carbon dioxide, are capable of ab-
      sorbing and trapping much more radiated heat.

Use repeated ideas
here to help you with
the main idea of para-
graph 8. Use new
ideas to help you with
the main idea of para-
graph 9.

            Just as industrialization has contributed to increased   9
      emissions of greenhouse gases, so too have the responses to
      the problem of feeding the world's rapidly growing popula-
90   **tion.** As agriculture has expanded, two specific forms of farming—
      cattle rearing and growing rice on artificial wetlands—have be-
      come significant sources of methane, a gas whose heat-trapping
      properties are approximately twenty times those of carbon dioxide.

            Deforestation has become a common policy in developing   10
95   countries, particularly those in the tropical zones of South Amer-
      ica, Africa, and Asia. By 1988, according to McNeill (1989), Ethio-
      pia had lost about 97 percent of the forests that existed forty years
      before. India had lost 72 percent of its forests since the turn of the
      century, while in Africa the proportion of trees being cut down to

Continue adding to
your simple cause-
effect diagram.

100   those being planted was 29 to 1. **Such deforestation, as well as**
      causing massive soil erosion and the extinction of thousands
      of natural species, releases significant amounts of carbon di-
      oxide into the air. In 1987, for example, the burning of the dense
      rain forest in the Amazon basin of Brazil produced emissions of
105   carbon dioxide larger than those of the entire United States for
      that year. In addition, as the magnificent forests shrink, so does
      the earth's capacity to absorb carbon dioxide from the air.

            During these one hundred years of industrialization and rapid   11
      population growth, there is also clear evidence that the earth has
110   become warmer. Jones and Wigley (1990) have rigorously analyzed
      temperature records going back to the 1850s and have established
      that the average global temperature has increased between 0.5°
      and 0.7° C over the last one hundred years. Other researchers have
      pointed to additional evidence to confirm the existence of a warm-
115   ing trend: an increase in the water temperature of Canadian lakes,
      a reduction in the amount of sea ice in the polar regions, and the
      retreat of inland glaciers.

Identify repeated and
new information in
this sentence. Use re-
peated information to
refresh your memory
of important ideas in
previous paragraphs.
Use new information
to help you with the
main idea of this
paragraph.

            However, at this time many scientists are reluctant to   12
      attribute the clear global warming trend of the last one hun-
120   **dred years to the buildup of greenhouse gases in the atmo-**
      sphere. Such a conclusion, they argue, is not justified by the pres-
      ent evidence, which merely shows that a slight global warming
      trend has occurred at the same time as concentrations of green-
      house gases in the atmosphere have been climbing. Another reason
125   for treating the causal link as unproven is that the warming trend
      has not been consistent; it was interrupted between 1945 and 1970,
      a period when global temperatures dropped so significantly that

some contemporary scientists were speculating on the approach of a new ice age! Such an interruption is not consistent with the global warming theory, which predicts that average temperatures should gradually rise as the concentration of heat-trapping gases in the atmosphere increases. In addition, the temperature increase of 0.5° C that has been established for the last one hundred years is at the lower end of the range of the increase predicted by proponents of the greenhouse theory. **This suggests to some scientists that, at the very least, the effects of the greenhouse gases on global climate have been exaggerated.**

Just as there exists some degree of scientific uncertainty about how to interpret the warming trend of the last one hundred years, there is also **doubt about the accuracy of predicting future climatic developments.** To carry out this task, teams of scientists use elaborate computer models that have been based on the assumption that the greenhouse gases in the atmosphere would double by around the middle of the twenty-first century. However, the different models have predicted temperature increases ranging from 1° C (2° F) to 5° C (9° F). The differences in predictions are problematic: An increase of one degree might cause little disruption to human activities; the effects of a five-degree increase, on the other hand, would be catastrophic.

3. Potential Effects of Climate Change

Some politicians and governments have used the lack of scientific certainty on greenhouse warming as a justification for not taking immediate action to control it. Their attitude is that we can't afford to worry about something that may not be a significant problem. **However,** the majority of scientists investigating global warming warn that it would be extremely risky to wait for greater certainty or conclusive evidence. If the world waits for another ten years, whatever warming occurs will be greater than the warming that would occur if effective measures were now taken to slow the rate at which greenhouse gases are accumulating in the atmosphere. The effects of the warming, therefore, will be greater, as will the costs of dealing with them. Moreover, there is a possibility that warming will accelerate the processes by which naturally occurring greenhouse gases are released into the atmosphere. In this case, warming would cause more warming and create a vicious cycle.

If we wait, and if the warming that occurs is in the middle or

Use repeated information in the first sentence of the next paragraph to help you summarize this paragraph.

As you read the rest of the paragraph, look for specific information about this difficulty.

Pay attention to this word as you read for the main idea of this paragraph.

Scan ahead to identify where the writer deals with these three types of consequences. Then come back, and continue reading this paragraph.

the upper part of the range predicted, **there will be extremely serious consequences for natural ecosystems, agriculture, and human settlements.** In the past, ecosystems have successfully adapted to slow and gradual temperature changes. For example, the belt of forest that runs across Canada and the northern United States has shifted slowly north from its original location farther south in the past ten thousand years in response to a slow increase (about .002° C annually) in temperature. However, the increase of 3° to 5° C that could occur in the next fifty years is approximately fifty times more rapid than the "natural" increase. In such circumstances, the forest belt would be under immense strain and is likely not to be able to adapt. The probable result of global warming in this case would be the destruction, on a massive scale, of the North American forests and of other ecosystems worldwide.

As you read, draw a simple cause-effect diagram to help you with the details.

Agriculture will also be seriously damaged by unchecked global warming. Higher temperatures in certain areas are likely to result in a faster evaporation of the moisture in the air. At the same time, higher temperatures could be accompanied in some regions by other climate changes, most significantly, a reduction in rainfall. In each case, the resulting new or increased demand for irrigation of crops may well exceed the supply of water available. One study cited by Schneider (1989) predicts that a 3° C climb in temperatures in the western and the Great Plains regions of the United States would bring with it a 33 percent reduction in the land available for crop production. While it is true that advances in agricultural science could produce larger harvests, it would be wildly optimistic to believe that these advances could offset such a large reduction in farmland. The impact on the supply of domestically produced food in the United States would be disastrous. Similar catastrophic effects on agriculture could be expected in other places on the globe.

As you read, draw a simple cause-effect diagram to help you with the details of this threat.

At the same time as climbing temperatures are damaging agriculture and destroying ecosystems as large as the North American forests, **coastal areas will face a different threat.** The higher global temperatures that are expected, especially in the higher latitudes, will begin to melt the polar ice caps as well as inland glaciers and bring about a rise in sea level. Again, predictions of the rise vary between 20 and 150 centimeters over the next one hundred years. While a rise in ocean level at the lower end of this range would have negligible effects, a rise of one meter would, for example, flood 15 percent of Bangladesh and force more than 10 million people to abandon their homes (Holdgate, 1991). It also would mean massive damage and disruption for the small, vulner-

210 able, low-lying island nations of the Pacific and Caribbean. Some
of them would simply cease to exist.

4. Responding to the Threat

As you read this section, look for solutions—general and specific—to the problem.

Thus, in the twenty-first century, global warming could in-   18
flict massive damage on the world and inevitably lead to large-
scale political and social disruption. Most environmental scientists
215 and an increasing number of politicians, therefore, advocate taking
swift action to reduce greenhouse gas emissions and thereby slow
global warming. They argue that we should see this as a form of
insurance against catastrophe, in this case the possibility that
global warming will eventually cause damage and disruption as
220 bad as or worse than the experts have predicted. If the catastrophe
occurs, the world will be better off than it would have been without
the insurance.

Taking the Lead

What does taking the lead *mean? Try to understand these words as you continue to read.*

How could an adequate reduction of greenhouse gas emissions   19
be accomplished? Most experts agree that to ensure an equitable
225 solution to the problem, the industrial countries of the world must
take the lead. After all, it is they who are to blame for most of the
greenhouse gases that accumulated in the atmosphere before the
1990s. In addition, their economic resources, their scientific knowledge, and technological expertise place them, initially at least, in a
230 better position to introduce measures to reduce greenhouse gas
emissions.

Scan forward in the text to identify where the writer describes other, more long-term strategies. Then begin reading here again.

An interim, short-term strategy must be to reduce the   20
use of energy produced by fossil-fuel burning. To accomplish
this, a first important step is for governments to introduce policies
235 that will encourage energy conservation. One specific measure is to
encourage recycling. Another is to introduce incentives for manufacturers to develop products with greater energy efficiency and for
consumers to purchase the new energy-efficient products. These incentives could include increased tax credits for the manufacturers'
240 costs of research and development and for consumers' costs of replacing old inefficient appliances with the new high-efficiency versions.

A second, more long-term strategy must be to replace fossil   21
fuels with environmentally safe, alternative sources of energy that
245 will be sustainable and will not deplete a region's natural resources. To accomplish this, governments will again need to introduce incentives for increased research into alternative energy

sources and for the development of affordable technology to exploit these sources.

Check back for what these policies are.
250

Conservation policies like those mentioned above are attractive because they have been effective in the past. For example, under pressure from the government's fuel economy standards of the 1970s and early 1980s, U.S. automobile manufacturers succeeded in making their products significantly more efficient without a loss in performance, size, or safety. During the same period of drastic increases in the price of oil, industrial production in Japan, Sweden, and West Germany became 40 percent more energy efficient. Therefore, the prospects are good that such policies will work in the future.
255

22

What is the other good news about conservation? Check back.
260

More good news for conservation is that technologies already exist today that are capable of significantly reducing energy consumption and greenhouse gas emissions—provided the right incentives are offered. For example, in the United States, the use of coal-generated electricity in residential and commercial buildings accounts for 34 percent of the country's carbon dioxide emissions. However, substantial energy savings are possible in this area if full use is made of the most energy-efficient appliances, materials, and building design. If the most efficient existing energy-saving technologies were utilized in new buildings and, where feasible, in existing buildings, it is estimated that a 40 percent reduction in energy consumption would be possible (Norberg-Blohm, 1991).
265

270

23

Draw simple cause-effect diagrams to clarify these other benefits.
275

Immediate action to reduce the threat of global warming is justified because it would bring **other benefits** unrelated to global warming. Its advocates point out that a reduction in the use of coal to generate electricity, for example, will cause a large decrease in the amount of carbon dioxide emissions. It will also help preserve our natural environment by drastically cutting down emissions of sulfur dioxide, the principal cause of the acid rain, which threatens the forests, lakes, and rivers of the United States and of much of northern and central Europe. Similarly, reduced burning of coal and gasoline, by cutting nitrous oxide emissions, will lower levels of air pollution in many cities.
280

24

Scan ahead to identify the places in the text where the writer deals with the drawbacks of the solution.
285

However, there is also bad news. First, a program of energy conservation has its costs. In addition to financing the incentives, the government will need to impose a substantial, if temporary, burden on the economy by increasing the price of energy to all consumers through user fees or higher taxes. Initial purchase incentives by themselves will not guarantee a reduction in energy consumption by consumers. If energy prices remain low while ap-

25

290   pliances become more efficient, consumers will respond in a pre-
dictable way; they will merely use the same amount of gasoline to
travel longer distances and the same amount of electricity and gas
to keep their homes warmer in winter and cooler in summer than
they did before. The direct costs of conservation measures will
295   therefore be high. Some economists have argued, for example, that
a 20 percent reduction in emissions of carbon dioxide by 2010 could
cost the United States between $800 and $3,600 billion[1] and would
slow economic growth by about 50 percent.

*As you read, draw a
simple cause-effect di-*   **Second, the gradual conversion to sustainable, environ-**   26
agram to explain why   300   **mentally friendly methods of generating electricity will also**
this is so.   **be enormously expensive.** Research and technology development
will be costly in themselves. Moreover, the conversion will place a
disproportionate burden on certain sections of society. As coal-fired
electricity generation is replaced, there will be social and economic
305   dislocation among those whose livelihoods depend, directly or indi-
rectly, on the coal industry. It will be government's responsibility
to provide programs that will compensate those affected members
of society for their losses and retrain them for employment in other
sectors of the economy.

Enabling Others to Follow

Scan ahead for who   310   **The responsibility for global warming, however, does**   27
else is responsible.   **not lie exclusively with the industrial world.** Domestic
Then come back, and   programs aimed at conservation and conversion to alternative
resume reading this   energy sources in these countries, therefore, are a necessary but
paragraph.   not a sufficient response to the threat of global warming. In their
315   attempts at rapid economic development, the developing countries
are beginning to produce greenhouse gas emissions equaling
those of the industrial countries (see Figure 4). In 1990, for example, 45 percent of global greenhouse gas emissions were from
the developing world. The beneficial effects of conservation pro-
320   grams in the industrial world are likely to be undermined, if not
completely negated, if the emission of greenhouse gases by developing nations continues to increase. And emissions will surely
continue to increase if these countries, under extreme pressure to
feed, house, educate, and employ their growing populations, con-
325   tinue to pursue economic development at any cost to the environment.

1. Cited in Council of Economic Advisers (1990).

People from different parts of the world view environmental issues—and each other's role in environmental problems—from different perspectives. (Scott Willis. Copyright 1989, Willis—*San Jose Mercury News*. Reprinted by permission.)

Under what circumstances? Check back and draw a simple cause-effect diagram to describe them.

Under these circumstances, the only realistic strategy for the industrial world is to ensure that developing nations are in a position to pursue responsible policies for development. To achieve this, it must first effectively address the problem of the massive debt carried by developing countries. According to the World Bank, this debt in 1988 was so great that the seventeen countries with the largest debts paid $31 billion more, mostly in interest to service this debt, than they received in aid from governments and other institutions in industrial countries. **It is partly because of the need to service this debt that developing countries are destroying their ecological resources, including their forests. It is no coincidence that the same fourteen developing countries (Speth, 1990) account for 50 percent of the Third World's external debt and about 70 percent of global deforestation.**

This paragraph has described a problem. What do you expect in following paragraphs?

By 1991, many experts were beginning to consider debt forgiveness an essential and inevitable component of any program for Third World debt relief. Debt forgiveness, however, need not be unconditional. It could take the form of a bargain negotiated be-

28

330

335

340

29

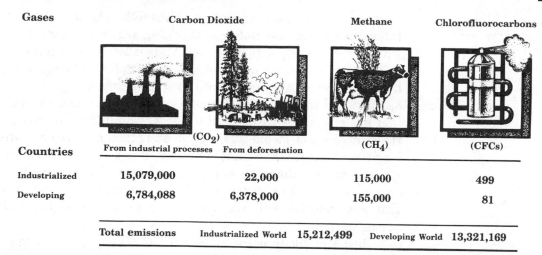

Gases	Carbon Dioxide		Methane	Chlorofluorocarbons
Countries	From industrial processes (CO_2)	From deforestation	(CH_4)	($CFCs$)
Industrialized	15,079,000	22,000	115,000	499
Developing	6,784,088	6,378,000	155,000	81

Total emissions	Industrialized World	15,212,499	Developing World	13,321,169

Figure 4. Greenhouse gas emissions in the industrial and developing worlds. (*Source:* World Resources Institute, *World Resources 1992–1993* [New York: Oxford University Press, 1992].)

345 tween Third World debtor nations and their industrial creditors. It could be offered, for example, in return for commitments by the developing nations to cease or severely restrict deforestation, to pass strict new environmental protection laws and to enforce them rigorously, and to pursue environmentally safe development policies.

Use the repeated ideas here to refresh your memory of what you've just read.

350 **In addition to resolving the debt crisis, however, the industrial world will need to provide increased aid to developing countries.** This aid will take the form of direct economic assistance, technical assistance, and better access to the newer technologies that will reduce greenhouse gas emissions. It will be 355 needed if developing countries are to attain their goals of economic development and a better standard of life for their people. Together with debt relief, such aid will permit developing countries to pursue policies of sustainable development and thus make their essential contribution to resolving the problem of global warming.

30

5. Rethinking Our Priorities

Rethinking something involves change. Scan ahead to identify where the writer describes a change. Then resume reading here.

360 In conclusion, then, this article is arguing that the problem of global warming cannot be effectively addressed without the decision, especially by industrial countries, to spend vast amounts of money. Some early estimates are that it could require annual global expenditures of as much as $150 billion.[2]

31

2. The figure is from Worldwatch Institute, cited by MacNeill (1989).

*Revolutions involve
change. As you read,
identify the specific
changes that the
writer thinks are nec-
essary.*

365   **In order to raise spending to these levels, a global revo-** 32
lution in public and political thinking will be necessary. We
will need to develop a global ecological perspective which then can
be used to reexamine our traditional attitudes, policies, and actions. This revolution will require both the public and politicians to
370   be convinced that the type of unsustainable economic development
that has characterized much of the last two hundred years and is
the root cause of global warming is a significant danger to their
long-term security. For many countries, if not all, it is a more significant danger than the military machines of traditionally un-
375   friendly nations. In addition, the global nature of the threat means
that any solution will then require unprecedented cooperation
among nations.

         Just how likely is such a revolution? There may be cause for 33
cautious optimism in indications that public and political thinking
380   has already started to change. There is evidence of a developing
public appreciation of the need to protect our global environment.
For example, opinion polls between 1981 and 1989 show that the
U.S. public is increasingly willing to give priority to the environment regardless of cost (see Figure 5). This is a trend that is also
385   evident in the other industrial democracies. Political leaders of the
Group of Seven, the world's major industrial democracies, have
spoken publicly about the need for sustainable development in general and have committed themselves to reducing greenhouse gas
emissions in particular. The governments of industrial nations
390   have also recognized that industry and agriculture in a completely
free market economy are not held accountable for their environmental costs, i.e., the ecological damage associated with the production, consumption, and disposal of their goods and services.
Governments are beginning to acknowledge that they have an obli-
395   gation to intervene in the market in order to balance these costs
and ultimately to eliminate them.

*Check back for the
meaning of the words.*

         A few actions have accompanied the words, for example, 34
the Montreal Protocol of 1990, by which fifty-nine nations agreed
to halt the use of CFCs by the year 2000. Similarly, during the
400   1992 United Nations Conference on Environment and Development (UNCED) in Rio de Janeiro—the so-called Earth Summit—
153 nations signed the Convention on Climate Change. This treaty
has the goal of stabilizing greenhouse gas emissions by the year
2000 at "earlier levels" and requires countries to set limits on the

*Do you expect to read
about the strengths or
weaknesses of the ac-
tions in the last para-
graph?*

405   emissions of greenhouse gases.
         However, it is very questionable how significant such 35

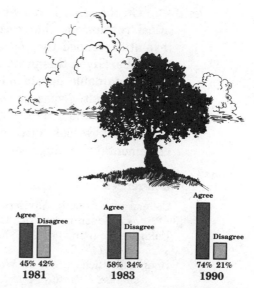

Figure 5. Public support for environmental protection, 1981–90. This figure shows the rate of response to the following statement: "Protecting the environment is so important that requirements and standards cannot be too high, and continuing environmental improvements must be made regardless of cost." (*Source:* CBS News/*New York Times* polls, as reported in R. E. Dunlap, "Public Opinion in the 1980s: Clear Consensus, Ambiguous Commitment," *Environment* 33.8 [1991]: 9–37.)

actions really are. The vague language of the Convention on Climate Change obliges the signing countries to make few concrete commitments. For example, the "earlier levels" to which green-
410 house gas emissions will be reduced by 2000 are not specified. Other agreements signed at the Earth Summit in Rio are similarly vague. For example, the discussions addressed the issues of sustainable development and increased aid to developing countries. Significantly, however, nowhere in the agreements did the wealth-
415 ier countries actually commit themselves to increasing their assistance to the developing world. Also of significance was the refusal of these wealthier countries at the Rio summit to grant debt relief to developing nations. In general, therefore, significant actions, either in the form of domestic policies or international treaties, have
420 been slower to appear than words of concern from the public and politicians. "I've seen glaciers mover faster" was how one scientific observer expressed his frustration with the slow pace of action on greenhouse warming.[3] We have yet to see the revolution that is required.

425   On the other hand, who in 1980 would have predicted the po-   36
litical revolutions that occurred between 1989 and 1991? These
revolutions ended the cold war and changed the political map of
the globe. Given this precedent and given the fact that the system
of unsustainable development that has been in operation for the
430   last few hundred years is obviously breaking down, perhaps people
will see that the time is right for another revolution. Perhaps the
world can now look forward to the needed global revolution in environmental thinking.

References

Council of Economic Advisers. (1990). *1990 economic report of the presi-
       dent*. Washington, DC: U.S. Government Printing Office.
Holdgate, Martin. (1991). The environment of tomorrow. *Environment*
       33(6), 14–42.
Houghton, Richard, A., & Woodwell, George M. (1989). Global climatic
       change. *Scientific American*, 260(4), 36–44.
Jones, Philip D., & Wigley, Tom M. L. (1990). Global warming trends.
       Scientific American, 263(2), 84–91.
Lorius, C., Jouzel, J., Raynaud, D., Hansen, J., & Le Treut, H. (1990). The
       ice-core record: Climate sensitivity and future greenhouse warming.
       Nature 347(6289), 139–145.
MacNeill, Jim. (1989). Strategies for sustainable economic development.
       Scientific American, 261(3), 155–165.
Monastersky, R. (1990). Time for action. *Science News*, 139, 200–202.
Norberg-Blohm, Vicki. (1991). From the inside out: Reducing CO_2 emis-
       sions in the building sector. *Environment* 33(3), 16–44.
Schneider, Stephen H. (1989). The changing climate. *Scientific American*,
       261(3), 70–79.
Speth, J. G. (1990). Toward a North-South compact for the environment.
       Environment 32(5), 16–43.

WORKING WITH THE MAIN READING

1. INTRODUCTION

A Closer Look

1. There is agreement among scientists that greenhouse warming is a
   serious problem.   T   F

   3. Cited by Monastersky (1991).

2. There is agreement among politicians on what should be done
about greenhouse warming.   T F

3. What are the important words and phrases in the text that helped you answer
questions 1 and 2?

Vocabulary in Context

Here are some words from section 1 that you may not have known. You either
guessed their meaning from context or from your knowledge of word families, or
you omitted the word and were still able to understand the sentence. Now check
and learn the meanings of the words. Use your dictionary to help you.

zone (line 1)	greenhouse (line 14, 18)
glacier (line 1)	inconclusive (line 18)
fiction (line 3)	debate (line 19)

2. FACTS AND UNCERTAINTIES

Main Idea Check

Here are the main ideas for this section of the article. Write the correct paragraph number beside its main idea.

_____ Scientists have established that the earth has become warmer in the last one
hundred years.

_____ The burning of tropical forests in developing countries is a major contributor of
carbon dioxide in the atmosphere.

_____ There is historical evidence that links increases in the earth's temperature to increased carbon dioxide and methane in the atmosphere.

_____ Computer models of future climate change have added to the uncertainty by
failing to agree on predictions of temperature increases.

_____ Intensive cattle rearing and rice growing in flooded fields are major factors in
the increase of methane in the atmosphere.

_____ Gases like carbon dioxide, methane, and CFCs could clearly produce a greenhouse effect because they allow sunlight through to warm the earth but prevent
the heat released by the earth from escaping into space.

_____ Any effects of greenhouse gases on climate will be felt worldwide and by future generations.

_____ Many scientists are not prepared to conclude that the warming trend of the last one hundred years is due to increased greenhouse gases in the atmosphere.

_____ Industrialization, not naturally occurring processes, accounts for much of the increase in greenhouse gases over the last one hundred years.

_____ Scientists have shown that the amount of greenhouse gases in the atmosphere has been increasing over the last one hundred years.

A Closer Look

1. In which way or ways does the burning of tropical forests contribute to the accumulation of greenhouse gases in the atmosphere?
   a. It causes the extinction of thousands of species.
   b. It sends massive amounts of carbon dioxide into the atmosphere.
   c. It causes problems of soil erosion.
   d. It reduces the earth's natural ability to absorb carbon dioxide from the atmosphere.

2. Here are some ideas from this section of the passage. Choose those ideas about which there is scientific disagreement.
   a. Industry and intensive agriculture are large contributors of greenhouse gases in the atmosphere.
   b. The earth has become warmer during the past one hundred years or so.
   c. Computer models have been able to give us accurate predictions of global climate in the middle of the twenty-first century.
   d. If greenhouse gases have an effect, it will be felt globally and more in the twenty-first century than today.
   e. The warming trend of the last one hundred years has been caused by the accumulation of greenhouse gases in the atmosphere.

3. What reason or reasons do some scientists have for rejecting the theory of greenhouse warming?
   a. There is evidence that glaciers are retreating and that there is less polar sea ice than there used to be.
   b. The general warming trend of the last one hundred years is not as consistent or as large as the greenhouse warming theory predicts.
   c. The present evidence does not show that the build-up of greenhouse gases caused the slight warming trend of the last one hundred years, but only that the two events occurred during the same period.
   d. Carbon dioxide, methane, and CFCs do not have the potential to warm the earth.

Vocabulary in Context

Here are some words from section 2 that you may not have known. You either guessed their meaning from context or from your knowledge of word families, or you omitted the word and were still able to understand the sentence. Now check and learn the meanings of the words. Use your dictionary to help you.

unanimous (line 28)	adjacent (line 57)
transparent (line 31)	decade (line 67)
radiation (line 33)	emission (lines 81)
to absorb (line 33)	polar (line 116)
to trap (lines 41, 62)	trend (line 119)
core (line 41)	to speculate (line 128)
to extract (line 41)	to exaggerate (line 137)
smog (line 53)	

3. POTENTIAL EFFECTS OF CLIMATE CHANGE

Main Idea Check

Here are the main ideas for this section of the article. Write the correct paragraph number beside its main idea.

_____ Higher temperatures will also probably have a very destructive impact on agriculture.

_____ The consequences for natural ecosystems will be extremely serious if we delay action and if temperature increases are 3° to 5° C.

_____ Higher temperatures will lead to a rise in ocean level, which may endanger vast areas of densely populated, low-lying land.

_____ Despite uncertainties about global warming, most scientists argue that we cannot afford to wait before taking steps to cut emissions of greenhouse gases.

A Closer Look

1. Some people believe that we should not do anything about greenhouse warming until we are certain about its effects.   T   F

2. Why does the writer use the example of the North American forest belt?
   a. to show the potential destructive effects of greenhouse warming on natural ecosystems

    b. to show that natural ecosystems have the ability to adapt to the expected temperature changes associated with greenhouse warming

    c. to show how greenhouse warming would affect agriculture and human settlements

3. Coastal areas of the world will escape the possibly catastrophic effects of global warming.   T F

4. The following diagram represents the possible relationship between greenhouse warming and agriculture. Reread the relevant paragraph(s), and then complete the diagram with ideas from the list below. Write only the correct letter in each box.

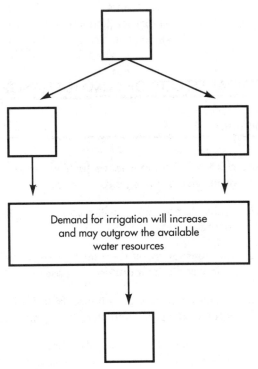

Demand for irrigation will increase and may outgrow the available water resources

    a. Rainfall will decline in certain areas.

    b. There could be a disastrous reduction in the amount of land available for growing crops.

    c. Temperatures will increase.

    d. Higher temperatures will accelerate evaporation.

Vocabulary in Context

Here are some words from section 3 that you may not have known. You either guessed their meaning from context or from your knowledge of word families, or you omitted the word and were still able to understand the sentence. Now check and learn the meanings of the words. Use your dictionary to help you.

vicious cycle (line 164)   unchecked/to check (line 181)
location (line 172)   to offset (line 193)
scale (line 179)

4. RESPONDING TO THE THREAT (Paragraphs 18–26)

Main Idea Check

Here are the main ideas for this section of the article. Write the correct paragraph number beside its main idea.

_____ We could reduce energy consumption and greenhouse gas emissions substantially with technology that already exists today.

_____ A major drawback of a program to reduce greenhouse emissions by energy conservation is its immense direct costs.

_____ Governments must also develop alternative, sustainable sources of energy to replace fossil fuels.

_____ Converting to alternative, environmentally friendly sources of energy will also be enormously expensive.

_____ The world's industrial nations should be the first to start programs to reduce greenhouse gas emissions.

_____ The majority of environmental scientists believe that we should insure ourselves against a future catastrophe by taking immediate action to cut greenhouse gas emissions.

_____ Conserving energy and reducing emissions would also contribute to the solution of other environmental problems.

_____ Governments must develop energy conservation policies that will reduce the demand for energy produced by fossil-fuel burning.

_____ Policies to reduce the consumption of energy were successful in the 1970s and 1980s.

A Closer Look

1. The writer believes that the world's leading industrial nations have a responsibility to start the process of reducing greenhouse gas emissions.   T   F

2. The following diagram represents the writer's ideas for a process that would reduce the contribution of industrial countries, especially the United States, to greenhouse warming. Scan to identify the relevant paragraphs, and reread them. Then complete this diagram with ideas from the list below. Write only the correct letter in each box.
   a. Greenhouse gas emissions are reduced.
   b. Industry and consumers have financial reasons to recycle.
   c. The global warming trend is slowed.
   d. Consumers have a reason to buy products that are more energy efficient.
   e. Alternative sources of energy and technologies to exploit them are developed.
   f. Industry is encouraged to develop products that are more energy efficient.

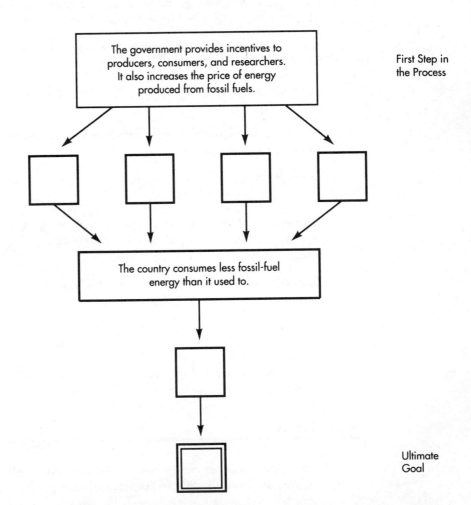

3. The diagram in question 2 does not show the negative sides of the solutions the writer proposes. Reread the relevant paragraphs, and then add these negative effects in the appropriate places in the diagram.

4. For what purpose or purposes does the writer want incentives such as tax credits to be used?
   a. to encourage research into alternatives to fossil fuels
   b. to encourage the development of more energy-efficient products
   c. to encourage consumers to purchase more energy-efficient products

5. Why does the writer include the examples of U.S. automobile manufacturers, Japan, Sweden, and Germany in paragraph 22?
   a. to show that Japan, Sweden, and Germany can manufacture cars more efficiently than the United States
   b. to show that policies aimed at conserving energy by improving energy-efficiency can be effective
   c. to show that major industrial countries are to blame for a large proportion of the greenhouse gases in the atmosphere

6. The writer believes that consumers should not have to pay higher prices for energy.   T   F

Vocabulary in Context

Here are some words from section 3 that you may not have known. You either guessed their meaning from context or from your knowledge of word families, or you omitted the word and were still able to understand the sentence. Now check and learn the meanings of the words. Use your dictionary to help you.

inflict (line 212)	residential (line 264)
to advocate (line 215)	feasible (line 269)
thereby (line 216)	conversion/to convert (line 299)
interim (line 232)	moreover (line 302)
appliances (line 241)	disproportionate (line 303)
drastic (line 256)	dislocation (line 305)
generated/to generate	livelihood (line 305)
(line 264)	sector (line 309)

4. RESPONDING TO THE THREAT (Paragraphs 27–30)

Main Idea Check

Here are the main ideas for this section of the article. Write the correct paragraph number beside its main idea.

_____ Debt forgiveness could be offered to developing countries that commit themselves to protecting the world ecology.

_____ Developing countries will also require increased economic and technical assistance.

_____ Actions by the industrial countries alone to reduce greenhouse gas emissions will not solve the problem of global warming if we ignore emissions of the same gases by developing countries.

_____ Industrial countries must solve the problem of Third World debt before developing countries will be able to pursue ecologically responsible policies for economic development.

A Closer Look

1. The diagram below represents how developing countries contribute to the buildup of greenhouse gases in the atmosphere. Scan to identify the relevant paragraph(s), and reread them. Then complete the diagram with ideas from the list below. Write only the correct letter in each box.

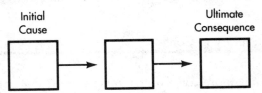

Initial Cause   Ultimate Consequence

   a. The top priority for developing countries is economic development, regardless of its cost to the environment.
   b. Developing countries have growing populations that need food, housing, education, and jobs.
   c. Emissions of greenhouse gases increase.

2. The diagram in question 1 is not complete. Paragraph 28 provides additional information you could use to add a fourth element at an appropriate place in the diagram. Reread this paragraph, and then complete the diagram appropriately *in your own words.*

3. What, according to the writer, could developing countries offer to do in return for debt forgiveness?
   a. to stop destroying their forests
   b. to negotiate trade agreements with their creditors
   c. to better protect the environment

4. The problem of greenhouse warming can be solved without the cooperation of developing countries.   T F

5. The diagram below represents the writer's idea of how the problem discussed in this section should be solved. Reread the relevant paragraph(s), and then

complete the diagram with ideas from the list below. Write only the correct letter in each box.

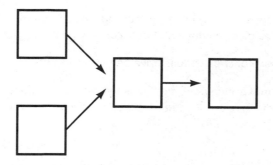

a. Emissions of greenhouse gases are considerably reduced.
b. The industrial countries give economic, technical, and technological assistance to the developing countries.
c. The industrial countries offer debt forgiveness to the developing countries.
d. Developing countries are able to adopt policies of sustainable development that cause much less harm to the environment.

Vocabulary in Context

Here are some words from section 4 that you may not have known. You either guessed their meaning from context or from your knowledge of word families, or you omitted the word and were still able to understand the sentence. Now check and learn the meanings of the words. Use your dictionary to help you.

debt (line 331)   bargain (line 344)
aid (line 334)   debtor (line 345)
coincidence (line 338)   creditor (line 345)

5. RETHINKING OUR PRIORITIES

Main Idea Check

Here are the main ideas for this section of the article. Write the correct paragraph number beside its main idea.

_____ Actions that really address the problem of greenhouse warming have been much slower to appear than words of concern about the problem.

_____ There is evidence that people and governments are beginning to give greater priority to environmental issues than before.

_____ The problem of global warming will not be resolved without massive expenditures.

_____ Perhaps the revolution in thinking about the environment can be expected because other fundamental political changes have occurred recently.

_____ A few concrete actions have been taken to protect the global environment.

_____ To make available the funds necessary to address the root causes of global warming, we will need to radically change our ways of thinking and conducting policy.

A Closer Look

1. The writer is absolutely certain that the problem of global warming will be solved.   T   F

2. What reason or reasons does the writer have for believing that the public and politicians are becoming more environmentally aware?
   a. Polls show that an increasing number of Americans feel we need economic development at any environmental cost.
   b. Politicians have agreed to reduce emissions of some greenhouse gases.
   c. The 1992 United Nations Conference on Environment and Development
   d. The Montreal Protocol of 1990

3. This section talks about a revolution in the way people and politicians think about the environment and economic development. It also suggests some necessary changes. In the list below, choose N ("New") for attitudes that would be typical if this revolution occurred. Choose O ("Old") for those attitudes that are typical of more traditional nineteenth- and twentieth-century thinking.

   a. Consuming and exhausting the world's natural resources is an acceptable policy of economic development.   N   O

   b. International cooperation is too difficult to achieve; each country should concentrate on its own development and protection.   N   O

   c. We need to spend more money on the environment than on our military forces.   N   O

   d. Governments should never interfere in the free market economy.   N   O

   e. Most economic development, as we have seen it over the past two hundred years, cannot be sustained.   N   O

   f. Unsustainable development is a greater danger to national security than the military machines of neighboring countries.   N   O

Vocabulary in Context

Here are some words from section 5 that you may not have known. You either guessed their meaning from context or from your knowledge of word families, or you omitted the word and were still able to understand the sentence. Now check and learn the meanings of the words. Use your dictionary to help you.

expenditures (line 364)   to stabilize (line 403)
to characterize (line 371) to specify (line 410)
to hold someone ac-
  countable (line 391)

Unit Five

Education and Family Life
in the United States

259

Text Study 1.
Recognizing Text Organization:
Comparison and Contrast

Read these three examples. The ideas in them will be familiar to you because they are from Units 1 and 4. As you read, try to answer these two questions:

What two things is the writer describing?

Does the writer focus on differences or similarities?

1. Both the wealthier industrial world and the developing world are having major problems with diseases that are quite easily prevented but that are difficult, if not impossible, to cure.

2. Industrial nations are concerned with providing the latest drugs and technology to treat that small section of the population who are ill. Here the focus is on the sophisticated treatment of conditions such as heart disease and cancer. Developing nations, on the other hand, are faced with the problem of providing for the majority of their population the clean water, the basic drugs, and the vaccines that the industrial world takes for granted. Here the priority is dealing with diseases that are widespread in the population because of unsanitary living conditions and the lack of basic health care.

3. Immense changes have occurred in the basin of the Aral Sea since the late 1950s. At that time, the sea covered sixty-six thousand square kilometers; now, in contrast, it has an area of only thirty-six thousand square kilometers. The salt content of the water now stands at 3 percent, whereas forty years ago it was 1 percent—perfect for supporting freshwater wildlife. Be-

261

fore 1960, commercial fishing flourished; today the boats lie abandoned because of lack of fish. The region within one hundred kilometers of the sea no longer produces cotton as its main agricultural crop. The climate used to be moderate enough to provide long summers without danger of frost, which were well suited to cotton growing. Now, however, the climate is more extreme and fewer frost-free days have caused major reductions in the production of cotton.

EXPLANATION

THE ELEMENTS OF COMPARISONS AND CONTRASTS

In the first example, the writer describes how industrial and developing nations are *similar* in one certain aspect. The basis for the comparison is the similarities in the diseases that are causing them problems—they are diseases that are much harder to cure than to prevent.

In example 2, the writer describes how the industrial nations and developing nations are *different* in another aspect. The basis for the contrast is the different challenges that face the health services of each group of nations.

In example 3, the writer describes how the Aral Sea of 1990 and the region around it are very *different* from how they used to be in 1950.

THE ORGANIZATION OF COMPARISONS AND CONTRASTS

Examples 2 and 3 are both are contrast paragraphs. However, the organization inside the paragraphs is different.

In example 2, the writer first completes the description of health-care problems in industrial countries (*a*); then the writer deals with the different problems in developing countries (*b*). We can label this method of organization *a, a, a* . . . ; *b, b, b* . . . .

In example 3, the organization is different. The writer deals with the size of the Aral Sea in 1950 and immediately contrasts it with its size in 1990; then the writer deals, one by one, with other characteristics of the Aral Sea—its salt content in 1950 and 1990, its fishing industry in 1950 and 1990, its climate in 1950 and 1990, and its cotton production in 1950 and 1990. We can label this method of organization *a-b, a-b, a-b* . . . .

Writers organize paragraphs in the same general ways to point out similarities or differences. They may also organize entire articles or sections of articles in the same ways. If you can identify the comparison-contrast method of organization when you see it, you will be able to read more efficiently.

MARKERS OF COMPARISON AND CONTRAST

Often a writer uses vocabulary that suggests to you, the reader, that you should expect to read a comparison or a contrast. This vocabulary includes nouns, verbs, and connecting expressions. We call this vocabulary *comparison-contrast markers*.

Read through the following list. Most, maybe even all, of the items will be familiar to you. If you need an explanation or example for an item that is not familiar to you, ask your instructor or check your English dictionary.

Describing Similarities

similar	to resemble
similarity	in common
identical	similarly
parallel	in the same way
comparable	likewise
common	like *X* . . .
equivalent	also

Describing Differences

to distinguish	in theory . . . in practice
distinction	but
difference	however
to differ	yet
to contrast	conversely
to oppose	in contrast (to *X*)
used to	unlike *X*
while	no longer . . .
whereas	once . . .
rather than	
on the one hand . . . on the other hand	
Any adjective in its comparative form, e.g., *larger than, more efficient than*	

READING STRATEGIES _____

1. While you are reading, be ready to identify words that tell you that the writer is examining similarities or differences.

2. Identify what in general is being compared or contrasted.

3. Identify the basis of the comparison or contrast.

4. Identify the method of organizing the contrast or comparison. Is it *a, a, a . . . ; b, b, b . . .* or *a-b, a-b, a-b . . .*? Knowing the organization will help you make connections and read more easily.

5. Identify the specific differences or similarities discussed by the writer.

EXERCISE _____

Practice your reading strategies as you read the following sentences or short paragraphs.

1. Identify any comparison-contrast markers.

2. Decide whether the writer is focusing on similarities or differences.

3. Identify the general subjects of the comparison or contrast.

4. Identify the basis of the comparison or contrast.

5. Look for any specific details of similarities or differences.

Example
Unlike Jim, his older brother, who is just under five feet six inches, Matthew is well over six feet tall.

Markers? *Unlike*

Focus? *differences*

General subject? *Jim & Matthew*

Basis of the comparison? *their height*

Details? *Jim — short*
Matthew — tall

1. The health-care systems of both industrialized and developing nations tend to give priority to the treatment of disease after it occurs.

2. While health care is available to all those in need of it in most modern industrial nations, it may reach only 20 percent to 30 percent of potential patients in the Third World.

3. Some of the problems facing privately funded health-care systems (e.g., like that of the United States) resemble those confronting publicly funded systems (e.g., like those of Sweden or Britain): access to health care is being reduced because of rapidly increasing costs.

4. The widespread unavailability of clear, uncontaminated water is one of the health-care problems faced by developing countries but not by the industrial world.

5. Children acquire perfect pronunciation in their native language, whereas most adults learning a second language never achieve perfect pronunciation in it.

6. The first major wave of immigration into the United States (1820–1890) brought for the most part inhabitants of northwest Europe to America. In contrast, the immigrants of the second wave (1890–1920) came mostly from the countries of central, southern, and eastern Europe.

7. Non-English-speaking immigrants to the United States show a pattern of language shift over two or three generations. New immigrants generally retain their native language, acquiring enough English for economic and social survival. Their children grow up bilingual, and their grandchildren are usually monolingual speakers of English. Contrast this with the language patterns of non-English-speaking groups who were already here when the first large waves of English-speaking settlers arrived—the native Americans, the Spanish speakers of the Southwest, and the French speakers of Louisiana. In general, these groups have retained their native languages while acquiring English. The resulting bilingualism has not shifted to the monolingual use of English after a generation or two; instead, it has persisted over many generations.

   How can we account for these two different patterns of language use?

8. Students in many countries are expected to sit quietly in class and absorb the information and ideas presented by the teacher. Rarely, if ever, do students ask questions. Questions would be seen either as a challenge to the teacher's authority or as a sign the student has not been paying attention. In the United States, on the other hand, teachers encourage students to ask questions. In fact, if a student never asks questions in class, the teacher may get the impression that the student is dull, inattentive, or uninterested in the class.

9. A question that may be perfectly appropriate and polite in one culture may be considered impolite, even insulting, in another culture. For many of us, for example, the question "How is your wife?" is a perfectly acceptable question to ask a friend or colleague. In another culture, however, the same question is hardly ever asked; it would suggest that the husband is not capable of taking care of his wife.

10. The language used by parents with their young children has properties that distinguish it from the speech used with older children and adults. It tends to be simpler and more transparent. Research has found, for example, that adults make their pronunciation temporarily more precise and distinct when they are talking with children of around two years of age. It has also been established that adults often repeat nouns rather than use a pronoun for them. In addition, they talk about actions that are occurring in the "here and now"—for example, "Now Mommy is going to the bedroom to get your shoes." They also select words and grammatical forms that they perceive to be more obvious in meaning than other forms.

11. When we say that children usually learn their native language from the adults around them, are we suggesting that these adults behave like second-language teachers? The answer is that there are only a few parallels between the traditional behavior of language teachers and that of adults caring for young children, say up to the age of four or five. Unlike second-language teachers, adults rarely, if ever, correct the grammar and pronunciation of young children even though their language is far from perfect in both these areas. Nor do adults deliberately give children practice in saying certain sounds or in using certain grammar rules. Where adults do resemble teachers is in their correction of children when they use a wrong vocabulary item, e.g., "Well, we don't call that a fork; we call it a spoon." They are also clearly acting like teachers when they attempt to build an awareness in young children of which speech forms are polite and acceptable and which are not.

For extra practice in reading texts with comparison-contrast organization, go back and reread paragraphs 1 and 2 in the Main Reading in Unit 1 and paragraphs 1 and 3–5 in Reading Passage 2.3. Complete a table like the one on page 264 for each paragraph.

Text Study 2.
Recognizing Text Organization:
Unfavored and Favored Views

EXPLANATION

A specific type of text organization by contrast occurs when a writer wants to present two views of an issue. One view may be quite common but it has flaws; this is the unfavored view. The second view is the one that the writer considers to be better; this is the favored view. Usually the unfavored view appears first. The favored view follows—either in the same paragraph or in a following paragraph. Here's an example:

(First) unfavored view

Negative assessment of first view
(Second) favored view

It seems to be a reasonable assumption that **the health problems of developing nations are very different from those that face the health-care systems in modern industrial countries.** *Yet we would be seriously mistaken if we were to accept this assumption.* **In fact, health-care systems throughout the world are facing many of the same general challenges and some of the same specific problems.** AIDS, for example, is a major threat in both industrial and developing countries. . . .

Some of the markers for the *unfavored-favored view* organization are the same as those for describing differences (see page 263). In addition, because such texts judge views, we also see words connected with believing and words containing positive or negative judgments. Use the following lists to review old vocabulary; there are only one or two new words.

Markers That Show Views

Verbs	*Nouns*
to believe	belief
to claim	claim
to imagine	

Verbs	Nouns
to conceive	conception
to analyze	analysis
to interpret	interpretation
to assume	assumption
to argue	argument
to perceive	perception
to conclude	conclusion
to regard	
to charge	charge
to allege	allegation
to accuse	accusation
to be supposed	
to seem	
to appear	
to convince	idea
to persuade	notion
	impression
	illusion
	fallacy
	myth

Assessment Markers

Nouns	Adjectives
accuracy	accurate/inaccurate
flaw	flawed/flawless
error	erroneous
weakness	weak
defect	defective
fault	faulty
shortcoming	
truth	true/untrue
mistake	mistaken
trap	
illusion	valid/invalid
fallacy	reasonable/unreasonable
myth	justified/unjustified
	warranted/unwarranted

READING STRATEGIES

1. Look for markers of (A) views, (B) contrast, and (C) negative or positive judgments.

2. Use markers A to identify beliefs.

3. Use markers *B* to identify where the second belief is introduced.

4. Use markers *C* to distinguish between the unfavored and favored beliefs.

EXERCISE

Practice the four new reading strategies while you read these short texts. As you read, you should:

1. Identify view markers, contrast markers, and assessment markers.

2. Identify the unfavored view.

3. Identify the favored view.

1.   Overpopulation, Poverty, and Family Planning

Some years ago, it was argued, usually by Western experts, that the overpopulation in Third World nations was one of the main causes of the widespread poverty in those countries. The failure of early birth-control pro-grams, however, showed that this analysis of the relationship between poverty and overpopulation was seriously flawed. People in poorer developing coun-tries had little incentive to use birth control; in fact, they needed large families to help them survive their poverty. Children could work to increase the fam-ily's income; children would also help support the parents when they were unable to work. In these circumstances, overpopulation was clearly the logical consequence of poverty, not its cause.

2.   Humans and the Nature Environment

Life in an advanced industrial society can lead us to believe that we are no longer dependent on our natural environment. It seems that we can escape from it when necessary or that we can modify it to meet our needs. When the weather cools down or warms up, for example, we can escape from its effects by switching on our heating or air-conditioning. When we need to produce more food, we have the power to turn arid, apparently useless land into pro-ductive farmland by means of irrigation, artificial fertilizers, and pesticides.

The idea that we can escape our dependence of the natural world, how-ever, is recognized by most scientists as a dangerous illusion. In our efforts to create our own environments, we are damaging the natural environments that have sustained humans for more than a million years. By burning coal to pro-duce electricity, we are causing potentially disastrous changes in the earth's climate patterns. By our overuse of irrigation and agricultural chemicals, we are reducing our supplies of the source of life—water. We may even, as in the case of the Aral Sea, change our environment to the point where it can no longer support us. We need, therefore, to acknowledge our dependence on the natural world. To imagine that we can survive without it is a mistake that may be fatal to the human species.

For more practice in reading texts with unfavored-favored view organization, go back and reread the following parts of earlier units:

paragraph 3 in Reading Passage 2.4
paragraph 4 in Reading Passage 2.5
paragraphs 11–12, 13–14, and 13 and 15 in the Main
Reading in Unit 2
paragraph 1 in Reading Passage 3.3
paragraph 14 in the Main Reading in Unit 4

Background Reading and Vocabulary Development

Family Structure and Society

Assume that the first paragraph is an introduction. Look for clear information about the topic of the article.

Throughout history, a priority for every known society has been to develop a reliable arrangement for the procreation and rearing of children, an institution where members also cooperate to give each other emotional and economic support and where children receive their socialization. This universal institution is the family. However, although the family performs a range of broadly similar functions in human societies, its form has varied widely according to the differing values and circumstances of those societies. **In this chapter, we will examine two very different family forms, the extended family and the nuclear family.**

Scan ahead, and mark where the writer discusses each form. How is the comparison organized?

The extended family, a pattern that was and is widespread in preindustrial societies, is a household consisting of related adults and married couples from different generations, their children, and their grandchildren. In extended families, child rearing is the responsibility of the entire network of older kin—cousins, aunts, uncles, and grandparents—and not just that of the natural parents. Members of extended families can look to a large number of relatives for support, companionship, and affection. There is often a division of labor between males and females, with the males doing most of the work on the family farm or in the family business and the females looking after the home and the children. However, the nature of this primary economic activity of the family means that

1

2

271

Family groups like these represent our ideas of how typical nuclear (*left*) and extended (*below*) families may look. (Photo Researchers)

females and even children are asked to become involved in it when extra help is needed. The head of such an extended family house-
25 hold is usually the oldest male.

Scan ahead, and mark where the writer discusses the same topic in a nuclear family system. Then come back, and resume reading here.

Societies in which extended families are the norm have   3
tended to develop systems of arranged marriages, where par-
ents play a significant role in the choice of a spouse for their
son or daughter. That such systems have developed is under-
30 standable. Consider a society in which a newly married couple is to
live under the same roof as the husband's parents. In such a case,
the family has an interest in avoiding situations in which their son
would feel compelled to take the side of his new wife in a dispute
with family members. This would be potentially very disruptive to
35 the family. It is important, therefore, that the new wife shares the
values of the household and can adjust to its rules. This in turn
makes it reasonable that senior members of the household have a
say in who joins the household. Their say can range from giving
or withholding approval of the son's choice to actually selecting
40 his future spouse, without consulting the son.

Sociologists (e.g., Talcott Parsons) have suggested that the   4
dominant family pattern in the United States and most western-
ized industrial societies is the so-called nuclear family. This family
type comprises a husband and wife who are economically indepen-
45 dent of and physically separated, to some extent isolated, from the
other members of their kin group (their siblings, parents, grandparents, uncles, aunts, cousins, nieces, and nephews). The husband
and wife are exclusively responsible for rearing their children and
for providing each other with companionship and affection. In the
50 traditional nuclear family, there is a strict division of labor; the
male spouse is the breadwinner, whose work takes him away from
the home; the female is the homemaker. However, like that of the
extended family, the structure is patriarchal; although he may listen to his wife's advice, especially in matters concerning home and
55 children, the husband has the ultimate authority to make decisions
concerning the family.

A behavior that is frequently associated with nuclear families   5
is the use of romantic love as the criterion for the choice of a
spouse. There are clear reasons why this is possible. Because of the
60 characteristic independence, even isolation, of the nuclear family,
the feelings of a person's birth family toward the intended spouse
need not be taken into account as much as in societies where extended families are the norm. While the birth family's approval
may be desirable, it is not essential. After all, since the new spouse
65 is not going to have to live under the same roof as the birth family,

What might be beneficial? Check back.

they don't need to be perfectly compatible. It is therefore possible for a young man or woman to base a choice of spouse solely on his or her feelings for the intended partner. **In some ways, it may even be advantageous and desirable to do so.** Romantic love
70 for an outsider weakens the ties to the birth family and enables young people to adapt to their own new, independent life and establish their own nuclear family.

Before you read, scan ahead for the organization of this contrast paragraph. Is it a, a, a . . . ; b, b, b . . . , or a = b, a = b, a = b . . . ? Or a mixture of the two?

Each of these two different family patterns seems suited   6
to a different type of society. In societies or communities where
75 a family's prosperity depends on the continued, permanent ownership of land that they farm and where few social services are provided by the government, the extended family is the norm. The efficient exploitation of the land requires more family members than would be available in a nuclear family. Similarly, without
80 government-funded retirement and child assistance programs, individuals need the support of a network of family members when they get old or lose a spouse. On the other hand, in a society where money is the basic form of wealth and where mobility—i.e., the ability to move where good jobs are available—is important, the
85 nuclear family tends to be prevalent. Thus we find the extended family system in societies with traditional agricultural economies and with few social services. In industrial or postindustrial societies, where the government provides a wide range of services, the nuclear family has tended to replace the extended family.

Main Idea Check

Here are the main ideas for this passage. Write the correct paragraph number beside its main idea.

_____ This paragraph gives us a definition and description of the nuclear family.

_____ In societies where the extended family system is dominant, arranged marriages are naturally very common.

_____ The extended family structure tends to be associated with preindustrial societies, whereas the nuclear family tends to dominate in industrial societies.

_____ This chapter will deal with the differences between two forms of the family, the nuclear family and the extended family.

_____ Romantic love is commonly the basis for marriage in societies where the nuclear family is predominant.

_____ This paragraph gives a definition and description of the extended family.

A Closer Look

1. From the following list, identify the characteristics that are typical of traditional extended families. Do the same for the characteristics that are typical of traditional nuclear families.
   a. They tend to have arranged marriages.
   b. The entire kin group is responsible for child rearing.
   c. The man's work is separate and distant from the family home.
   d. Newly married couples set up their own independent households.
   e. A married couple look to the larger kin group for emotional support and material assistance.
   f. They tend to base marriage on feelings of love between the two individuals who are centrally involved.
   g. It may be desirable but it is not essential for the family to agree with an individual's choice of marriage partner.
   h. Father and mother have exclusive responsibility for bringing up the children.
   i. Husband and wife are dependent on each other for support.
   j. The nature of the way the husband earns his livelihood means that his wife and children may sometimes become involved in it.
   k. The family must approve the choice of a spouse before a marriage takes place.
   l. New couples usually make their home in the same house as the husband's family.

2. According to the passage, what feature or features do traditional extended families and traditional nuclear families have in common?
   a. Wives are usually subordinate to their husbands.
   b. Child rearing is a cooperative activity that is shared by the child's mother and other relatives such as aunts, cousins, and grandparents.
   c. Their structure is usually patriarchal.

3. The following diagram describes the connection between the type of society and the type of family structure that society finds most suitable. From the list below and from your reading of the article, complete the diagram. Write only the correct letter in each box.
   a. No child assistance programs are provided by the government.
   b. The welfare of the family depends on the husband's ability to find suitable work.
   c. There is less need for the support of relatives.
   d. The extended family is seen as more suitable.
   e. The nuclear family is seen as more suitable.
   f. There is a need for family members to support the elderly.
   g. The government or other agencies provide a wide range of social services for the young and for the elderly.
   h. The family's welfare depends on its success in working its land.
   i. The government provides no retirement benefits.

j. There is a need for smaller families to ensure better mobility.

k. There is a need for a number of trusted people to work on the family farm.

l. There is a need for support from relatives for the task of child rearing.

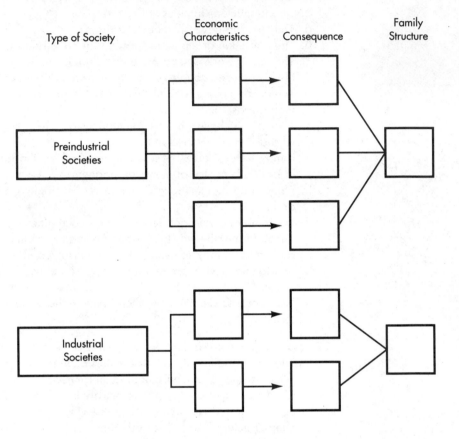

What Do You Think?

Think about the type of family you were brought up in. Would you describe it as extended or nuclear? Why? Are there any types of families that do not seem to fit either of these two structures?

Vocabulary in Context

Here are some words from the passage that you may not have known. You either guessed their meaning from context or from your knowledge of word families, or you omitted the word and were still able to understand the sentence. Now check and learn the meanings of the words. Use your dictionary to help you.

procreation (line 2)   siblings (line 46)
kin (line 15)   patriarchal (line 53)
to have a say in (line 37)   to take into account (line 62)
to withhold (line 39)   solely (line 67)
spouse (line 40)   tie (line 70)

READING PASSAGE 5.2

Divorce*

This is an excerpt from a sociology textbook. In such books, writers often show what is wrong with popular beliefs about life and society. As you read, look for popular views that the writer describes and challenges.

That American society has been successful in promoting marriage as a way of life is clear from American marriage statistics. Nine out of ten people in America get married at least once in their lives—and they do it fairly early in life. The median age for marriage among women is slightly over 22, and for men, it is between 24 and 25 years (U.S. Bureau of the Census, 1980). But what happens to all of those marriages that start out with so much love and so many high hopes? Unfortunately it is very difficult to know for certain what does happen.   1

To begin with, it is almost impossible to come up with a satisfactory definition of what constitutes happy and unhappy marriages. And without such a definition, we cannot expect to come up with figures concerning how many of each kind occur. And even if we rely on information that seems to be measurable—for instance, the number of marriages that end in divorce—the task remains very complicated.   2

The Difficulty of Measuring Divorce

This sentence seems to contradict the title of the section. Try to explain the contradiction as you read.

Measuring the divorce rate would seem to be an easy job. Just count up the number of divorces granted in any one year and compare that statistic with the number of marriages performed in the same year. For example, in 1979, there were 1.1 million divorces and 2.2 million marriages (U.S. Bureau of the Census, 1980), for a divorce rate of roughly 50 percent.   3

*Reprinted from Donald Light, Jr., and Suzanne Keller, *Sociology*, 3rd ed., 1982, pp. 385–387. Copyright © 1982 by McGraw-Hill, Inc., and used with permission.

*Is the writer going to
accept or reject the
ideas of the previous
paragraph? Read on
to test your answer.*

25

It seems simple, but the wrong things are being com-   4
**pared, and, in fact, we are learning nothing about the rate of
divorce.** A valid divorce rate must compare the number of divorces
in one year with the total number of marriages that exist in that
year. Thus when you compare the more than 48 million marriages
existing in 1979 with the 1.1 million divorces in that year, the
divorce rate turns out to be only about 2 percent.

30

*As you continue to
read, check to see if
the writer accepts or
rejects this idea.*

Many observers would like to use this divorce rate, as   5
**compared with a lower divorce rate in a preceding era, to
show that today marriage is passé and that the institution of
the family is in a state of decay.** But interpreting divorce statistics is tricky, especially when comparing those of two eras. Say we

35

were to compare the rate of divorce today with that in 1920. One
problem would be that divorce rates then were unreliable estimates based on records from half the states of the U.S. Moreover,
in 1920 there were more inhibitions about getting a divorce: it was
costlier, there were fewer grounds on which to sue for divorce, and

40

there was greater social condemnation of divorce than there is today. Finally, life expectancy was considerably shorter then, which
meant that some marriages were dissolved by death before they
could be dissolved by divorce. So, for various reasons, there were
many couples that stayed married in 1920 that would obtain di-

45

vorces if they lived today. This is why divorce rates alone are an
inaccurate indicator of the health and happiness of family life
(Crosby, 1980).

*Did you understand
the first problem?
If not, reread
paragraph 5.*

50

Another problem with a general rate of divorce, like our   6
2 percent figure, is that it reveals nothing about the marriages
that ended in that year. How many lasted more than three years?
How many more than ten? More than twenty? Comparing these
figures would tell us more about the stability of marriage than we
learn from the simple fact that 2 percent of existing marriages
ended in divorce.

55

How then should we measure divorce? One method that   7
would solve some of these problems is the longitudinal study: a
researcher could follow a representative sample of Americans from
the year they marry to the end of their lives. Such a study would
yield several kinds of data: average age at marriage, average dura-

60

tion of the group's marriages, rate of remarriage, and so forth. A
number of such studies done over different periods of time would
reveal a great deal more about divorce in America than a simple
"rate" statistic can ever tell us.

Quickly scan ahead for general information about how to account for divorce rates.

65

Quickly scan ahead, and mark where these factors are discussed. Then come back, and continue reading. Draw simple cause-effect diagrams for yourself as you read these paragraphs.

70

75

Explaining Divorce Rates

Although it is difficult to calculate current divorce rates and to compare them with those of earlier periods, most social scientists conclude that divorce is more prevalent in America today than during any other time in our history. The rates do seem to be going up. **Besides psychological reasons, the major explanations are all social factors, all involving change—in values, in institutions, and in the position of women.**

8

The major change in values involves a shift from a philosophy of self-sacrifice to one that emphasizes individual happiness. The principal reason for getting married today is to satisfy one's psychological needs ("romantic love"); failure to have these needs met now leads to dissolution of the marriage rather than an attempt to stay together "for the children's sake." Instead of all divorces being regarded as a sign of personal failure (as in past eras), some divorces today are viewed as a sign of psycho-emotional health, of personal growth, and of the ongoing struggle for self-fulfillment (Crosby, 1980, p. 57).

9

80

Institutions affecting family life have also changed. For instance, most churches now recognize divorce. In addition, the legal apparatus for obtaining divorces has been made less complex; 47 states now have some form of no-fault divorce laws, and free legal aid is available for those wishing to obtain a divorce (Melville, 1980). Finally the change in the position of women has contributed to increasing divorce rates in two ways: (1) it has made women less economically dependent on men, and therefore freer to opt out of marriage (Kephart, 1977); and (2) in promoting the general equality of the sexes, it has made it easier for people who are not married to adjust socially (Glick, 1975).

10

85

90

References

Crosby, John F. "A Critique of Divorce Statistics and Their Interpretation." *Family Relations,* vol. 29 (January 1980), 51–58.

Glick, Paul C. "A Demographer Looks at American Families." *Journal of Marriage and the Family,* vol. 37 (February 1975), 15–26.

Kephart, William M. *The Family, Society, and the Individual* (4th edition). Boston: Houghton Mifflin, 1977.

Melville, Keith. *Marriage and Family Today.* New York: Random House, 1980.

U.S. Bureau of the Census. *Current Population Reports,* Series P-20, No. 349, "Marital Status and Living Arrangements: March 1979." Washington, D.C.: U.S. Government Printing Office, 1980.

Main Idea Check

Here are the main ideas for paragraphs 3–10 of this passage. Write the correct paragraph number beside its main idea.

_____ It might be possible to calculate the divorce rate by comparing the annual number of marriages with the annual number of divorces.

_____ A more informative method to investigate marriage and divorce would be to collect data from the same sample of Americans from their first marriage until their death.

_____ Divorce figures have been affected by the increasing accessibility of divorce and the growing independence and equality of women.

_____ Since the divorce rate does not identify the length of the marriages that end in divorce, it does not reveal much about how stable marriages are.

_____ A better way to calculate the divorce rate is to compare the annual number of divorces with the total of existing marriages in the same year.

_____ The modern emphasis on personal happiness and fulfillment has led more people to end unsatisfactory marriages by getting a divorce.

_____ Because of differences in historical circumstances, it is difficult to simply conclude from increases in the divorce rate that the institution of marriage is in decline.

_____ In spite of the problems obtaining reliable divorce statistics, there is general agreement that divorce is becoming more common.

A Closer Look

1. The divorce rate is a scientifically adequate method of measuring the health of the institution of marriage.   T   F

2. For what reason or reasons is it unscientific to conclude from rising divorce rates today that modern marriages are less happy than those in an earlier era, say in 1920?
   a. The divorce statistics available for 1920 are not reliable.
   b. It is financially and legally easier to obtain a divorce now than it was in 1920.
   c. There is greater opposition to and disapproval of divorce today than in 1920.
   d. In 1920, the death of a partner may have intervened more often than today before a divorce could end the marriage.

3. Which present method of calculating the divorce rate does the writer prefer?
   a. comparing the number of divorces per year with the number of marriages performed in the same year
   b. comparing the number of divorced people with the number of people in the total population
   c. comparing the number of divorces in a year with the number of existing marriages in the same year

4. According to the article, the divorce rate has been affected by changing values in the individual. What change or changes does the writer refer to?
   a. a growing belief that marriage should be primarily for the purpose of bringing happiness and fulfillment to the individual
   b. a growing willingness to remain married for the sake of the children
   c. a growing belief that divorce is a sign of failure

5. Why does the writer mention the fact that most churches now recognize divorce?
   a. as evidence to show how the position of women has changed
   b. as an example to support the claim that changes in social institutions have contributed to a rising divorce rate
   c. as an example to show how the philosophy of self-sacrifice is becoming more acceptable and popular

Vocabulary in Context

Here are some words from the passage that you may not have known. You either guessed their meaning from context or from your knowledge of word families, or you omitted the word and were still able to understand the sentence. Now check and learn the meanings of the words. Use your dictionary to help you.

median (line 4)	duration (line 59)
to come up with (line 10)	apparatus (line 83)
roughly (line 22)	

VOCABULARY PRACTICE

Same or Different?

Writers sometimes express the same ideas with very different grammar and vocabulary. This exercise will help you identify such occurrences.

Read the first sentence in each example carefully. Then read each of the two following sentences to decide whether they are the same or different in meaning to the first sentence. Choose S when the sentence expresses the same idea as the first sentence. Choose D when it expresses a different idea.

1. Today people feel fewer inhibitions about divorce than they did seventy years ago.

   a. People are more comfortable with getting divorced and less ashamed of it today than they were seventy years ago.   S D

   b. Fewer people are opting for divorce today than seventy years ago.   S D

2. It is undisputed that a child needs to have frequent contact with affectionate adults in order to develop normally.

   a. There is unanimous agreement that successful child rearing depends on the presence of caring and loving adults in the child's environment.   S D

   b. Raising a child to be a caring, loving adult is a goal everyone agrees on.   S D

3. We have no option; we need to consult a lawyer about the problem.

   a. One of our alternatives is to talk to a lawyer about the problem.   S D

   b. The only thing we can do is talk the problem over with a lawyer.   S D

4. What criteria did you use to assess each applicant's suitability for the job?

   a. Whom did you consult in order to decide on the suitability of each applicant for the job?   S D

   b. On what basis did you judge how well each applicant was suited to the position?   S D

5. So far no politician has identified how to reverse or even halt the process of decay in American inner cities.

   a. As yet no American politician has come up with a way to stop, let alone turn around, the deterioration of the inner city.   S D

   b. So far no politician has been consulted about ways to reverse or even stop the decaying of inner cities in the United States.   S D

6. Roughly two hundred people were arrested by the police for blocking the entrance to the nuclear power plant.

a. The police acted roughly in their arrest of two hundred people who were blocking the entrance to the nuclear power plant. S D

b. The police arrested approximately two hundred people who were preventing traffic from entering or leaving the nuclear power plant. S D

7. Seventy years ago, the prevailing view among the general public was that divorce should be avoided for the sake of the children.

a. Seventy years ago, most people felt that people having trouble in their marriage should stay together because that would be best for the children. S D

b. Seventy years ago, it was generally felt that the dissolution of a marriage was in the best interest of the children. S D

8. The newspaper is charging that the politician withheld information that might help the police in their investigation.

a. The newspaper is saying that the politician cooperated with the police and gave them information that could help them in their investigation. S D

b. According to the newspaper, the politician failed to give the police information that could assist the police in their inquiries. S D

Making Connections

Each example in the exercise has a lead sentence and two sentences (a and b) that might or might not logically follow the lead sentence. Read the lead sentence, and ask yourself what kind of idea you could expect in the next sentence. Then read sentence a. Decide whether it can follow the lead sentence and make good sense. Choose Y for "Yes" or N for "No." Do the same for sentence b. *Remember:*

1. Look for the ideas that make a logical connection between each pair of sentences.

2. This is also a vocabulary learning exercise. If you have problems with any new words, check their meanings as you work.

1. Married women today are able to pursue a much wider range of career options than in the 1950s.

    a. Males still constitute the vast majority of doctors and lawyers and continue to dominate in the engineering profession.   Y N

    b. The era when women were expected to sacrifice their careers for child rearing has clearly ended.   Y N

2. This apartment building has fallen into decay in the last five years.

    a. In fact, the structure has deteriorated so badly that it now constitutes a danger to those living in it.   Y N

    b. In an attempt to compel them to carry out some basic repairs, the residents are withholding their rental payments and have brought a lawsuit against the building's owners.   Y N

3. The committee is having a lot of trouble coming up with applicants who meet the minimum criteria for the position.

    a. Ten out of twelve people who applied for the job have the desired experience and qualifications.   Y N

    b. The prevailing view is that the committee has set its standards unrealistically high.   Y N

4. Before the wedding, many people had doubts about the compatibility of the two movie stars, Rose Thorn and Rogue McMann, and expected their marriage to be of short duration.

    a. People with very close ties to the couple felt that Rose had found in Rogue a spouse who would fulfill her need for affection and companionship.   Y N

    b. There was little shock when Rose announced, five months later, that she was suing for a dissolution of the marriage.   Y N

5. What constitutes a successful marriage?

    a. A first step toward answering this question might be to consult married people and establish the criteria they used to judge their own marriages.   Y N

    b. One objective, but ultimately unsatisfactory, criterion for identifying a successful marriage is its duration.   Y N

Background Reading and Vocabulary Development

READING PASSAGE 5.3 _____

In your opinion, are the effects going to be good or bad? Quickly scan ahead to check your hypothesis.

The Effects of Divorce on Children*

I asked Peter when he had last seen his dad. The child looked at me blankly and his thinking became confused, his speech halting. Just then a police car went by with its siren screaming. The child stared into space and seemed lost in reverie. As this continued for a few minutes, I suggested that the police car had reminded him of his father, a police officer. **Peter began to cry and sobbed without stopping for 35 minutes** (quoted in Wallerstein and Kelly, 1980, p. 72).

Sometimes a writer decides to begin with an example. Look for the interpretation of the example as you read on.

This interview with a young boy whose parents had separated several years earlier, and who saw his father only once every few months, confirms adults' worst fears about the effects of divorce on children. Conventional wisdom holds that children are usually devastated by the dissolution of their parents' marriage. Often they feel personally abandoned by the parent who has left the home. Confused, grief-stricken, even fearful that the divorce was somehow their fault, the children of separating parents find their world severely shaken.

With the growing incidence of divorce in recent years, social scientists feel an increasing urgency to understand the nature and

*Reprinted from Donald Light, Jr., and Suzanne Keller, *Sociology,* 3rd ed., 1982, pp. 390–91. Copyright © 1982 by McGraw-Hill, Inc., and used with permission.

What does In part *cause you to expect? All bad effects? Or some positive effects as well as negative ones?*

20 extent of the impact that divorce has on children. **In part, their findings agree with what common sense suggests: divorce is usually a very painful experience for children.** In one study of 131 children of divorcing parents, from nursery school age to ado-lescence, almost all clung to the hope that their parents would

25 somehow be miraculously reconciled (Wallerstein and Kelly, 1980). Even five years after their parents' separation, over a third of these children remain intensely unhappy with their new family life. Many were moderately to severely depressed and lonely, and a substantial number were angry much of the time.

Do you expect positive or negative effects of divorce in this para-graph? Continue read-ing to test your hypothesis.

30 **But investigation into the effects of divorce on children** 3 **has also uncovered some encouraging facts.** First, the passage of time helps. Within a year after their parents separate, most chil-dren no longer experience the intense pain and despondency they felt initially. Instead, they have become resigned to the change in

35 their family structure, even if reluctantly so (Kelly and Waller-stein, 1976). Second, when both parents are consistently supportive, understanding, and affectionate, children of divorce adjust much more readily. Sometimes one unusually caring parent can make up for another who is uninterested and aloof. But this is relatively

40 rare. Typically a continuing close relationship with both parents is necessary for good adjustment (Wallerstein and Kelly, 1980). Moreover, if the custodial parent is relatively secure financially and making a healthy psychological transition to his or her new social status, the adjustment of the children is usually even better

45 (Lamb, 1977).

Do you expect positive or negative effects of divorce in this para-graph? Continue read-ing to test your hypothesis.

All these findings challenge the popular assumption that 4 **divorce is necessarily bad for children.** Maintaining a hostile and conflict-ridden marriage can be more damaging to a child than ending that marriage (Kurdek and Siesky, 1980). Especially when

50 a parent is rejecting or abusive toward a child, his or her removal from the house can hardly do much further harm. In such circum-stances, divorce may actually be beneficial to children, particularly if the remaining parent subsequently forms a close relationship with a much more caring person (Lamb, 1977). **On the other**

Are you still satisfied with the hypothesis you formed after sen-tence 1 of this para-graph?

55 **hand, it is equally wrong to assume that divorce is neces-sarily good for the children if it is good for the adults in-volved.** Children of divorce can continue to suffer even when their parents are happy. As one nine year old thoughtfully commented a year after her mother and father separated: "Divorce is better for

60 my parents, but not better for me" (quoted in Kelly and Waller-stein, 1976, p. 30). In short, the effects of divorce on children are very complex and depend greatly on the individual circumstances.

There are no inevitable emotional or psychological consequences of divorce.

Sources

Kelly, Joan B., and Judith S. Wallerstein. "The Effects of Parental Divorce: Experiences of the Child in Early Latency." *American Journal of Orthopsychiatry*, vol. 46 (1976), 20–32.

Lamb, Michael E. "The Effect of Divorce on Children's Personality Development." *Journal of Divorce*, vol. 1, no. 2 (Winter 1977), 163–174.

Kurdek, Lawrence A., and Albert E. Siesky. "Children's Perception of Their Parents' Divorce." *Journal of Divorce*, vol. 3, no. 4 (Summer 1980), 339–378.

Wallerstein, Judith S., and Joan B. Kelly. "California's Children of Divorce." *Psychology Today*, vol. 13, no. 8 (January 1980), 67–76.

Main Idea Check

Here are the main ideas for this passage. Write the correct paragraph number beside its main idea.

_____ Research into the effects of divorce on children also offers evidence that children can adjust fairly well to life after their parents get divorced.

_____ The conventional view is that divorce has an extremely negative affect on the psychological health of children.

_____ The apparently contradictory findings of research into the effects of divorce on children suggest that these effects will vary as the circumstances of each child vary.

_____ Many research studies support the commonsense assumption that divorce causes serious emotional harm to children.

A Closer Look

1. The example at the beginning of the article illustrates how divorce can benefit children.　　　　T　F

2. According to the writer, what is the popular view of the effect of divorce on children?
   a. It is usually an extremely painful experience for children.
   b. It is often a very beneficial development for children.
   c. It normally has no significant effects on children.

3. This article fully supports the popular view of how divorce affects children.　　　　T　F

4. According to this article, what factor or factors can help children adjust to life after their parents get divorced?
   a. The child sees only one parent and is able to forget about the other.
   b. time
   c. school
   d. The parent with whom the child is living is adjusting well to life after divorce.

5. According to this article, divorce has serious negative effects on all children.   T   F

Vocabulary in Context

Here are some words from the passage that you may not have known. You either guessed their meaning from context or from your knowledge of word families, or you omitted the word and were still able to understand the sentence. Now check and learn the meanings of the words. Use your dictionary to help you.

to sob (line 6)   readily (line 38)
interview (line 9)   aloof (line 39)
common sense (line 21)   custodial/custody (line 42)
to cling to X (line 24)

READING PASSAGE 5.4 _____

Find out the meaning of comparing apples and oranges. *As you read, look for this kind of comparison.*

Evaluating U.S. Education: Comparing Apples and Oranges

Since the Soviet Union launched its first satellite, Sputnik 1, in 1957, the United States has witnessed a continuing debate about the quality of its educational system. Many prominent figures in the political and academic worlds have warned that our education system is deteriorating and that it is shortchanging both its students and the country.

The present debate, just as when it started after the shock of Sputnik, has an international dimension. A 1983 U.S. government report painted an alarming picture of the United States losing its dominant position in science and technology because of declining educational standards:

Our Nation is at risk. Our once unchallenged preeminence in commerce, industry, science and technological innovation is being over-

15   taken by competitors throughout the world. . . . International comparisons of student achievement completed a decade ago reveal that on 19 academic tests American students were never first or second and, in comparison with other industrialized nations, were last seven times.[1]

20   Since 1983, a number of more recent reports have shown that American students routinely rank lower than students of the same age from other industrialized nations, especially in tests of mathematical and scientific knowledge. The low rankings of our students have convinced many politicians, educators, and the media that our education system is woefully deficient.

Check back for the meaning of such judgments.

25   **I have learned, however, to treat such judgments with caution, especially when they attempt to make comparisons across cultures.** I am reminded of a German college student whom I had taught while I was working in Germany. I met her again when she was studying for a year at a minor state university in the United States. The student was profoundly uncomfortable with her U.S. college experience. Her roommates, two years younger than she, seemed immature and showed little or no interest in the intellectual aspects of college life. Their overall behavior and attitudes reminded her of younger German high-school students. By the time I ran into her, during the New Year break, she had decided that U.S. college students were inferior to their German counterparts; she was far from eager to start her second semester.

30

35

3

What kind of information do you expect in the next paragraph? Read on to check your answer.

40   Let us assume that the small sample of U.S. students on which she based her judgments was a representative one and that, in fact, U.S. college students in general are somehow less academic than their German counterparts. **What would account for this difference?**

4

A comparison-contrast paragraph. Take simple notes on how the two countries differ.

45   **One source of the difference becomes evident when we consider what proportion of the population in each of these countries moves on to higher education after high school.** The figures are strikingly different. Today, while approximately 32 percent of German secondary school graduates are in higher education, a full 63 percent of their American peers are attending college.[2] The figures suggest that higher education in Germany and the United States serve rather different sections of their popula-

50

5

1. National Commission on Excellence in Education, *A nation at risk: The imperative for educational reform* (Washington, D.C.: U.S. Government Printing Office, 1983), pp. 5, 8.
2. Figures from the World Bank, *World development report* (New York: Oxford University Press, 1992).

tions. In Germany, college students are a rather small, more elite group; levels of educational achievement within the group fall within a narrow range and are at the high end of the scale. In the United States, on the other hand, college students constitute a majority of high-school graduates and obviously must represent a wider range of ability and educational achievement than their German counterparts. While the best U.S. college students will probably be the equals of the best German students, the average U.S. college student must of necessity be less academically prepared, maybe even less academically interested, simply because a higher proportion of their age group is admitted to college.

The difference in proportions of secondary school graduates enrolled in German and U.S. colleges is clearly significant. It suggests that the two cultures do not agree on what a college education should be or on what section of the population should be served by such an education. It suggests that, on the contrary, our conception of the form and function of a high-school or college education may vary extensively from culture to culture.

In the United States and Canada, in comparison with most other industrialized nations, education tends to be inclusive; it seeks to retain students longer in general high-school education. To obtain a basic high school graduation certificate, for example, students must usually attend classes until they are eighteen years old. Subsequently, as we have seen, a majority of these students are admitted to college. In other countries, the systems tend to be more selective; they often separate academically promising students into academically oriented high schools. Students who wish to start work or job training or attend vocational schools are permitted to leave secondary school at fifteen, sixteen, or seventeen with an appropriate certificate. Those who remain in the secondary schools for the last two, sometimes three, years of secondary education are thus a select group who are not representative of their entire age group. In these countries, those students who go on to higher education are therefore also more of a select group and less representative of their full age group than are their U.S. and Canadian peers (see Figure 1).

In a very real sense, therefore, my German student was suffering the effects of culture shock. She had arrived with her own culturally determined criteria for how college students should be and behave. She had naturally fallen into the trap of assuming that the U.S. and German education systems share the same goals and methods and should produce the same results. Because her expectations clearly had not been fulfilled by the students she had

Check back for this difference in proportions if you don't remember it.

Another comparison and contrast paragraph. Scan for its organization before you continue reading.

6

7

8

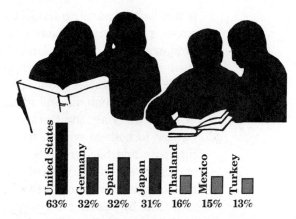

Figure 1. Percentages of secondary school graduates in higher education: United States and other selected nations. (*Source:* World Bank, *World Development Report 1992* [New York: Oxford University Press, 1992].)

*What is this trap?
Check back.*

What opinion do these writers share? Check back if you need to.

This is the second part of a comparison. If you need to, check back to refresh your memory of the first part.

95 met, she was now beginning to evaluate them and the system they were part of negatively. **I suggest that some educational researchers and those who use their findings may fall into the same trap.**

     Of the same opinion are Husen[3] and Rotberg,[4] who point   9
100 out that the international comparisons of the 1960s and early 1970s neglected to consider what percentage of the age group was attending the final years of secondary school in each country. At the time of testing, a mere 20 percent of the age group in Europe were enrolled in the upper level of secondary school, and this 20
105 percent was composed of the students with the highest levels of academic achievement. **In the United States, on the other hand, 80 percent of the age group were still attending high school.** Thus the international evaluations compared the average scores of a full 80 percent of U.S. students with the average scores of the top
110 9 percent of students in then West Germany, the top 13 percent in the Netherlands, and the top 45 percent in Sweden. These are scientifically flawed comparisons; yet they were cited in *A Nation at Risk* as one indicator of the failure of U.S. education and have attracted a great deal of uncritical media publicity.

115   It seems clear, therefore, that we should not jump to conclu-   10
sions about the quality of U.S. education on the basis of superficial international comparisons. This does not mean, of course, that all

3. T. Husen, Are standards in U.S. schools really lagging behind those in other countries? *Phi Delta Kappan*, March 1983, pp. 455–461.
4. I. C. Rotberg, I never promised you first place, *Phi Delta Kappan*, December 1990, pp. 296–303.

is well with American schools, especially in their teaching of mathematics and science. Nor does it mean that we should disregard
120   comparisons of how the United States and other countries educate their populations. It does suggest, however, that comparing international test scores is not the most scientific way to diagnose our educational problems and identify solutions to them.

By the way, the German student returned for her second se-   11
125   mester to college where, from all reports, she met students with interests and backgrounds more compatible with hers. The effects of culture shock diminished, and she began to enjoy and appreciate her college experience in the United States. Perhaps she even realized that by making her own comparisons between United States
130   and German college life, she was comparing apples and oranges. I'm sure that she would be amused to know how today's experts and media opinion-shapers are making similar mistakes.

Main Idea Check

Here are the main ideas for this passage. Write the correct paragraph number beside its main idea.

_____ A much smaller percentage of young people attend college in Germany than in the United States. This means that the average German college student is academically better prepared than the average American college student.

_____ In interpreting the results of international tests carelessly, experts are making the same type of mistake as the German student who came to a premature conclusion about U.S. college students.

_____ Researchers have shown that international studies make a basic mistake. They compare U.S. students with students in school systems that retain much smaller proportions of the given age group than U.S. schools do.

_____ In the United States and Canada, high-school and college education is intended for a much larger proportion of the population than in other industrial countries.

_____ The writer introduces an example of a German student who, on the basis of her initial experiences here, decided that U.S. college students were intellectually inferior to German college students.

_____ International test scores, therefore, are not the best way to assess the quality of American education.

_____ The German student who reacted negatively to American students was making the mistake of expecting the U.S. education system to be the same as the system in Germany.

_____ American students rank consistently low on international tests of school achievement. This leads many people to believe that the educational system has major problems.

_____ The differences in college-enrollment patterns between the United States and Germany suggests that different cultures can have different ideas about high-school and college education.

_____ How can we explain the differences between U.S. and German college students—assuming that the differences are real?

_____ In a long debate about the quality of U.S. education, many American political and academic leaders have been saying that the educational system has problems.

A Closer Look

1. Many influential people in the United States believe that American schools are inferior to those in other industrialized countries.   T   F

2. What impression or impressions did the writer get of the young German student when they met during her stay in the United States?
   a. She seemed immature and uninterested in the intellectual aspects of college life.
   b. She was suffering from culture shock.
   c. She felt that U.S. college students were less mature and less academically interested than students back home.

3. More than half of high-school graduates attend college in both the United States and Germany.   T   F

4. The list below contains characteristics of the U.S. educational system and the German education system. Identify the characteristics of each educational system?
   a. It tends to be inclusive.
   b. It keeps the vast majority of students in school until the age of eighteen.
   c. It is more elitist.
   d. It permits students to leave school from the age of fifteen to seventeen.
   e. It is more egalitarian.
   f. It tends to be selective.

5. What is the writer's position in the debate on the quality of American education?
   a. It is risky to assume that U.S. education is inferior solely because American students rank low on international academic comparisons.
   b. The American educational system is actually superior to the systems of other countries.

c. U.S. education is not as good as the education received by students in other industrialized countries.

What Do You Think?

Find out some more information about the U.S. education system by asking specific questions of your instructor. Then from your own experience, discuss in what ways the education system in your country is different from or similar to the U.S. education system.

Vocabulary in Context

Here are some words from the passage that you may not have known. You either guessed their meaning from context or from your knowledge of word families, or you omitted the word and were still able to understand the sentence. Now check and learn the meanings of the words. Use your dictionary to help you.

to launch (line 1)	oriented (line 78)
innovation (line 13)	vocational (line 79)
woefully (line 24)	to evaluate (line 95)
overall (line 33)	to diminish (line 127)
scale (line 54)	amused (line 131)

READING PASSAGE 5.5

Before you read the article, examine the illustrations. What changes in the American family do you see there?

In what part of an introduction are you likely to find the most help about the topic of the passage? Pay special attention to that part.

5

10

The Changing American Family

In 1951, the sociologist Talcott Parsons used the term   1
***isolated nuclear family* to describe the typical U.S. family of the period.** The family comprised a husband and breadwinner, a wife and homemaker, and one or more children. This is also the family form that is used most frequently in magazine advertisements and television commercials and in popular television shows. According to a *Newsweek* poll in 1989,[1] it is the form that a substantial majority of Americans apparently support. The poll found that 68 percent of those responding felt that it was important for couples to make financial sacrifices to allow one parent to stay at

1. Reported in J. R. Footlick, What happened to the family? *Newsweek*, Special Edition, Winter/Spring 1990, 14–19.

*Do you expect the
writer to accept the
nuclear family as a
description of the typi-
cal U.S. family?*

home to raise the children. As we will see, however, what is seen
as desirable as an ideal is often not attainable in practice. **The
concept of the isolated nuclear family, we will see, represents
an enduring idealization of American family life rather than
its reality.**

15

Early research studies investigating the validity of Parsons's   2
description found that American families were not as isolated from
their kin group as Parsons had proposed. In fact, many nuclear
families, both working class and middle class, maintained close
20 ties to the kin group. In this respect, the families resembled traditional extended families. However, although many lived in the
same neighborhood as their kin group, they did not live under one
roof. Nor did the close and frequent contact with the kin group
seem to interfere with the autonomy of each family. In one study,[2]
25 76 percent of families living independently reported giving or receiving assistance within their kin group during an illness; a full
83 percent reported giving or receiving financial support, while 46
percent reported giving or receiving help with child care. To some
researchers, therefore, such families merit the label of *modified ex-*
30 *tended families*. Other studies have shown that more affluent and
geographically mobile nuclear families keep in close contact with
their kin group despite the distances between them. These nuclear
families tended to look to their extended families for emotional
support rather than for material assistance.

*As you read, look for
details of this compar-
ison. Will these details
be differences or sim-
ilarities?*

35   **Today the idealized nuclear family appears to reflect**   3
**reality even less accurately that it did forty, or even twenty,
years ago.** For one thing, despite the general affection found by
the *Newsweek* poll for having a stay-at-home parent, in reality this
version of the family is fast disappearing. As shown in Figure 1,
40 married women are returning to work earlier than they used to. In
1991, almost 56 percent of wives and mothers with children less
than one year old were working outside the home; this figure represents a roughly 83 percent increase over the equivalent rate in
1975. Then as their offspring become older, more women enter or
45 reenter the labor force. In 1991 again, almost 67 percent of married
women with children under eighteen reported that they were employed or seeking employment.

Yet the typical American family is undergoing even more   4
dramatic and radical changes than the increasing employment of
50 wives and mothers. In a growing number of cases, families are liv-

2. Marvin B. Susman, The isolated nuclear family: fact or fiction? *Social Problems*
6 (1959): 333-340.

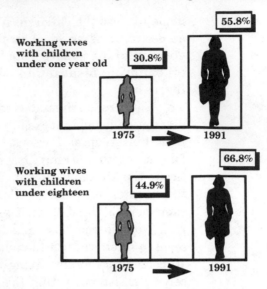

Figure 1. Working wives and mothers, 1975–91. (*Source:* U.S. Bureau of the Census, *Statistical Abstract of the United States: 1992,* 112th ed. [Washington, DC: GPO, 1992].)

ing with only one parent. Between 1960 and 1990, the proportion of children living with two parents fell from 88 percent to 73 percent, while the percentage living with one parent rose from 9 percent to 25 percent (see Figure 2).

55   These single-parent families, of course, are the consequence of   5
a variety of different circumstances. **However, the increase in the number and proportion of such families can be associated with two clear social trends.** The first of these is the rising divorce rate, which has occurred as the stigma associated with di-
60   vorce has virtually disappeared from U.S. society. Americans, it seems, have become much more willing to seek in divorce a solution to marital dissatisfaction or discord. As shown in Figure 3, between 1960 and 1990, there was a steep (400 percent) rise in the ratio of divorced persons to married persons living with their
65   spouses.
        Even more striking is a second trend, namely, the increasing   6
number of Americans who voluntarily accept single parenthood without ever being married. During the same period (1960–1990), the total number of children living with an unwed parent climbed
70   to almost 5 million.
        In addition to the increase in single-parent families, the num-   7
ber and proportion of stepfamilies have also grown—as a result of

Quickly scan ahead, and mark where the writer discusses these trends. Then continue reading from here.

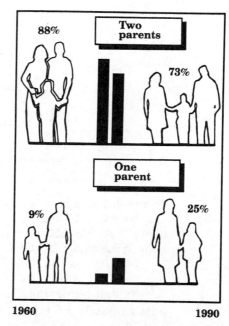

Figure 2. Two-parent and single-parent families, 1960–90. (*Source:* U.S. Bureau of the Census, Current Population Reports, Series P-20, No. 450, *Marital Status and Living Arrangements: March 1990* [Washington, DC: GPO, 1991].)

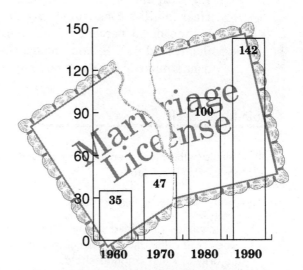

Figure 3. Divorce rate in the United States, 1960–90 (divorced persons per 1,000 married). (*Source:* U.S. Bureau of the Census, Current Population Reports, Series P-20, No. 450, *Marital Status and Living Arrangements: March 1990* [Washington, DC: GPO, 1991].)

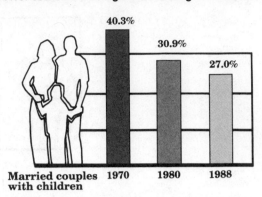

Figure 4. Two-parent families as a percentage of U.S. households, 1970–88. (*Source:* U.S. Bureau of the Census, Current Population Reports, Series P-20, No. 450, *Marital Status and Living Arrangements: March 1990* [Washington, DC: GPO, 1991].)

divorce and remarriage. According to U.S. Census Board statistics, approximately 9.6 million children in 1990 were living with a biological parent who had remarried. In the five years between 1980 and 1985, the number of such children grew by 11.6 percent.

Check back to refresh your memory of these trends. How many are there? What are they?

The social trends described above are transforming American society. Part of this transformation, it seems, is that the heyday of the nuclear family, defined as a married couple living with one or more biological children, is past. In fact, such nuclear families constituted only 27 percent of all households in 1988, a drop of 33 percent in eighteen years (see Figure 4). If it ever dominated in U.S. households, there is little doubt that today Parsons's nuclear family is no longer the prevalent form.

Main Idea Check

Here are the main ideas for this passage. Write the correct paragraph number beside its main idea.

_____ The proportion of single-parent families is increasing in the United States.

_____ The changes described in this article are radically altering American society. One result is that the concept of the nuclear family no longer is applicable to the majority of American households.

_____ The increase in the number of single-parent families is also linked to an increase in the number of people who think it is acceptable to have children without being married.

_____ The conception of the typical American family as an isolated nuclear family does not reflect the realities of present-day U.S. society.

_____ Stepfamilies are becoming increasingly common in the United States.

_____ One major difference between the idealized nuclear family and present reality is that a majority of wives and mothers have jobs outside the home.

_____ The increase in the number of single-parent families can be related to the rise in the rate of divorce.

_____ Studies show that nuclear families have enough contact with their kin group to call into question the validity of describing them as "isolated" or "nuclear."

A Closer Look

1. Apparently a majority of Americans still believe that the traditional form of the nuclear family (where the wife works in the home) is preferable to other family forms.   T F

2. According to research, in what way or ways may modern American families be similar to traditional extended families?
   a. They keep in frequent and close contact with the kin group.
   b. They often live in the same house as the other members of the kin group.
   c. They give both emotional and material support to and receive it from members of the kin group.

3. In the United States, a majority of people feel that divorce brings disgrace to the people involved in it.   T F

4. What social phenomenon or phenomena have become more widespread in the United States during the last thirty years or so?
   a. living in a traditional nuclear family
   b. divorce
   c. single parenthood
   d. stepfamilies

5. The traditional nuclear family appears to be maintaining its strong position in U.S. society.   T F

What Do You Think?

This article does not consider any problems that new American families (families with two working parents, single-parent families, and stepfamilies) might have to face. Discuss what these problems could be. Also discuss how they could be solved.

Vocabulary in Context

Here are some words from the passage that you may not have known. You either guessed their meaning from context or from your knowledge of word families, or you omitted the word and were still able to understand the sentence. Now check and learn the meanings of the words. Use your dictionary to help you.

to comprise (line 3)	marital (line 62)
in this respect (line 20)	discord (line 62)
autonomy (line 24)	voluntarily (line 67)
mobile (line 31)	unwed (line 69)
offspring (line 44)	heyday (line 79)

VOCABULARY PRACTICE

Same or Different?

Writers sometimes express the same ideas with very different grammar and vocabulary. This exercise will help you identify such occurrences.

Read the first sentence in each example carefully. Then read each of the two following sentences to decide whether they are the same or different in meaning to the first sentence. Choose *S* when the sentence expresses the same idea as the first sentence. Choose *D* when it expresses a different idea.

1. The United States ranks first among the affluent industrial nations in the proportion of children born to unwed teenage mothers.

   a. The United States and the other wealthy industrial nations are trying to reduce the proportion of babies who are born to unmarried females in their teens.   S D

   b. The United States has a higher percentage of births to unmarried teenage women than the other wealthy industrial countries.   S D

2. The student's mind went blank during the entire examination.

   a. For the duration of the examination, the student was unable to think or remember anything.   S D

   b. The student became very despondent and remained so for the entire examination.   S D

3. Many eminent scientists are saying that the government is disregarding the important domestic dimension of what causes global warming.

a. According to many well-known and respected scientists, the government feels that it is important to examine the domestic causes of global warming.   S   D

b. Many well-known and respected scientists are charging the government with ignoring how much we here at home contribute to global warming.   S   D

4. John has no doubts about the wisdom of his decision to resign from his present job.

a. John is sure he is correct in deciding to give up his current position.   S   D

b. Wisely, John is resigned to being dismissed from his present job.   S   D

5. The majority of witnesses interviewed by the committee saw little merit in the government's new plan for health care.

a. Most of those who testified to the committee were very critical of the government's new health-care plan.   S   D

b. In their statements to the committee, most witnesses supported the government's new health-care plan.   S   D

6. The incidence of tuberculosis is rising, especially among the poorest people in some inner cities.

a. Cases of tuberculosis are becoming more common, particularly among the most impoverished residents of some inner cities.   S   D

b. Tuberculosis is spreading, particularly among the elite of some inner cities.   S   D

7. The workers' interest in a lawsuit against the company diminished dramatically when they learned that the courts had rejected a similar case some years ago.

a. When the workers heard that a lawsuit similar to theirs had failed in court some years ago, they became much less eager to sue the firm.   S   D

b. The desire on the part of the workers to bring a lawsuit against the company began to weaken rapidly after they heard how a similar one had been unsuccessful some years ago.   S   D

8. In June 1990, the U.S. government assessed the risk of Iraq's launching a large-scale attack on Kuwait as negligible.

   a. According to the U.S. government's evaluation of the situation in June 1990, the likelihood of an invasion of Kuwait by Iraq was very low.   S D

   b. In the judgment of the U.S. government in 1990, only a miracle would prevent a large-scale strike against Kuwait by Iraq.   S D

9. In the 1980s, government neglect had a devastating effect on America's inner cities and their residents.

   a. America's inner cities and the people living there have endured in spite of a lack of interest and action by the government during the 1980s.   S D

   b. America's inner cities and their people have suffered terribly as a result of the government's disregard for their welfare during the 1980s.   S D

10. The political situation in the northern region of the country has been transformed by the growing enthusiasm among its residents for autonomy.

   a. A radical political change is occurring in the northern region of the country as residents become increasingly eager to gain a degree of independence.   S D

   b. A profound and fundamental political shift in the northern part of the country is being brought about by a growing desire on the part of its residents for some level of independence.   S D

Making Connections

Each example in the exercise has a lead sentence and two sentences (*a* and *b*) that might or might not logically follow the lead sentence. Read the lead sentence, and ask yourself what kind of idea you could expect in the next sentence. Then read sentence *a*. Decide whether it can follow the lead sentence and make good sense. Choose *Y* for "Yes" or *N* for "No." Do the same for sentence *b*. *Remember:*

1. Look for the ideas that make a logical connection between each pair of sentences.

2. This is also a vocabulary learning exercise. If you have problems with any new words, check their meanings as you work.

1. The members of the basketball team appeared more despondent than reporters had ever seen them before.

   a. The loss of two key players had had a devastating effect on them.   Y N

   b. Only a miracle, it seemed, could restore their confidence and desire to win.   Y N

2. According to public-opinion polls, the majority of Americans feel that ideally one parent should stay at home during the early child rearing years.

   a. Many would eagerly and readily take time off work if they could afford to because they believe that young children are shortchanged in two-career households.   Y N

   b. How can we reconcile this finding with the fact that the number of stay-at-home parents is declining steeply?   Y N

3. The past forty years in the United States have witnessed a dramatic reduction in the stigma attached to divorce.

   a. A clear indication of this is the striking decline in the divorce rate since the 1950s.   Y N

   b. One clear benefit of this is that people no longer have to continue to endure marriages with abusive spouses because they fear society's disapproval.   Y N

4. The modern nuclear family comprises a married couple and their children living autonomously and in some degree of isolation from the other members of their kin group.

   a. In this respect, it has a radically different structure from that of the extended family.   Y N

   b. It is routine, in nuclear families, to find several generations of related adults and their offspring living under the same roof.   Y N

5. The government is profoundly disturbed by the dramatic rise in the incidence of adolescent crime.

   a. Yet, in its new crime prevention program, it completely disregards the issues of parental neglect and abuse, factors that appear in the background of most young offenders.   Y N

   b. Over the last five years, the figures show a 40 percent overall increase in the number of crimes committed by people in the eighteen to thirty age range.   Y N

6. Historically, it is the most affluent nations of the world that have contributed most to the problem of global warming.

   a. Their contribution has been diminishing over the last decade.　　Y　N

   b. Today, however, this situation has been transformed because developing countries now rank among the major producers of greenhouse gas emissions.　　Y　N

7. In the United States, some undergraduate students are beginning to feel that they are being shortchanged by their research-oriented universities.

   a. A few are resigned to this; others are seeking radical changes in the way their universities treat undergraduate students.　　Y　N

   b. They are paying considerable tuition for classes which, in elite universities, are taught mostly by teaching assistants, not by the prominent professors these universities mention in their public-relations literature.　　Y　N

8. The idea of the isolated nuclear family is an idealized notion of the typical American family of today.

   a. As a realistic picture of the majority of U.S. households, however, it is woefully inaccurate.　　Y　N

   b. About 70 percent of households in the U.S. merit the label "nuclear."　　Y　N

Synonyms and Paraphrases

Review the meanings of the words to the left of each paragraph below. Find out how to use these words by studying examples from the Vocabulary Study and from the reading passages of this unit. Then read each paragraph for its details. Replace the words in boldface with the correct new words. Sometimes you will need to change the grammar of the sentence so that the new word or expression fits into it correctly.

readiness
in many respects
marital
alarming
spouse
dimension
counterpart
profound
autonomy

1. Another **aspect** of the **great** changes in the family that the United States has **seen** in the past two or three decades is the rise in the number of single-parent families. Such families, **comprising** one parent, usually but not always the mother, and one or more children, are becoming more common for a number of reasons.

   To a small extent, the increase is due to the number of single women who **wish** to have children but who do not wish to give up their personal **independence** by taking a **husband**.

   Another proportion of the increase can be attributed to the increased

discord
to consist of
unwed
to witness
to desire
to seek
temporarily

willingness of Americans to **try to find** in divorce a solution to **problems (1) in their marriage (2).** Higher divorce rates create more single-parent families, at least **for a time.**

Perhaps the most significant factor in the increase of single-parent families, however, is the growing numbers of young **never-married** mothers, often still in their teenage years, who have few job skills and who therefore have to become dependent on welfare to support themselves and their children. **In many ways,** this third trend is **of the most concern** to society. Children born in these circumstances generally have a much more difficult time developing into productive citizens than their **peers** in families where the parents (or parent) are more mature and economically secure.

transformation
desirable
voluntarily
labor force
affluent
ideal
option
to rear
to diminish
to seek

2. Most Americans still believe that the **best** environment for **bringing up** children is provided when one parent remains at home, especially during the crucial early years. However, what people feel to be **preferable** in theory may in fact be unattainable in real life. Economic circumstances, for example, may be such that parents feel they do not have any **alternative** except for both to **look for** work outside the home. This seemed to be true in many parts of the United States in the early 1990s. Between 1980 and 1990, many fairly **prosperous** areas of the country experienced a **radical change** in their economic structure. They lost large numbers of well-paid manufacturing jobs as industries in trouble from overseas competition cut back the **numbers of employees** or moved elsewhere. As family earnings **declined,** many women took employment outside the home not **because they wanted to** but because of economic necessity.

to abuse
offspring
subsequent to
to seek
to propose
to shortchange
to disregard
eminent
to neglect
radical

3. Some of the most **important and well-respected** experts on violent crime are **suggesting** that we make a **fundamental** change in our approach to this growing social problem. They say we must **make it our goal** to prevent people from becoming criminals in the first place, rather than focus on punishment and correction **after** the crime. According to these experts, we cannot afford to **ignore** the fact that the majority of violent criminals have been **cheated of certain things they had a right to** in their childhood. For example, they have **not received proper care from** their parents; in many cases, they have been **treated cruelly and violently.** According to these experts, therefore, we need to find ways to reduce the tendency of some adults to neglect and abuse their **children** instead of building more prisons.

Using New Vocabulary

Review the meanings of these words. Use the examples in the Vocabulary Study and in your ESL dictionary to learn how to use them in sentences.

to witness	to seek
to neglect	to reconcile
miracle	radical
to devastate	to endure
to disregard	

Now finish each of the following sentences in a way that seems appropriate and interesting to you. You may wish to add a second sentence after your first one to make the context more complete. You may also want to use ideas connected with your readings in this unit or in earlier units.

1. In his long life from 1900 to 1992, the writer witnessed . . .

2. Anyone who witnessed . . .

3. The police neglected to . . .

4. It was a miracle that . . .

5. The city was devastated . . .

6. We were absolutely devastated by . . .

7. The investor disregarded . . .

8. The United States is seeking . . .

9. Leading environmental scientists are seeking to . . .

10. It is very difficult to reconcile . . .

11. There has been a radical . . .

12. I couldn't endure . . .

Main Reading

PREREADING THE ARTICLE: GETTING A FIRST IDEA

Read the main title of the article, and answer the following questions. Justify your answers by referring to the text.

1. The writer will argue that the family has been growing stronger.   Y N

2. The writer is concerned about the developments he sees taking place in the family.   Y N

3. The writer will suggest ways to counteract recent developments in the family.   Y N

4. What overall pattern of organization do you expect for this article?
   a. comparison-contrast
   b. problem-solution
   c. cause-effect

Check through the section titles of the article to answer these questions:

5. In what section of the article do you expect to find the solution to family decline?
   a. Paragraphs 1–17
   b. Paragraphs 18–24
   c. Paragraphs 25–34

6. Look for confirmation of your answer in the first paragraph of the section you chose in question 5. Note any "solution markers" you see.

7. Think about your answers to questions 5 and 6. What do you expect the remainder of the article (the paragraphs you didn't choose in question 5) in general to deal with? Are there any specific topics you expect to be discussed in the remainder of the article?

MAIN READING

Breakup of the Family:
Can We Reverse the Trend?*

by David Popenoe

As a social institution, the family has been "in decline" since   1
the beginning of world history. It gradually has been becoming
weaker through losing social functions and power to other institutions such as church, government, and school. Yet, during the past
5 twenty-five years, family decline in the United States, as in other
industrialized societies, has been both steeper and more alarming
than during any other quarter-century in our history. Although
they may not use the term *decline,* most scholars now agree—
though for many this represents a recent change of viewpoint—
10 that the family has undergone a social transformation during this
period. **Some see "dramatic and unparalleled changes," while
others call it "a veritable revolution."**

I believe, in short, that we are witnessing the end of an epoch.   2
Today's societal trends are bringing to a close the cultural domi-
nance of the traditional nuclear family—one situated apart from
both the larger kin group and the workplace, and focused on procreation. It consists of a legal, lifelong, sexually exclusive, heterosexual, monogamous marriage, based on affection and companionship, in which there is a sharp division of labor (separate spheres),
20 with the female as full-time housewife and the male as primary
provider and ultimate authority. Lasting for only a little more
than a century, this family form emphasized the male as "good
provider," the female as "good wife and mother," and the paramount importance of the family for childbearing. (Of course, not all
25 families were able to live up to these cultural ideals.) During its
heyday, the terms family, home, and mother ranked extraordi-
narily high in the hierarchy of cultural values.

In certain respects, this family form reached its apogee in the   3
middle of the twentieth century. By the 1950s—fueled in part by
30 falling maternal and child mortality rates, greater longevity, and a
high marriage rate—a larger percentage of children than ever before were growing up in stable, two-parent families. Similarly, this

*Before we can appreci-
ate the changes to X,
we need to know the
original form of X.
Check for this in the
next paragraph.*

*David Popenoe, "The Breakup of the Family: Can We Reverse the Trend?" Re-
printed from *USA Today Magazine,* May, 1991. Copyright © 1991 by the Society
for the Advancement of Education.

period witnessed the highest-ever proportion of women who married, bore children, and lived jointly with their husbands until at
35 least age fifty.

*Quickly scan ahead,
and mark where the
writer deals with each
of these four trends.
Then resume reading
here.*

In the 1960s, however, four major social trends emerged 4
**to signal a widespread "flight" from both the ideal and the
reality of the traditional nuclear family: rapid fertility decline, the sexual revolution, the movement of mothers into**
40 **the labor force, and the upsurge in divorce.** None of these
changes was new to the 1960s; each represents a tendency that
already was in evidence in earlier years. What happened in the
1960s was a striking acceleration of the trends, made more dramatic by the fact that during the 1950s they had leveled off and, in
45 some cases, even reversed direction.

First, fertility declined in the United States by almost 50 per- 5
cent between 1960 and 1989, from an average of 3.7 children per
woman to only 1.9. Although births have been diminishing gradually for several centuries (the main exception being the two de-
50 cades following World War II), the level of fertility during the past
decade was the lowest in U.S. history and below that necessary for
the replacement of the population.

A growing dissatisfaction with parenthood is now evident 6
among adults in our culture, along with a dramatic decrease in the
55 stigma associated with childlessness. Some demographers predict
that 20–25 percent of today's young women will remain completely
childless, and nearly 50 percent will be either childless or have
only one offspring.

*The author does not
explain this concept.
However, you could
get an idea of it by
looking for how Amer-
ican attitudes to sex
have changed.*

Second, **the sexual revolution** has shattered the association 7
60 of sex and reproduction. The erotic has become a necessary ingre-
dient of personal well-being and fulfillment, both in and outside of
marriage, as well as a highly marketable commodity. The greatest
change has been in the area of premarital sex. From 1971 to 1982
alone, the proportion of unmarried females in the United States
65 aged fifteen to nineteen who engaged in premarital sexual inter-
course jumped up from 28 to 44 percent. This behavior reflects a
widespread change in values; in 1967, 85 percent of Americans
condemned premarital sex as morally wrong, compared to 37 percent in 1979.

70 The sexual revolution has been a major contributor to the 8
striking increase in unwed parenthood. Nonmarital births jumped
from 5 percent of all births in 1960 (22 percent of black births) to
22 percent in 1985 (60 percent of black births). This is the highest
rate of nonmarital births ever recorded in the United States.

75 Third, although unmarried women long have been in the la- 9

bor force, the past quarter-century has witnessed a striking movement into the paid work world of married women with children. In
1960, only 19 percent of married women with children under the
age of six were in the labor force (39 percent with children between
80   six and seventeen); by 1986, this figure had climbed to 54 percent
(68 percent of those with older children).

Fourth, the divorce rate in the United States over the past   10
twenty-five years (as measured by the number of divorced persons
per 1,000 married persons) has practically quadrupled, going from
85   35 to 130. This has led many to refer to a divorce revolution. The
probability that a marriage contracted today will end in divorce
ranges from 44 percent to 66 percent, depending upon the method
of calculation.

Quickly check back
to refresh your
memory of what these
trends are.

These trends signal a widespread retreat from the tradi-   11
90   tional nuclear family in its dimensions of a lifelong, sexually exclusive unit, focused on children, with a division of labor between husband and wife. Unlike most previous change, which reduced family
functions and diminished the importance of the kin group, that of
the past twenty-five years has tended to break up the nucleus of
95   the family unit—the bond between husband and wife. Nuclear
units, therefore, are losing ground to single-parent households, se-
rial and stepfamilies, and unmarried and homosexual couples.

What generalization
does this example sup-
port? Check back.

The number of single-parent families, for example, has   12
grown sharply—the result not only of marital breakup, but also
100   of marriage decline (fewer persons who bear children are getting
married) and widespread male abandonment. In 1960, only 9 percent of U.S. children under eighteen were living with a lone parent; by 1986, this figure had climbed to nearly one-quarter of all
children. (The comparable figures for blacks are 22 percent and 53
105   percent). Of children born during 1950–54, only 19 percent of
whites (48 percent of blacks) had lived in a single-parent household
by the time they reached age seventeen. For children born in 1990,
however, the figure is projected to be 70 percent (94 percent for
blacks).

You can expect this to
be a then-now com-
parison. Note the de-
tails as you read.

The psychological character of the marital relationship   13
110   **also has changed substantially over the years.** Traditionally,
marriage has been understood as a social obligation—an institution designed mainly for economic security and procreation. Today,
marriage is understood mainly as a path toward self-fulfillment.
115   One's self-development is seen to require a significant other, and
marital partners are picked primarily to be personal companions.

Check back for the meaning of this shift.

Put another way, marriage is becoming deinstitutionalized. No longer comprising a set of norms and social obligations that are enforced widely, marriage today is a voluntary relationship that individuals can make and break at will. As one indicator of **this shift,** laws regulating marriage and divorce have become increasingly more lax.

As psychological expectations for marriage grow ever higher, dashed expectations for personal fulfillment fuel our society's high divorce rate. Divorce also feeds upon itself. With more divorce, the more "normal" it becomes, with fewer negative sanctions to oppose it and more potential partners available. In general, psychological need, in and of itself, has proved to be a weak basis for stable marriage.

As you read, mark and number the ways in which the family has been weakened.

Trends such as these have dramatically reshaped people's lifetime connectedness to the institution of the family. **Broadly speaking, the institution of the family has weakened substantially over the past quarter-century in a number of respects.** Individual members have become more autonomous and less bound by the group, and the latter has become less cohesive. Fewer of its traditional social functions are now carried out by the family; these have shifted to other institutions. The family has grown smaller in size, less stable, and with a shorter life span; people are, therefore, family members for a smaller percentage of their lives. The proportion of an average person's adulthood spent with spouse and children was 62 percent in 1960, the highest in our history. Today, it has dropped to a low of 43 percent.

The outcome of these trends is that people have become less willing to invest time, money, and energy in family life. It is the individual, not the family unit, in whom the main investments increasingly are made.

These trends are all evident, in varying degrees, in every industrialized Western society. This suggests that their source lies not in particular political or economic systems, but in a broad cultural shift that has accompanied industrialization and urbanization. In these societies, there clearly has emerged an ethos of radical individualism in which personal autonomy, individual rights, and social equality have gained supremacy as cultural ideals. In keeping with these ideals, the main goals of personal behavior have shifted from commitment to social units of all kinds (families, communities, religions, nations) to personal choices, lifestyle options, self-fulfillment, and personal pleasure.

Social Consequences

How are we to evaluate the social consequences of recent fam- 18
ily decline? Certainly, one should not jump immediately to the con-

Quickly scan ahead,
and mark where the
writer discusses these
positive aspects. Then
come back, and re-
sume reading here.

160 clusion that it is necessarily bad for our society. **A great many
**positive aspects to the recent changes stand out as notewor-
thy. During this same quarter-century, women and many minorities clearly have improved their status and probably the overall
quality of their lives. Much of women's status gain has come
165 through their release from family duties and increased participation in the labor force. In addition, given the great emphasis on
psychological criteria for choosing and keeping marriage partners,
it can be argued persuasively that those marriages today which do
endure more likely than ever before to be true companionships
170 that are emotionally rewarding.

This period also has seen improved health care and longevity, 19
as well as widespread economic affluence that has produced, for
most people, a material standard of living that is historically unprecedented. Some of this improvement is due to the fact that peo-
175 ple no longer are dependent on their families for health-care and
economic support or imprisoned by social class and family obligation. When in need, they now can rely more on public care and
support, as well as self-initiative and self-development.

If you need to, check
back to refresh your
memory on these posi-
tive aspects.

Despite these positive aspects, the negative consequences 20
180 of family decline are real and profound. The greatest negative effect of recent trends, in the opinion of nearly everyone, is on children. Because they represent the future of a society, any negative
consequences for them are especially significant. There is substantial, if not conclusive, evidence that, partly due to family changes,
185 the quality of life for children in the past twenty-five years has
worsened. Much of the problem is of a psychological nature, and
thus difficult to measure quantitatively.

Perhaps the most serious problem is a weakening of the fun- 21
damental assumption that children are to be loved and valued at
190 the highest level of priority. The general disinvestment in family
life that has occurred has commonly meant a disinvestment in children's welfare. Some refer to this as a national "parent deficit."
Yet, the deficit goes well beyond parents to encompass an increasingly less child-friendly society.

This is an idea that
the writer has already
introduced. If you
don't understand it,
check back.

195 **The parent deficit** is blamed all too easily on newly working 22
women. Yet, it is men who have left the parenting scene in large
numbers. More than ever before, fathers are denying paternity,
avoiding their parental obligations, and are absent from home. (At

the same time, there has been a slow, but not offsetting, growth of
the "house-father" role.)

200

The breakup of the nuclear unit has been the focus of much 23
concern. Virtually every child desires two biological parents for
life, and substantial evidence exists that child rearing is most successful when it involves two parents, both of whom are strongly

205 motivated to the task. This is not to say that other family forms
cannot be successful, only that, as a group, they are not as likely
to be so. This also is not to claim that the two strongly motivated
parents must be organized in the patriarchal and separate-sphere
terms of the traditional nuclear family.

210

Regardless of family form, there has been a significant 24
change over the past quarter-century **in what can be called the
social ecology of childhood.** Advanced societies are moving ever
further from what many hold to be a highly desirable child-rearing
environment, one consisting of a relatively large family that does

215 a lot of things together, has many routines and traditions, and
provides a great deal of quality contact time between adults and
children; regular contact with relatives, active neighboring in a
supportive neighborhood, and contact with the adult world of work;
little concern on the part of children that their parents will break

220 up; and the coming together of all these ingredients in the development of a rich family subculture that has lasting meaning and
strongly promulgates such values as cooperation and sharing.

*This seems a strange
use of the word* ecol-
ogy. *As you read, look
for the writer's expla-
nation of it.*

Agendas for Change

*Look for possible solu-
tions (recommended
and not recom-
mended) as you read
this section.*

*Scan ahead. Mark
where the writer dis-
cusses each of these
solutions. Then come
back, and resume
reading here.*

What should be done to counteract or remedy the nega- 25
tive effects of family decline? This is the most controversial

225 question of all, and the most difficult to answer. Among the
agendas for change that have been put forth, two extremes stand
out as particularly prominent in the national debate. **The first is a
return to the structure of the traditional nuclear family characteristic of the 1950s; the second is the development of ex-**

230 **tensive governmental policies.**

Aside from the fact that it probably is impossible to return to 26
a situation of an earlier time, the first alternative has major drawbacks. It would require many women to leave the work force and,
to some extent, become "de-liberated," an unlikely occurrence in-

235 deed. Economic conditions necessitate that even more women take
jobs, and cultural conditions stress ever greater equality between
the sexes.

As you continue read-ing, identify these weaknesses.

        In addition to such considerations, the traditional nu-   27
clear family form, in today's world, may be fundamentally
240 flawed. As an indication of this, one should realize that the young
people who led the transformation of the family during the 1960s
and 1970s were brought up in 1950s households. If the 1950s families were so wonderful, why didn't their children seek to emulate
them? In hindsight, the 1950s seem to have been beset with prob-
245 lems that went well beyond patriarchy and separate spheres. For
many families, the mother-child unit had become increasingly isolated from the kin group, the neighborhood and community, and
even from the father, who worked a long distance away. This was
especially true for women who were fully educated and eager to
250 take their place in work and public life. Maternal child rearing
under these historically unprecedented circumstances became highly
problematic.

Use the repeated idea here to help you with the main idea of the previous paragraph.

        Despite such difficulties, the traditional nuclear family   28
is still the one of choice for millions of Americans. They are
255 comfortable with it, and for them it seems to work. It is reasonable,
therefore, at least not to place roadblocks in the way of couples
with children who wish to conduct their lives according to the traditional family's dictates. Women who freely desire to spend much
of their lives as mothers and housewives, outside of the labor force,
260 should not be penalized economically by public policy for making
that choice. Nor should they be denigrated by our culture as second-
class citizens.

        The second major proposal for change that has been stressed   29
in national debate is the development of extensive governmental
265 programs offering monetary support and social services for families, especially the new "nonnuclear" ones. In some cases, these
programs assist with functions these families are unable to perform adequately; in others, the functions are taken over, transforming them from family to public responsibilities.

What path have they followed? Check back.

270 This is the path followed by the European welfare   30
states, but it has been less accepted by the United States than
by any other industrialized nation. The European welfare states
have been far more successful than the United States in minimizing the negative economic impact of family decline, especially on
275 children. In addition, many European nations have established policies making it much easier for women (and increasingly men) to
combine work with child rearing. With these successes in mind, it
seems inevitable that the United States will (and I believe should)
move gradually in the European direction with respect to family

280 policies, just as we are now moving gradually in that direction
with respect to medical care.

*What has major dis-
advantages? Check
back.*

There are clear drawbacks, however, in moving too far 31
down this road. If children are to be served best, we should seek
to make the family stronger, not to replace it. At the same time
285 that welfare states are minimizing some of the consequences of decline, they also may be causing further breakup of the family unit.
This phenomenon can be witnessed today in Sweden, where the
institution of the family probably has grown weaker than any-
where else in the world. On a lesser scale, it has been seen in the
290 United States in connection with our welfare programs. Fundamental to successful welfare state programs, therefore, is keeping uppermost in mind that the ultimate goal is to strengthen
families.

*If you don't remember
what these alterna-
tives are, check back
in the text. Also, as
you read these last
paragraphs, look for
the writer's own solu-
tion.*

While each of the above alternatives has some merit, I 32
295 **suggest a third one.** It is premised on the fact that we cannot
return to the 1950s family, nor can we depend on the welfare state
for a solution. Instead, we should strike at the heart of the cultural
shift that has occurred, point up its negative aspects, and seek to
reinvigorate the cultural ideals of family, parents, and children
300 within the changed circumstances of our time. We should stress
that the individualistic ethos has gone too far, that children are
getting woefully shortchanged, and that, over the long run, strong
families represent the best path toward self-fulfillment and personal happiness. We should bring again to the cultural forefront
305 the old ideal of parents living together and sharing responsibility
for their children and for each other.

What is needed is a new social movement whose purpose is 33
the promotion of families and their values within the new con-
straints of modern life. It should point out the supreme importance
310 to society of strong families, while at the same time suggesting
ways they can adapt better to the modern conditions of individualism, equality, and the labor force participation of both women and
men. Such a movement could build on the fact that the overwhelm-
ing majority of young people today still put forth as their major life
315 goal a lasting, monogamous, heterosexual relationship that includes the procreation of children. It is reasonable to suppose that
this goal is so pervasive because it is based on a deep-seated human need.

*Check back for the
meaning of this
goal.*

The time seems ripe to reassert that strong families con- 34
320 cerned with the needs of children are not only possible, but necessary.

WORKING WITH THE MAIN READING

PARAGRAPHS 1–3

Main Idea Check

Here are the main ideas for this section of the article. Write the correct paragraph number beside its main idea.

_____ This paragraph gives a description of the traditional nuclear family, which in the author's view is no longer dominant.

_____ The American family has undergone a radical change since the mid-1950s.

_____ The traditional nuclear family was strongest in the United States in the mid-twentieth century.

A Closer Look

1. Historically, the power and position of the family first began to decline approximately twenty-five years ago.   T F

2. What feature or features does the writer mention as being characteristic of the traditional nuclear family?
   a. It was based on a stable marriage.
   b. It encouraged divorce as a solution to an unhappy marriage.
   c. Its central role was to provide an environment for bearing and raising children.
   d. The wife was the homemaker; the husband was the breadwinner.

3. There is general agreement among scholars that radical changes in the American family have occurred since about 1955.   T F

Vocabulary in Context

Here are some words from the passage that you may not have known. You either guessed their meaning from context or from your knowledge of word families, or you omitted the word and were still able to understand the sentence. Now check and learn the meanings of the words. Use your dictionary to help you.

monogamous (line 18)   hierarchy (line 27)
paramount (line 23)   jointly (line 34)
to live up to (line 25)

PARAGRAPHS 4–10

Main Idea Check

Here are the main ideas for this section of the passage. Write the correct paragraph number beside its main idea.

_____ A change in attitudes means that for an increasing number of Americans, sex is no longer closely associated with marriage and having children.

_____ In the last thirty years, the U.S. birthrate has almost been cut in half.

_____ The U.S. divorce rate has increased by 400 percent in the last twenty-five years.

_____ The changes in attitudes toward sex have been a very significant factor in the increase in children being born to unmarried parents.

_____ The nuclear family began to decline in the 1960s because of rising divorce rates, changes in sexual behavior, a decline in the birthrate, and an increase in the number of working women.

_____ In the last twenty-five years, the number of mothers working outside the home has increased very rapidly.

_____ Two social trends linked to the decline in birthrates are a decreasing interest in becoming a parent and a growing acceptance of people who do not have children.

A Closer Look

1. In the United States, mothers first began taking jobs outside the home in the 1960s.   T F

2. What would be the effect on the U.S. population figures if fertility rates remained at the same level as when this article was written?
   a. They would stabilize.
   b. They would fall.
   c. They would gradually rise.

3. According to the text, American society used to regard people who had no children more negatively that it does today.   T F

4. What does the writer see as the consequence or consequences of the so-called sexual revolution that occurred in the United States between the 1950s and the 1990s?
   a. More young unmarried females are having sex before marriage.

       b. Married couples are having larger families.

       c. More children are being born to unwed mothers.

       d. Considerably fewer people think premarital sexual intercourse is immoral than did in the 1960s.

5. How would you describe American divorce rates in the period 1955–1990?

       a. They stabilized at a higher level.

       b. They increased slightly.

       c. They climbed dramatically.

       d. They declined between 44 percent and 66 percent.

Vocabulary in Context

Here are some words from the passage that you may not have known. You either guessed their meaning from context or from your knowledge of word families, or you omitted the word and were still able to understand the sentence. Now check and learn the meanings of the words. Use your dictionary to help you.

upsurge (line 40)   to shatter (line 59)

the level of (line 50)   to quadruple (line 84)

PARAGRAPHS 11–17

Main Idea Check

Here are the main ideas for this section of the article. Write the correct paragraph number beside its main idea.

_____ The changes of the last twenty-five years have considerably reduced the strength of the family as a social institution.

_____ The four crucial social developments of the last twenty-five years have tended to damage the center of the nuclear family, i.e., the relationship between the marriage partners.

_____ In Western industrial societies, there is a general cultural trend toward interest in the individual. A decreased commitment to the family is part of this general trend.

_____ The substantial increase in the number of single-parent families shows how much the husband-wife nucleus has been damaged by social trends.

_____ The new attitude toward marriage is associated with the rising divorce rates.

_____ Today marriage has become a voluntary, not an obligatory, arrangement that people enter into to pursue their own happiness and fulfillment.

_____ People are more interested in working for their own success as individuals than for the success of the family group.

A Closer Look

1. Today the nuclear family is becoming a more common type of household while the proportion of single-parent, step-, unmarried, and homosexual families is falling.   T   F

2. What prediction does the writer include about children and single-parent families in the United States?
   a. After 1990, 70 percent of all children would be living in single-parent families.
   b. Seventy percent of the children born in 1990 would be born into single-parent families.
   c. Of the children born in 1990, 70 percent would experience living in a single-parent family at some time.

3. What evidence does the writer have for claiming in paragraph 14 "psychological need, in and of itself, has proved to be a weak basis for stable marriage"?
   a. Current American divorce rates are high.
   b. People are now spending much less of their lives in family-related activities.
   c. The U.S. birthrate has fallen.

4. Scan to identify where this section compares society's attitudes to marriage and the family in 1990 with its attitudes twenty-five years ago. Then read carefully for the following general tendencies of the two time periods. Identify each tendency as typical of 1950 or 1990 as appropriate.
   a. People tend to invest more time, energy, and money in things connected with family life.
   b. The family is smaller.
   c. Individuals are more independent, less dependent on the family.
   d. Marriage tends to be considered a social obligation rather than a voluntary arrangement between two individuals.
   e. Society is fulfilling many of the functions the family has at times performed.
   f. The major part of an adult's life is spent with his or her family.
   g. There is a greater emphasis on individualism.
   h. The goal of marriage is personal fulfillment rather than economic security and raising children.

Vocabulary in Context

Here are some words from the passage that you may not have known. You either guessed their meaning from context or from your knowledge of word families, or you omitted the word and were still able to understand the sentence. Now check and learn the meanings of the words. Use your dictionary to help you.

bond (line 95)   to reshape (line 130)
to lose ground to (line   cohesive (line 135)
  96)   to invest/investment (line 144)
at will (line 120)   supremacy/supreme (line 153)
lax (line 122)   in keeping with (line 153)
sanction (line 126)

SOCIAL CONSEQUENCES (Paragraphs 18–24)

Main Idea Check

Here are the main ideas for this section of the passage. Write the correct paragraph number beside its main idea.

—— Parents and society in general no longer give the highest priority to the interests of children.

—— This paragraph describes some of the desirable family conditions for bringing up children, conditions that are becoming rarer in the United States and other advanced societies.

—— Men who abandon their children are more to blame than working women for the problem of inadequate parenting.

—— Today's unprecedented standard of living in Western societies is due in part to a lessening of family responsibilities and obligations.

—— The quality of life for children has deteriorated as a result of family decline.

—— The recent social changes that have brought about family decline also have had a positive impact on society.

—— Child rearing is more likely to be effective when two good parents are available to care for the children.

A Closer Look

1. According to the writer, the decline in the social position of the family has had consequences that are uniformly negative.   T F

2. According to the writer, children are the people most seriously affected by the changes in the American family.   T F

3. The writer believes that the traditional nuclear family—with the wife as homemaker and with the husband as breadwinner and ultimate decision-maker—provides the best environment for bringing up children.   T F

4. According to this article, what factor or factors will contribute positively to the atmosphere in which children are raised?
   a. adults who spend a lot of time with their children
   b. an emphasis on competitiveness among individuals in the family
   c. opportunities for children to see the world in which the adults work
   d. an absence of anxiety among children about the stability of their parents' marriage.
   e. little contact between children and other relatives and neighbors

Vocabulary in Context

Here are some words from the passage that you may not have known. You either guessed their meaning from context or from your knowledge of word families, or you omitted the word and were still able to understand the sentence. Now check and learn the meanings of the words. Use your dictionary to help you.

to jump to the conclusion that (line 159)	to leave the scene (line 196)
noteworthy (line 161)	to deny (line 197)
longevity (line 171)	paternity, paternal (line 197)
initiative (line 178)	on the part of (line 219)
disinvestment (line 191)	ingredient (line 220)

AGENDAS FOR CHANGE (Paragraphs 25–33)

Main Idea Check

Here are the main ideas for this section of the article. Write the correct paragraph number beside its main idea.

_____ Some welfare programs provided by governments, however, may be weakening the family, not strengthening it.

_____ A second proposed solution to family decline is for government to offer increased financial support and social services for families.

_____ Two very different solutions have been proposed to the problem of family decline.

_____ A return to the nuclear family is also problematic because the traditional nuclear family clearly has major defects that make it unsuited to a modern society.

_____ The United States should follow the example of European nations by offering more government support for families.

_____ We need a new social movement that convinces people that strong families are essential for a healthy society and that the family can adapt to the needs of modern society.

_____ However, there should be support for people who want to organize their families in the traditional way.

_____ The author's solution is to modernize and strengthen the family by showing people that living together in a close family is best for parents and children alike.

_____ Going back to the traditional nuclear family is problematic because it is unlikely that working women could or would want to leave their jobs.

A Closer Look

1. The writer advocates a return to the traditional nuclear family pattern of the 1950s.   T   F

2. The writer believes that the traditional nuclear family should be completely abandoned as a way to organize family life.   T   F

3. In what way or ways, according to the writer, have European nations counteracted the negative impact of family decline on children?
   a. by offering welfare programs that assist people to perform their parental functions
   b. by passing laws that make it more difficult to obtain a divorce
   c. by helping people combine work and parenting
   d. by trying to ensure that children in nontraditional families don't suffer economically.

4. From your reading of the text, which country do you think has a more extensive system of social services for families—the United States or Sweden?

5. What is the author's response to the decline of the family?
    a. He accepts it as an inevitable development that cannot be resisted.
    b. He feels that an expansion of government support programs will help stop the decline.
    c. He suggests that there needs to be a new social movement that will emphasize the need for and the benefits of stable two-parent families.

What Do You Think?

The writer claims that welfare can weaken the family but does not explain or support his claim. What is welfare? Who gets it? How could it contribute to the decline of the traditional two-parent family?

Vocabulary in Context

Here are some words from the passage that you may not have known. You either guessed their meaning from context or from your knowledge of word families, or you omitted the word and were still able to understand the sentence. Now check and learn the meanings of the words. Use your dictionary to help you.

to counteract (line 223)	with respect to (X) (line 279)
agenda (line 226)	premise (line 295)
aside from (line 231)	to reinvigorate (line 299)
to emulate (line 243)	constraint (line 308)
maternal (line 250)	pervasive (line 317)
roadblock (line 256)	ripe (line 319)
to penalize (line 260)	to reassert (line 319)
to denigrate (line 261)	

Vocabulary Study

This Vocabulary Study contains many of the words in the book that high-intermediate ESL students like you may not already know. The words belong to the category of general, nontechnical academic vocabulary, i.e., words you will meet in academic reading and listening or even when you are watching a documentary or news program on television. Unlike technical words, which are usually explained by the speaker or writer, this general vocabulary would not need to be explained for native speakers of English.

The words are listed by reading passage and in order of their appearance in the passage. After words are introduced in a given reading passage, they appear again in the Vocabulary Practice in the main reading of that unit. You will also see many of these words in the later units of the book.

When you come to learn new vocabulary, there are a number of strategies that you may find helpful.

STRATEGIES FOR VOCABULARY LEARNING

1. Work for short periods—maybe even as short as five minutes at a time. Work only for as long as you can really concentrate. Then stop and do something else. Come back to the vocabulary later, review the words from your first session, and work on new words for another short period.

2. Learn the meaning of a word by studying as many examples as you can. Look for examples in these pages, in the reading passage of the section, and in your ESL dictionary.

3. If you translate into your language, translate the same word from a number of different English examples. You will find that sometimes you will have to change your translation as the example changes.

4. Review regularly and frequently the vocabulary you have already learned. Research shows that the more you see a word, the better you understand and remember it.

5. Try to think of words you already know that seem to have a similar meaning or an opposite meaning to the new word. Look for ways in which the similar words might be slightly different in meaning from the new word.

6. Learn the grammatical category of the new word or expression—noun, verb, adjective, adverb, connector, or prepositional phrase.

7. Learn what kinds of words often go together with the new word by studying examples in your reading.

If the word is an adjective, what kind of nouns can it describe?

If the word is a verb, what kind of nouns can be its subject; what kind of words can be its object?

8. Learn important grammatical patterns that are associated with the new word—again by studying the new word in context. You need this knowledge for writing and speaking; even if you don't use the words yourself, knowing the grammar patterns will help your reading.

If the word is a verb, is it transitive (+ object) or intransitive (no object) or both?

If the word is a verb, what verb pattern or patterns can follow it?

If a preposition is associated with the word (e.g., depend *on*, wish *for*, interested *in*, tired *of*), learn the preposition at the same time as you learn the new word.

VOCABULARY STUDY: READING PASSAGE 1.1

to associate (*X* with *Y*) (verb); **association** (noun)   to connect *X* with *Y*
     Examples   Scientists have found evidence that smoking is associated with lung cancer.
           However, cigarette producers do not accept that there is an association between lung cancer and cigarette smoking.

stress (noun)   1. emphasis; 2. pressure (often pressure that comes from difficulties in your life)
     Examples   In the word *discover,* the stress is on the second syllable. We say dis*cov*er. In the word *driver,* the stress is on the first syllable. We say *driv*er.
           John is under a lot of stress at the moment. He is out of work; his wife is ill, and they don't have enough money to pay all their monthly bills.

nutrition (noun)   1. food and its effect on the body; 2. the scientific study of food and its effects on the body

Examples Experts agree that good nutrition is necessary for health. If you eat the wrong types of food, your health will suffer.

U.S. schools often employ people who have studied nutrition at the university. Their job is to plan healthy meals for the schoolchildren.

expert (noun)   a person who has a lot of knowledge or skill in a certain subject; **expertise** (noun)   the knowledge or skill that an expert has

Examples Agricultural experts from other countries often visit Canada and the United States. They come to learn about the farming methods that are used in North America.

These people want to increase their expertise in order to better solve agricultural problems in their own countries.

to emphasize (verb); **emphasis** (noun)   to place more importance on X (than on other things), to stress; *to place emphasis on X:* to emphasize X

Examples The speaker emphasized his important ideas by repeating them and speaking louder.

In some countries, governments do not place enough emphasis on education. They spend a lot more money on less important things.

aware (adjective)   *to be aware:* to know; *to become aware:* to realize

Examples The student was not aware that the parking lot was only for police cars, so he parked his car there. When he returned, he found a parking ticket on his car.

More and more people in the United States are becoming aware that exercise is important for health. They are beginning to run, swim, or play other sports regularly.

to tend (verb); **tendency** (noun)   something that tends to occur is something that often or usually happens

Examples Smokers tend to have more health problems than non-smokers.

Although we are aware of the connection between illness and the way we live, there is still a tendency for people to think about their health only when they become sick and have to see a doctor.

sufficient (adjective)   Enough X; synonym: **adequate** opposites: **insufficient, inadequate, deficient** (adjective)   *to be deficient in* X: not to have as much of X as is needed

Examples Children of poor Third World families sometimes suffer from malnutrition. Their diets are deficient in certain essential vitamins, or they simply do not get sufficient food to keep healthy.

A few people, including the cigarette producers, still claim that there is insufficient evidence that smoking causes cancer and other lung diseases.

to rely on X (verb); **reliable** (adjective)   to depend on X; to trust

Examples I'm sorry I have to leave now. Friends of mine are relying on me to get them to the airport in time for their 6:00 P.M. flight.

My first car was old and uncomfortable, but it was very reliable. It always started and got me where I needed to go.

mere(ly) (adjective and adverb)   nothing more than X; only X and nothing more

Examples Research studies have shown that people do not need to train like Olympic runners in order to improve their health. People who normally do not exercise can reduce their chances of heart disease merely by walking thirty minutes a day.

For healthy nutrition, it is not sufficient merely to choose food with low cholesterol. You also need to reduce the amount of fat in your meals.

to treat (verb); **treatment** (noun)   to behave toward someone in a certain way; to give medical care to someone or to a condition

Examples The passengers who had missed their connecting flight were treated quite well by the airline. They were each given a hotel room for the night, a free return ticket to wherever the airline flies. They were also able to leave on the first flight the next morning.

The standard treatment for flu is to give the patient plenty of liquids to drink and plenty of rest.

diet (noun)   1. the types of food that a person or a group normally eats; 2. a limited list or amount of food that a person is allowed to eat

Examples   Researchers now believe that the typical U.S. diet contains too much animal fat. They are advising people to eat less red meat, butter, and cheese.

Lots of people attempt to lose weight merely by going on a diet. They do not understand that exercise is an important part of a healthy weight-loss program.

habit (noun)   behavior that often occurs, especially behavior that you can't stop although you may want to

Examples   Smoking is an unhealthy habit that many people are trying to give up.

Parents try to teach their children good health habits. For example, they teach them to always wash their hands before they eat or touch food. They hope that washing their hands will become a habit for the children if they repeat it enough times.

to benefit (verb); **benefit** (noun)   to be helpful or useful to someone; to get an advantage from something

Examples   The new tax law is not going to benefit us. You need to be making over $200,000 before you benefit from it.

The student did not get much benefit from his vacation. He was ill for ten of the fourteen days.

regular (adjective)   describes something that happens again and again with the same time, more or less, between occurrences; opposite: **irregular** (adjective)

Examples   Doctors say that exercise is important for health, but it must be regular exercise. In other words, you have to exercise every day, or every second day.

The student's attendance in class was very irregular. Some weeks he didn't come to class at all; other weeks he came to class 40 percent to 60 percent of the time.

VOCABULARY STUDY: READING PASSAGE 1.2 _____

rate (noun)   Any number, amount, or value that is calculated in relation to another number, amount, or value; speed

Examples   The divorce rate in the United States is very high. Today, according to statistics, one out of every three new marriages will end in divorce.

Death rates among children in the Third World are extremely high. For example, thirty-five thousand children below the age of one year die every day in developing countries.

to alarm (verb and noun); **alarming** (adjective)   to cause a feeling of fear or anxiety in a person

Examples   Don't let the fire bell alarm you when it sounds today. It is only being tested.

Humans are using up the world's natural riches at an alarming rate. There is now great concern about what kind of a world we will leave our children and grandchildren.

urgent (adjective)   describes something that needs to be dealt with immediately or without much delay

Examples   After the 1989 earthquake in Armenia, there was an urgent need for medicine, food, and shelter for the victims of the disaster. Many countries sent help immediately.

"Your sister just phoned and wanted to talk with you. She said it was urgent. She asked you to call her back as soon as possible."

to finance (verb)   to provide money that is needed for *X*; **financial** (adjective)   connected with money
    Examples   The World Bank often finances health programs in developing countries; these countries cannot afford to pay for the programs themselves.

           This company is in good financial health. It has made a profit of more than $4 million in each of the last five years.

enormous (adjective)   very large
    Examples   John's parents are very wealthy. They live in an enormous house with ten bedrooms and eight bathrooms!

           The new equipment costs over $2 million. Not all hospitals can afford to spend an enormous amount of money like this for just one piece of equipment.

surgery (noun)   medical treatment in which the doctor cuts into a patient's body in order to improve the patient's condition; **surgeon** (noun)   a doctor who performs surgery
    Examples   You do not always need to go to the hospital for minor surgery. Often your doctor will be able to perform it in his or her own office.

           Modern medicine has saved the lives of many people. Today surgeons can perform operations that were not possible thirty years ago.

technology (noun)   the use of scientific discoveries to produce better machines and equipment
    Examples   There has been great progress in computer technology in the last fifteen years. Now very small computers are more powerful than older computers that were as big as an office.

           Modern technology allows us to do many things that were impossible twenty years ago. For example, we can now produce energy from the sun quite cheaply.

advance (noun)   One example of progress
    Examples   In the last twenty years, there have been a number of important advances in the treatment of heart disease. Doctors are now able to help many more patients than they used to.

           Advances in computer technology are now enabling companies to produce very small computers that are more powerful, much smaller, and cheaper than the computers of twenty years ago.

operation (noun)   a piece of work, especially the work of a doctor who cuts into a person's body to treat a health problem; **to operate** (verb)   to work; to cause something (e.g., machinery) to work
    Examples   The operation was long and difficult. The doctors had to repair some damage to the patient's heart. But it was successful, and the patient is now better.

           We have a new computer in our office, but I don't have enough expertise to operate it properly. I think I'll take a computer class next semester.

to perform (verb)   to do a piece of work (e.g., an operation or a function)
    Examples   The doctor who performed the heart operation yesterday has a lot of experience. He has performed more than two hundred similar operations.

           The Red Cross organization performs extremely important services, especially in times of disasters or war. For example, it provides food and shelter to the homeless.

advantage (noun)   a useful quality of something; opposite: **disadvantage** (noun)
    Examples   One advantage of a smaller car is that it doesn't consume a lot of gasoline. You can operate it quite cheaply.

           One disadvantage of a small car is that it is uncomfortable for longer journeys.

to recover (verb)   1. to get something back again (which you had earlier); 2. to become healthy again (after an illness, an operation, etc.)
    Examples   The police recovered the stolen car. They found it ten miles away from where it disappeared.

           My sister was seriously ill last month, but she is now recovering well. She hopes to go back to work next week.

to conclude (verb); **conclusion** (noun)   to decide that something is true because of evidence that is
         available; to end, finish; **conclusive** (adjective)   describes something (e.g., evidence)
         that X is true
   Examples   From the fall in the number of smokers in the United States, we can conclude that the
         public is paying attention to the warnings about the dangers of tobacco.
         Medical experts believe that there is conclusive evidence of the damage smoking can
         do to your health. The tobacco companies, of course, do not believe that the evi-
         dence proves tobacco is a health risk.

VOCABULARY STUDY: READING PASSAGE 1.3

gene (noun); **genetic** (adjective)   the parts of cells that we get at birth from our parents and that
         control our growth, appearance, and other characteristics
   Examples   Genetic engineering attempts to change the genes of plants and animals in order to
         bring benefits to people
         Scientists who are conducting genetic research are now able to identify the genes that
         carry certain serious diseases. Children can inherit these genetic diseases from
         their parents or grandparents.
defect (noun); **defective** (adjective)   something wrong, a fault in a person or a thing
   Examples   Because of a small defect in this piece of furniture, I was able to buy it for half the
         normal price.
         Scientists have discovered that some serious illnesses are genetic; they are caused by
         defective genes.
to inherit (verb)   to receive X from someone who has died, or who is your parent, or who was in a
         position before you
   Examples   Mike inherited $50,000 from an uncle who died last year. His uncle left Mike the
         money because he was his favorite nephew.
         Often a new government will say: "Don't blame us for the country's problems. We
         inherited them all from the last government. We didn't create these problems."
normal (adjective) usual; opposite: **abnormal** (adjective)   unusual (and often bad)
   Examples   After the operation, the patient felt very tired, but the doctors weren't worried. They
         knew that this was merely a normal reaction to the surgery.
         April last year was abnormally cold here. Usually the weather in April is quite warm,
         but last year we had frost and quite a lot of snow!
to diagnose (verb); **diagnosis** (noun)   To identify what is wrong (usually in a patient who is ill)
   Examples   In order to diagnose a health problem, a doctor will start with the patient's symptoms,
         e.g., the presence of a fever, pains, headaches, dizziness, etc. After that, if the doc-
         tor is in doubt, he or she may do some tests to complete the diagnosis.
         An expert diagnosed my computer problems as being caused by a virus.
to threaten X (verb); **threat** (noun)   to be a possible danger to X; to say that you will cause damage or
         harm to someone
   Examples   In 1936, Hitler threatened to invade Czechoslovakia unless the German-speaking pop-
         ulation there were treated better.
         The threat of atomic war has not disappeared but has decreased since the fall of the
         Soviet Union.
immune (adjective); **to immunize** (verb); **immunity** (noun)   *to be immune to* X: to have protection
         from *X; to immunize:* to put a substance into a person's body which will protect him or
         her from a certain disease

Examples   Polio is a very dangerous disease that attacks children. In the 1950s, U.S. scientists developed a vaccine for it. Now children in many countries are immunized against polio at an early age.

Sometimes, if you have already had a certain illness, for example, measles, you become immune to it. Your immunity may last your entire life. If so, you will not catch the illness again.

to infect (verb); **infectious** (adjective)   to give a disease to a person

Examples   If you cut yourself, be sure to clean the cut carefully. If you leave dirt in the cut, it can become infected.

Colds and flu are very infectious. If one person in an office catches a cold or flu, he or she will usually infect others in the same office.

effective (adjective)   describes something that gives good results, that has the effect you want

Examples   This medicine is quite effective for colds. If you take it before you go to bed, you sleep well and feel better in the morning.

The government's economic program has been very effective. It has reduced unemployment from 10 to 7.5 million. It has also encouraged new businesses to develop.

fatal (adjective)   describes something that causes death, disaster, or other very negative results

Examples   There was a fatal accident on the freeway last night. Three people were rushed to the hospital; one was dead on arrival.

The company made the fatal mistake of hiring a person was an expert in her subject but who could not work with other people.

caution (noun); **cautious** (adjective); **to caution** (verb)   great care; very careful (to avoid problems, danger, mistakes, etc.); to warn someone to be careful

Examples   People should drive with great caution when there is ice or snow on the roads.

The police stopped the driver and cautioned him not to drive so close to the car in front.

to eliminate X (verb)   to cause X to disappear or not to be part of another thing any longer

Examples   Some people believe that medical science will soon be able to eliminate all diseases from the world, but doctors know that this will be impossible. New diseases are discovered almost every year.

Our soccer team was beaten 4–1, so we were eliminated from the competition. That was our last game this season.

physical (adjective)   describes something which you can touch or see, or something which is connected with a person's body (not with his mind); opposite: **mental** (adjective)   describes something that is connected with a person's mind

Examples   This map shows the physical features of the country: the mountains, the rivers, the lakes, and so on.

Medical science is beginning to understand more about mental illness. However, we still cannot treat this type of illness as successfully as we can treat some physical diseases.

ethical (adjective)   describes something that is connected with our ideas of good and bad or something that is honest and good; synonym: **moral**

Examples   Should we give abortions to women? This is an ethical question. Our answer will depend on our ideas of morality, our beliefs about right and wrong.

The minister of education gave a lot of government business to a company owned by his brother. For most people, this sort of behavior is not ethical.

abortion (noun)   an operation to end a woman's pregnancy

Examples   Abortion is used as a method of birth control in some countries. But many doctors believe that repeated abortions can damage a woman's health.

There is a lot of disagreement about abortion in the United States. Some people believe that it is a type of murder. Others believe that a woman has the right to end her pregnancy if she wants to.

VOCABULARY STUDY: READING PASSAGE 1.4 _____

ultimate(ly) (adjective and adverb)   describes something that occurs at the end of a process; final
> *Examples*   Most medical researchers believe that science will ultimately find ways to prevent or cure diseases like cancer and AIDS.
>
> The research program is making progress, but it is still a long way from reaching its ultimate goal—to develop a convenient method of birth control that is also completely safe and effective.

priority (noun)   something that needs attention before other things; **prior to** (preposition)   before
> *Examples*   After the bus accident, the doctors at the small hospital could not treat everyone at once. The gave priority to the people who were badly hurt. The people who were not seriously injured could afford to wait.
>
> Prior to the plane's landing in New York, the cabin crew passed out immigration and customs forms to the passengers.

to establish (verb)   to start something; to set something up; to show or prove that something is true
> *Examples*   According to scientists, the earliest European settlement in North America was established by Scandinavians in the eleventh century.
>
> Finally the cause of the accident has been established. A severe weather condition called wind shear caused the plane to lose speed and crash before landing.

to transmit (verb); **transmission** (noun)   to pass or send something to some other place or person (intentionally, e.g., a radio message; or unintentionally, e.g., a disease)
> *Examples*   Nowadays thanks to satellites, television news companies can transmit pictures of events as they actually happen to the other side of the world.
>
> The most common means of transmission for the cold virus is the human hand. Washing your hands frequently will reduce your risk of becoming infected during cold season.

to contaminate (verb); **contaminated** (adjective)   to make something unhealthy and dangerous to living things
> *Examples*   The explosion at the Chernobyl atomic reactor contaminated a large area around the plant with radioactivity.
>
> Drinking water in many areas of the developing world is contaminated with bacteria. It's not safe to drink but often it is the only water available to people.

annual (adjective)   in one year
> *Examples*   The annual celebration of Thanksgiving in the United States takes place in late November.
>
> This magazine appears three times annually, in January, May, and September.

case (noun)   one occurrence of X (e.g., a disease or a crime); *In this case:* if this happens
> *Examples*   The health authorities in the city are very worried; in the last three days, there have been twenty-five cases of serious food poisoning.
>
> It is possible that the weather will force us to cancel the soccer game tomorrow. In this case, we will play the game next week.

global (adjective)   describes something that affects the whole world; **globe** (noun)   the earth; a model of the earth
> *Examples*   Pollution is often a global problem, not merely a local, regional, or national one.
>
> This 1985 globe shows the main physical features of the earth, but some of the political information on it is now out-of-date.

catastrophe (noun); **catastrophic** (adjective)   a disaster; an event that causes much suffering and/or destruction

Examples   World War II was a catastrophe for most of the nations of Europe. It destroyed their economies and killed enormous numbers of their people.

The war's impact on the population of the then Soviet Union was especially catastrophic. It is believed that 20 million lost their lives in the war against Nazi Germany.

to estimate (verb); **estimate** (noun)   to calculate something approximately; to guess

Examples   There are no reliable official figures for the number of AIDS cases in some countries. So, the World Health Organization has to estimate the number.

Before you get your car repaired, you should ask for an estimate of how much the repairs will cost.

mass (noun and adjective); **massive** (adjective)   a large amount of material; a large number of people or things

Examples   If we use methods of mass production, we can make goods for the lowest possible price.

When we reached the movie theater, there was a mass of people outside it. They were all waiting for tickets, so we decided to leave and try to see the movie later.

vaccine (noun)   a substance that is put into the body and that causes the body to develop its own protection against a certain disease

Examples   Scientists have successfully developed vaccines for many diseases. These vaccines have even eliminated some diseases in certain parts of the world.

Some vaccines can be dangerous. A small number of people have bad reactions to them. Scientists are working to develop safer vaccines, especially for children.

simple (adjective)   describes something that is easy to do or understand or something that is not highly developed; opposite: **complex** (adjective)   describes the opposite

Examples   Often simple equipment is better than high-tech equipment. The complex high-tech equipment tends to break down more often and can only be repaired by an expert.

When students begin to write English, they usually write very simple sentences. Later they begin to write more complex sentences, with more than one clause.

incentive (noun)   something that encourages you to act in a certain way

Examples   People who own a house have an incentive to keep it in good repair. If you look after the house well, its value will normally increase.

As an incentive to people to save more and spend less, the government is reducing income tax rates on the interest that you earn on your savings.

to be reluctant (to do X) (adjective); **reluctance** (noun)   unwilling; not wanting to do something; not enthusiastic about doing it

Examples   Although there are major problems with the U.S. health-care system, the government is reluctant to change it—perhaps because it could lose the support of people who like the present system.

Many parents feel uncomfortable talking to their children about sexual behavior. This reluctance could mean that important messages about AIDS may not be reaching many young people.

VOCABULARY STUDY: READING PASSAGE 1.5 ⎯⎯⎯⎯⎯⎯⎯⎯⎯

capable (adjective)   to be able to do *X;* opposite: **incapable** (adjective)

Examples   Mary was not satisfied with her B on the test. She knew that she was capable of much better work, so she decided to study harder.

Before his operation, the patient was incapable of walking a mere ten yards. Now he can walk two miles a day without help.

to prolong (verb)   to make something longer in time
  Examples   Probably you can prolong your life if you exercise regularly and eat properly.
  We planned to end the meeting at 5 P.M., but we had to prolong it. There were still many things that had to be discussed. We didn't finish until 7 P.M.

conscious (adjective)   describes someone who is awake and who is able to understand what is happening around him; opposite: **unconscious** (adjective)
  Examples   Although the driver was badly hurt in the accident, she was still conscious. She was able to pull herself out of her car before it exploded.
  During the soccer game, Ali fell and hit his head. He was unconscious for about five minutes. As a precaution, we decided to take him to the hospital and have a doctor look at him.

to function (verb)   to work; **function of X** (noun)   the purpose of X; the work that X intended to do
  Examples   Clearly the U.S. health-care system is not functioning as it should. Over 30 million Americans are without health insurance.
  The human brain performs a number of important functions; for example, it controls all the movements of the body.

drug (noun)   1. medicine, medication; 2. a substance that people take for pleasure; it becomes a habit and often damages a person's health
  Examples   Doctors use modern drugs to fight infections in their patients.
  Aspirin is a drug, but it is not the type of drug that becomes a habit. Examples of problem drugs are opium, heroin, and cocaine.

to consider (verb)   to think (carefully) about X; **considerable** (adjective)   large enough to be important; **to reconsider** (verb)   to think about X again (with a possibility of changing your mind)
  Examples   People in this area are really angry with a local chemical company. It dumped large amounts of chemicals into the river without considering the possible effects on the environment.
  Experts say that the company's dumping of the chemicals will cause considerable damage to the river's ecology.
  Kate informed her boss that she was leaving her job. Her boss asked her to reconsider her decision; he did not want to lose her. He even offered her a 25-percent salary increase.

regardless of X (prepositional phrase)   in spite of X; X does not matter; without considering X
  Examples   The law of the United States declares that people must be treated equally regardless of their color, sex, religion, or national origin.
  This person is really very inconsiderate; he does what he wants regardless of how it might affect other people.

alternative (noun and adjective)   something that you can do or use instead of something else
  Examples   We need to solve the problems of the health-care system. We have no alternative. If we don't, health care will be available only to the wealthiest members of society.
  In many parts of the United States, people drive their cars to work because they have no alternative way to get to work. Public transport is nonexistent in many places.

circumstances (noun, usually plural)   the general situation; the conditions that can have an effect on something at a certain time
  Examples   After an accident, the police make inquiries about the circumstances of the accident. For example, how fast were the cars going? Was there rain or snow on the road? How much other traffic was there on the road?

Usually students must register for classes before the beginning of the semester. However, in certain circumstances, for example, if a foreign student can't get here on time, the student is permitted to register late.

to contribute (to X) (verb)   to help cause X; to join with others to give money, help, etc., to X
> *Examples*   Engine failure was not the only cause of the plane crash last month. Another factor that contributed to the disaster was the lack of experience of the pilot and first officer.
>
> Many people contribute to the Red Cross and other organizations that help people in trouble.

VOCABULARY STUDY: READING PASSAGE 2.1 _____

pattern (noun)   the way something usually (repeatedly) happens or is organized
> *Examples*   Scientists who study the behavior of animals first try to identify types of behavior that occur repeatedly. Once they have identified some behavior patterns, they are better able to explain the behavior.
>
> You can see patterns in academic writing. For example, a general claim that something is true is often followed by detailed examples that support the claim.

significant (adjective); **significance** (noun) opposite: **insignificant;**   important; large enough to be important or worth considering
> *Examples*   Primary health-care programs have brought about a significant improvement in people's health in some Third World countries.
>
> The significance of this research should be emphasized; it shows clearly that diets that are rich in fat are related to heart disease.

to complain (verb); **complaint** (noun)   to say that you are unhappy or dissatisfied about someone or something
> *Examples*   The weather has been very hot and dry for six weeks; almost everyone, especially the farmers, are complaining about it.
>
> Usually big companies have a department that handles customer complaints. Write to this department if you're having a problem with a product.

frustration (noun); **frustrated** (adjective)   the angry and upset feeling you get when you cannot do what you want to do
> *Examples*   You can experience a lot of frustration in health-care work: You see the problems of the people; you know they can be solved, but the government refuses to spend money where it is most needed.
>
> Sometimes you can get quite frustrated when you are trying to communicate with someone in English but you don't have the right words.

constant (adjective); **constantly** (adverb)   describes something that does not change or does not stop over time
> *Examples*   If you drive at a constant speed on the highways, you get more miles from your gasoline.
>
> It seems that the president is being criticized constantly in the newspapers.

culture (noun)   the shared way of life (customs, ideas, values, traditions, etc.) of a group of people
> *Examples*   Although the cultures of the United States and Britain are similar in some ways, there are also some differences that can cause problems when natives of the two cultures work together.

One value of U.S. culture is that children should be trained to be independent at an early age, an age that other cultures might find too young.

task (noun)   a piece of work that you must do

Examples   The task of the class in this test is to identify the main idea of each paragraph.

In the experiment, the subjects' task was to listen to people speaking English voices and then guess their social class on the basis of their language.

to interpret X as Y (verb)   to decide that X means Y; **to misinterpret** (verb)   to give the wrong meaning to something (In general *mis-* at the beginning of a word means something was done wrongly, for example, *to misjudge* and *to mislead*.)

Examples   After you do some research and obtain results, you need to interpret these results, in other words, decide what the results mean for a specific theory or hypothesis.

It is easy to misinterpret what a person is saying if she is speaking in a language that is not your native language.

process (noun); **to process** (verb)   a set of actions that happen naturally or are performed by someone to achieve some result

Examples   Louis Pasteur, the French scientist, developed a process for taking dangerous bacteria out of milk.

Modern computers can process certain types of information much faster than humans can.

to adjust (verb); **adjustment** (noun)   to change something (or yourself) so that it is better for a specific situation

Examples   If a person's hair appears green on your television, you probably need to adjust the color control.

Driving in the United Kingdom, where you have to drive on the left, requires some adjustments by U.S. visitors, who are used to driving on the right side of the road.

to remove (verb)   to take something away; to take something off

Examples   Before you hang new wallpaper, it is important to remove the old wallpaper and make any necessary repairs to the surface of the wall.

In some cultures, it is considered polite behavior to remove your shoes when you enter a person's home.

emotion (noun); **emotional** (adjective)   a feeling like love, anger, hate, fear, pity, etc.

Examples   When people have to make an important decision, they usually want to be influenced as little as possible by their emotions.

In some cultures, it is not really acceptable to show an emotional reaction in public.

to condemn (verb)   to say very strongly that something is bad

Examples   Every politician condemns the violence that occurs at professional soccer games, but no one has suggested a realistic way of preventing it.

You shouldn't condemn an entire country just because you've had problems with a few people from that country.

VOCABULARY STUDY: READING PASSAGE 2.2

successive (adjective); **in succession**   describes things that follow each other in time without interruption

Examples   The six successive days of heavy rain last week have caused major problems in the low areas of the state.

The local baseball team is doing well right now; they have won thirteen games in succession.

to flow (verb); **flow** (noun)   to move in an uninterrupted way (like the water of a river)
Examples   Traffic was flowing very freely on the highway this morning. I had no trouble getting to the airport in time for my plane.
In the United States, there is always a flow of people to areas of the country where more jobs are available.

to decline (verb); **decline** (noun)   to decrease (in number, size, strength, quality)
Examples   Overpopulation is a major problem in parts of Africa and Asia. In Europe, however, the population of some countries is declining.
A lot of people believe that U.S. education standards are declining. They complain about high-school graduates who sometimes cannot read.

to oppress (verb); **oppression** (noun)   to treat people cruelly and unfairly
Examples   Political oppression is still a major problem in many countries of the world. In these countries, the governments want no opposition.
Even in countries that seem free, some people—for example, women and racial minorities—feel oppressed.

prejudice (noun); **prejudiced** (adjective)   an opinion that you have formed without adequate information and that you then use to judge something or someone unfairly
Examples   In order to be a fair judge, you should eliminate as many of your prejudices as possible.
Carlos thinks soccer is a better game than football. He's prejudiced, however, because he grew up in Europe and played soccer all the time.

transition (noun)   a change from one condition to a different one
Examples   Newtown is a city in transition. It used to be a manufacturing city; now its economy is more dependent on research and service industries.
Moving to a new country is a difficult transition for many people.

to integrate (verb)   (to cause people) to become part of a group; opposite: **to disintegrate** (verb)   to break into many small pieces
Examples   Most people in the United States believe in integrated schools, where people of both sexes and all races can learn together.
The explosion caused the plane to disintegrate in the air near Ireland. There were no survivors.

sacrifice (noun); **to sacrifice** (verb)   something valuable that you give up in order to do something else
Examples   It seems that some people are prepared to sacrifice their family life and even their health for success in their jobs.
Many immigrants to the United States made sacrifices so that their children and grandchildren would have a better life.

prosperous (adjective); **prosperity** (noun)   wealthy and successful
Examples   This used to be a prosperous neighborhood, but then people and jobs began to move to other parts of the country.
The prosperity of Detroit depends a great deal on the automobile industry.

visible (adjective); **visibility** (noun)   able to be seen
Examples   Viruses and bacteria are not visible to the eye. We need a microscope to see them.
The plane could not take off because of poor visibility at the airport. There was dense fog that made it impossible to see more than twenty yards.

symbol (noun); **to symbolize** (verb)   something that represents something else
Examples   In the 1989 revolution, the people of Rumania cut the star out of their flag. It was for them a symbol of the political oppression of the communist government they wanted to eliminate.
The stars in the flag of the United States symbolize the fifty states of the country.

diversity (noun)   a number of different types
> *Examples*   One of the most noticeable features of U.S. society is the diversity of its people. You
> see Americans of every race, religion, and geographical origin.
> Fortunately, this is not a city that depends on one industry for its economic health. In
> fact, there is a wide diversity of business and industry here.

VOCABULARY STUDY: READING PASSAGE 2.3

to pursue (verb); **pursuit** (noun)   to follow (but the exact meaning depends on the object)
> *Examples*   My friend stopped his university studies to pursue (= start and try to build) a career
> as a professional musician.
> The pursuit (attempt to achieve) of happiness is a basic human right, according to the
> U.S. Bill of Rights.

background (noun)   facts about a person's life (e.g., family, education, etc.) before a certain time in
his or her life; facts that help to explain something
> *Examples*   Many people find it unbelievable that you can buy a gun in many of the United States
> without even a check into your background.
> In order to really understand the violence that occurred last week, you need some
> background information.

proportion (noun)   number or amount of X (usually in relation to a number or amount of Y)
> *Examples*   Most people would like to save a proportion, say 10 percent, of what they earn each
> month, but many find it impossible to do this on a regular basis.
> The proportion of nonsmokers to smokers in the United States has changed. Non-
> smokers now outnumber smokers.

to challenge (verb); **challenge** (noun)   to question whether something that has been claimed is really
true; something new and difficult that demands great effort or thought to do successfully
> *Examples*   John is finding his new job a real challenge; he is working in areas where he has little
> experience.
> The idea that smoking can cause serious illness has been challenged by some scien-
> tists, but most of them have connection to the tobacco industry.

thorough (adjective)   describes something that is done as completely and carefully as possible or
someone who is very careful and pays attention to details
> *Examples*   The student wrote a very thorough analysis of the topic and got an A for his paper.
> You can have confidence in Sue's work. She is very thorough.

to analyze (verb); **analysis** (noun)   to examine something (especially by dividing it into parts) in
order to understand it
> *Examples*   In order to find a solution to a problem, you really need first to analyze the problem
> and its causes.
> In research, it is often essential to conduct a statistical analysis of your results.

ethnic (adjective)   connected with a social group, often of the same national or racial background,
which has its own different cultural traditions
> *Examples*   "Ethnic cleansing" is an expression that came into the English language in the 1990s
> from the former Yugoslavia. It means to eliminate members of an ethnic group
> from an area of the country so that members of a different ethnic group can live
> there by themselves.

In a fair and free society, it is important to protects the rights of minority ethnic groups so that they are not oppressed by the majority group.

network (noun)   a large number of things or people that are connected with each other

Examples   The U.S. telephone network is one of the most advanced in the world.

The university has bought a new computer network. Now every office will be able to send and receive messages from other offices by computer.

source (of X) (noun)   a person, place, or thing from which you get X or which causes X

Examples   When you write a research paper, you must mention the sources of all ideas that are not your own.

Some toxic substances have been found in a river near here; scientists are trying to identify the source of the pollution.

to compete (verb); **competition** (noun)   to try to get or win something for yourself

Examples   If two or more companies are competing with each other for customers, this tends to keep the price of their products low.

The World Cup is a soccer competition that takes place every four years.

hostility (noun); **hostile** (adjective)   unfriendly; behaving like an enemy

Examples   John and Peter do not like each other. You can feel the hostility between them when they meet.

The politician got a very hostile reaction from the factory workers who had lost their jobs and who blamed the government.

to resent (verb); **resentment** (noun)   to feel angry because you think you've been treated unfairly

Examples   There is a lot of resentment among the female workers in this factory. They get lower wages than male workers for what they feel is the same type of work.

A few people resent the presence of foreign students in the United States. They feel that their tax dollars are helping support these students.

VOCABULARY STUDY: READING PASSAGE 2.4 _____

to commit yourself to X (verb); **committed to** (adjective)   to decide and promise (usually publicly) that you will do X

Examples   This company has committed itself to a policy of equal opportunity for all, regardless of race, color, religion, or national origin.

The government is committed to not increasing taxes. However, few experts feel that they can raise the money they need for new programs without breaking this commitment.

to preserve (verb)   to prevent something from being damaged or destroyed

Examples   There was a plan to destroy this old church to make way for a new highway. However, a group of citizens pressured the city government to preserve it because of its historic significance.

One of the tasks of the United Nations is to preserve world peace.

policy (noun)   a set of ideas that controls the way people (e.g., a government, an office) deals with specific situations

Examples   The government's economic policy is failing. It is creating more unemployment, not getting people back to work.

It is the policy of this university to admit students regardless of their racial or national origins

controversy (noun); **controversial** (adjective)   a public discussion or disagreement between two groups about a specific subject

Examples   The controversy about abortion has been going on in the United States for more than twenty years.

U.S. television networks usually avoid controversial programs because companies will not buy time for commercials during these programs.

to respond (verb); **response** (noun)   to answer; to react

Examples   The patient is responding well to this new drug. He's out of danger, and the doctors are expecting him to recover fully.

The company offered the workers a 2-percent pay raise. The response of the employees was to threaten to stop work if the offer were not raised to 5 percent.

to favor X (verb); **to be in favor of** (verb)   to treat someone better than others; to support something; opposite: **to be opposed to**

Examples   The government's new tax plan is being criticized; it seems to favor the wealthy while it raises taxes on the poor.

I haven't met anyone who is in favor of the new tax plan. Everyone seems to be opposed to it.

empirical (adjective); **empirically** (adverb)   describes something that is connected to our direct practical experience of life

Examples   We have a great deal of empirical evidence that learning perfect pronunciation in a second language is difficult or impossible. The clearest type of evidence is the different foreign accents we can hear in English.

In psychological research, theories have to be empirically tested with human subjects.

to approve of X (verb); **approval** (noun)   to be in favor of something; to consider X good, right, suitable, etc.; opposite: **to disapprove** (verb)

Examples   Members of older generations often do not approve of the behavior of younger people. Among other things, they criticize their clothes, their music, and their hair styles.

The crowd at the soccer game showed their disapproval of the referee's decision by booing and whistling.

likely (adjective); **likelihood** (noun)   probable; or probably true

Examples   Because of lots of publicity about the dangers of smoking, it's likely that the proportion of smokers in the general population will continue to decline.

According to the weather forecast, there is a likelihood of heavy rain this afternoon. You'd better take an umbrella to school with you.

to retain X (verb); **retention** (noun)   to keep X; not to lose X or give it up

Examples   People with photographic memories are able to retain information they have only seen once.

First-generation immigrants to the United States typically retain their native language and many of the cultural values of their native country. This sometimes leads to problems between them and their children, who are exposed to U.S. culture and its often different rules of behavior

to adapt (verb); **adaptation** (noun)   to change X or yourself in order to deal with a new situation

Examples   When people settle in a new country, they have to adapt to the new culture.

For some people, this process of adaptation can be long and difficult.

to assimilate to/into (verb); **assimilation** (noun)   to become like the things or people around you

Examples   It often takes two or three generations for immigrants to assimilate into their new society.

Assimilation is a process that most immigrants to the United States have gone through successfully.

VOCABULARY STUDY: READING PASSAGE 2.5 _____

potential (adjective); **potential** (noun) possible; the possibility that something or someone will develop in a given way

  Examples Although nuclear energy is of great potential benefit to society, many people are frightened of it because of the disaster at Chernobyl.

  Most experts agreed that Smith had the potential to become an Olympic athlete; but a succession of serious injuries forced her to retire before she achieved this.

to tolerate (verb); **tolerant** (adjective) to be willing to accept things (ideas, behavior) in other people which are strange and which you may not approve of); opposite: **intolerance** (noun)

  Examples Although there is prejudice in the United States, it is generally a fairly tolerant country. Many Americans agree with the saying "live and let live" and believe that people should be able to live and think as they wish as long as they don't harm others.

  The English settlers who came to the United States in the seventeenth century left England because of the religious intolerance that existed there. They could not follow their religion without problems from the government.

to persist (verb); **persistent** (adjective) to continue to exist; to continue to do something although conditions are against it

  Examples A cough is usually nothing to worry about unless it persists for ten days or more. In this case, you should see your doctor.

  In spite of lots of evidence contradicting it, there is a persistent belief that Western high-tech medicine will solve the health-care problems of the Third World.

objective (noun) a goal, or something you wish to achieve; **objective** (adjective) describes views or people who are fair and not influenced by emotions and prejudices.

  Examples One of the objectives of this book is to show you some strategies that might help you with your English reading. Another objective is to teach you vocabulary.

  Newspaper reports of events should be as objective as possible. However, reporters find it difficult to always keep their feelings out of their stories.

to minimize (verb) to keep something as small as possible; opposite: **to maximize; minimum** (noun or adjective) the smallest number or amount possible; opposite: **maximum**

  Examples We can't hope to eliminate prejudice completely, but we can work to minimize it.

  Normally, interstate highways have a minimum as well as a maximum speed. It is just as dangerous to drive too slowly on an interstate as it is to drive too fast.

to cite (verb); **citation** (noun) to mention information from another source (usually to support your own views)

  Examples If you use ideas or information from another person in a research paper, you must cite your sources.

  You should list all your citations in a special list at the end of your research paper.

to determine X (verb) to find the facts about something; to have control and influence over something

  Examples The government ordered an official inquiry into the plane crash in order to determine what caused it.

  The amount of money you make determines how much tax you pay every year.

to perceive (verb); **perception** (noun) to use your senses and mind to form a picture of some reality outside yourself

  Examples One of the interesting questions that psychology tries to answer is the following: How can two people see the same thing and still perceive it differently?

Perceptions are extremely important in politics. It doesn't matter if a politician is honest or not as long as people perceive him or her to be honest. Appearances are often more important than reality.

to assume (verb); **assumption** (noun)   to believe that something is true without proof that it really is true

Examples   This reading textbook is intended for high-intermediate students. It assumes that students already have some knowledge of English vocabulary and grammar.

It is a mistake to make the assumption that two people watching the same event will perceive that event similarly.

to contradict (verb); **contradiction** (noun)   to say or show that a person or idea is wrong; to be in disagreement with an idea

Examples   The evidence we have seems to contradict the view that everyone can learn a second language well. We have found many cases of people whose English is still poor after twenty-five years in this country.

There are often contradictions between what people say and what they do.

superior to X (adjective)   higher in quality, numbers, or position; opposite: **inferior**

Examples   Many people believe that Japanese cars are superior to American cars. That's the main reason why so many Japanese cars are sold here.

There's a saying in English: "You get what you pay for." This means if you pay less than normal for some job, then the work will probably be inferior.

rational (adjective)   describes a person who uses logic, or ideas and actions that are based on reason or logic; opposite: **irrational**

Examples   Let's stay calm and think about the problem rationally. Anger and fear will get us nowhere!

Politicians often use emotional rather than rational arguments to win support for their actions and ideas.

VOCABULARY STUDY: READING PASSAGE 3.1 _____

impression (noun)   a feeling or idea produced in your mind by someone or something

Examples   Movies and television shows tend to give a rather false impression of life in the United States. They make it appear more exciting or more dangerous than it really is.

When you see the number of new cars and the prosperous-looking neighborhoods, you get the impression that the economy of this city is strong.

uniform (adjective)   not varying in any way; even

Examples   The goods produced by this company are not of uniform quality. Some are excellent; other are full of defects.

The results of the three public opinion polls were fairly uniform. In all three, 50 percent to 52 percent of the public approved of the government's economic policy.

version (noun)   a different form of the same basic thing (e.g., a story)

Examples   One driver in the accident claimed that he stopped at the stop sign. The second driver's version was different; he said the first driver had failed to stop.

The first jet airliner, the *Comet,* suffered a number of fatal crashes in its first years of service. Later versions of the *Comet,* however, flew millions of miles without further problems.

to vary (verb); **variation** (noun); **variety** (noun); **various** (adjective)   to be different; the fact that something is different; difference(s)

Examples   The rent for an apartment in this town varies according to the neighborhood.

There is great variation between day and night temperatures in the Sahara. During the day, temperatures can rise to above 100°; at night, they can fall to near freezing.

to observe (verb); **observation** (noun)   to watch carefully; to notice (formal)

Examples   One of the first steps of science is to observe the thing you wish to study and then to record what you see.

Although the driver seemed uninjured after the accident, her doctors decided to keep her in the hospital overnight for observation.

to extend (verb)   to stretch; to make X longer or greater; **extensive** (adjective)   large; covering a large area; **to some extent** (adverb phrase)   partly

Examples   The storm caused extensive damage to the Southeast. Very few places were left undamaged.

To some extent, political oppression was a factor in European immigration to the United States. The main cause, however, was economic hardship.

standard (noun); **standard** (adjective)   the level of quality that is considered to be acceptable and that you use to judge someone or something

Examples   This professor has very high standards. You'll need to work very hard to pass her class.

Standard American English is the kind of English that is spoken and written by well-educated people in the United States.

formal (adjective)   describes something which is correct and suitable for official situations; opposite: **informal**

Examples   Students of English need to learn the difference between formal and informal English vocabulary so that they can speak in a way that suits the situation.

John has been told unofficially that he is going to be promoted; however, he hasn't received formal notification of this yet.

label (noun)   a piece of paper attached to something in order to identify it or give information about it; **to label** (verb)   to give a name to something or someone

Examples   When you travel by air, make sure that you write your name, address, and phone number on labels and attach the labels to your baggage.

One of the first things that children do with language is to label objects in their environment.

role (noun)   the function of someone or something in a certain situation

Examples   The book examines the role of aircraft in World War I. Its conclusion is that aircraft had little effect on the fighting.

In some countries, the roles of men and women are clearly different. Men are expected to earn money, while women work at home and raise the children.

interaction (noun)   speaking or working together; **to interact** (verb)   to have an effect on each other

Examples   To try to identify important factors in the process of language acquisition, researchers are studying the interaction between babies and their parents.

Scientists believe that a large number of factors interact to determine how well a person learns a second language.

relevant (adjective); **relevance** (noun)   connected with the topic being discussed; opposite: **irrelevant** (adjective)

Examples   When you write an academic paper, you have to decide what is relevant and what is irrelevant. You omit what is irrelevant.

The meeting was a waste of time. We spent almost all of the time talking about things of no relevance.

VOCABULARY STUDY: READING PASSAGE 3.2 _____

competence (noun); **competent** (adjective)   the ability to do something which is required of you; opposite: **incompetent**
    Examples   Before foreign students begin their academic studies, they usually need to show their competence in English by taking a test of English.
        The worker was dismissed by his employer for incompetence.

to comprehend (verb)   to understand; **comprehensible** (adjective)   possible to understand; opposite: **incomprehensible; comprehensive** (adjective)   thorough; including (almost) everything
    Examples   The telephone connection was so poor that the reporter's words were almost incomprehensible to the listeners.
        This book is interesting but it is not a comprehensive examination of the research. That would take a much longer book.

to investigate (verb); **investigation** (noun)   to attempt to find all the relevant facts about something (e.g., a crime, a person, an event)
    Examples   A team of government experts is sent to investigate all accidents involving commercial aircraft in the United States.
        Scientists investigating heart disease have been able to identify a number of factors that contribute to the disease.

component (noun)   one of the parts that make up something (a machine or a system)
    Examples   This is a Japanese car, but many of its components were manufactured in the United States.
        Scientists see language as having three major components: a sound component, a grammar component, and a meaning component.

to modify X (verb); **modification** (noun)   to change something (usually slightly)
    Examples   The automobile company has modified the engines on last year's cars in order to meet the government's new standards for fuel efficiency.
        After some safety modifications, the company began to market its children's car seats again.

sequence (noun)   a number of things that follow each other in succession; the order in which things follow each other
    Examples   Subject-verb-object is the basic sequence of elements in an English sentence.
        After he recovered consciousness, the driver was not able to remember the sequence of events that led up to the accident.

to involve X (verb)   to require X as a necessary part of something; to cause X to be connected with something
    Examples   John decided not to accept the new job because it involved a lot of traveling overseas. He did not wish to spend so much time away from his family.
        It is probably good advice not to get involved in arguments between your friends.

random (adjective); **at random** (adverbial phrase)   without any meaningful plan or pattern
    Examples   Random guessing will not help people pass examinations.
        This public opinion poll was conducted with adults selected at random from the local telephone book.

provided (that) (connecting phrase)   only if; on condition that
    Examples   Banks will lend you enough money to buy a house provided that you convince them you will be able to pay it back.
        You have been given conditional admission by the university. This means that you can start your studies provided you pass the English language test.

to refer to X (verb)   to mean; to mention or speak about X
Examples   In English, we use the pronouns *he* and *she* to refer to people. The pronoun *it* refers to
things.
In her speech, the politician did not refer to the latest opinion polls showing that only
25 percent of people approved of her policies.

element (noun)   simple, basic things that combine to form other things
Examples   The elements of an English utterance are the sounds and the words that combine to
produce the meaning.
Oxygen and hydrogen are elements; when they combine in certain proportions, they
form water.

concept (noun)   an idea; **to conceive** (verb)   to think or imagine
Examples   As they grow, children need to learn such concepts as past and future, distance and
time.
Some people find it difficult to conceive of ways of thinking that are different from
those of their own culture.

VOCABULARY STUDY: READING PASSAGE 3.3

to reinforce X (verb)   to make X stronger
Examples   The results of this new study reinforce the findings of earlier studies that exercise
improves people's general level of health.
Unfortunately, news stories about crime in immigrant communities may reinforce
prejudice against immigrants.

error (noun); **erroneous** (adjective)   a mistake
Examples   The investigators concluded that mechanical failure, not human error, was the cause
of the plane crash.
There is a popular but erroneous belief that health care is free in Britain. It is not.
People pay for it through extra taxes they pay to the government.

crucial (adjective)   extremely important
Examples   Collecting reliable data is crucial to any scientific experiment. Without good data, our
conclusions will not be defensible.
Clean water and adequate sanitation are crucial factors in improving the health of
people in many developing countries.

document (noun)   an official piece of paper giving some information; **to document** (verb)   to record
or prove something with a document
Examples   Your passport and school certificates are important documents. You should keep them
in a safe place.
The history researcher is having problems because the question he is investigating is
not well documented. He has only found two reliable sources of information.

accurate (adjective); **accuracy** (noun)   correct and exact
Examples   This student's English is grammatically accurate but it does not sound natural. He
needs to spend more time talking and listening to English speakers than studying
grammar.
Newspaper reporters should check the accuracy of their stories before they are published.

genuine (adjective)   real; exactly what it appears to be or is claimed to be; honest
Examples   These shoes can't be made of genuine leather. The price is too low.

Mary's surprise when she walked into the party was completely genuine. She had no idea that her friends had been planning a surprise party for her birthday.

to apply (verb)   to formally request something in writing (usually admission or permission); to use; to be relevant

Examples   If you want to start your university classes next semester, you should apply now. The admission process takes some time.

Applied linguistics is that field of study that tries to apply knowledge from more theoretical research in linguistics in order to answer questions and solve problems that have some practical connection to language.

The automobile company is warning drivers that there is a potentially dangerous defect in their Model S cars. The warning applies only to Model S cars produced in 1991.

data (noun)   facts and information collected for scientific investigation

Examples   The student wanted to investigate people's attitudes toward language, but he wasn't sure about how best to collect the data. He asked his professor for advice.

After they analyzed the data, the researchers were able to establish a connection between diet and heart disease.

relative (adjective)   refers to a description of something or someone that is true when you compare it to similar things

Examples   Mary is a relative newcomer to this part of the country. She moved here three years ago. The rest of us have been here for fifteen years or more.

After the first test, which 50 percent of them had failed, the students found the second test relatively easy. About 80 percent of them passed.

to assess X (verb); **assessment** (noun)   to consider and judge X

Examples   Tests are one way for a teacher to assess how much a student has learned.

One expert predicted that war would break out soon between the two countries. However, others disagreed with his assessment of the situation.

to conform (to X) (verb)   to satisfy the established standards or rules

Examples   Cars imported into the United States must conform to U.S. safety and antipollution standards.

In any group, there is pressure on people to conform—to dress, act, and think like others.

to accomplish (verb); **accomplishment** (noun)   to achieve; to succeed in doing or finishing something

Examples   I was in the office for eight hours yesterday, but I feel I wasn't able to accomplish very much. I was constantly being interrupted.

It is quite an accomplishment to complete a university degree at the same time as working in a full-time job.

VOCABULARY STUDY: READING PASSAGE 3.4 _____

to resemble (verb); **resemblance** (noun)   to look like; to be similar to

Examples   Many words in English resemble French words. This is because French speakers brought their language with them to England in 1066 and influenced the development of English.

John and Mary are brother and sister, but I can see little family resemblance.

mature (adjective)   fully developed; opposite: **immature**

Examples   A mature oak tree can reach a height of 110 feet or more.

I believe you can rely on this student to do good work for you. Although she is only nineteen, she is very mature for her age.

range (noun); **to range** (verb)   the limits within which something can vary

Examples   At $25,000 this car is not in my price range. I can't afford to pay more than $18,000.

The ages of the students range from eighteen to thirty-six.

vague (adjective)   not clear; not clearly described or established; opposites: **clear, distinct, definite, precise, exact**

Examples   After he recovered from his head injury, the driver only had a vague memory of how the accident had happened.

Often politicians give deliberately vague answers to questions; they feel that such answers will satisfy everyone and offend no one.

sample (noun)   a small quantity of X that is intended to show you what the whole of X is like

Examples   If a public opinion poll is to be accurate, then it must be based on a random sample of people.

Sometimes companies will give free samples of products in order to win new customers.

stage (noun)   a period or a point in a process

Examples   The discussions between the company and the workers have reached a crucial stage. We should know soon if the workers are going to strike or to accept the company's wage offer.

Some researchers argue that culture shock has three stages: the honeymoon stage, when everything is new and interesting; the crisis stage, when the newcomer is very uncomfortable; the resolution stage, when the newcomer either goes home or begins to adapt and feel better.

to substitute X for Y (verb); **substitute** (noun)   to replace Y with X; to use X instead of Y

Examples   In order to reduce fat in their diet, doctors are recommending that people substitute margarine for butter.

Many teachers believe there is no substitute for hard work when you want to learn a second language.

consistent (adjective)   not changing (behavior or attitudes); not contradictory; opposite: **inconsistent**

Examples   The student's performance in class was very inconsistent; one day her performance was excellent; the next day her work would be very poor.

Scientific theories have to be consistent; they must not contain any contradictions.

capacity (noun)   ability; the amount or number something can contain or produce

Examples   Many scientists believe that humans are born with a special capacity to learn language.

The room was filled to capacity for the popular speaker. All the seats were occupied; people were even standing and sitting on the floor.

to imitate (verb)   to copy someone's behavior

Examples   If you observe children, it will be clear that children often imitate the actions of adults.

One of the best ways to learn to ski is to imitate the movements of an expert skier.

to possess (verb); **possessions** (noun)   to have something (as a quality); to own

Examples   Early immigrants used to arrive in the United States with all they possessed in one or two suitcases.

The family lost all their possessions when there was a fire in their apartment building. Fortunately, they had insurance.

to construct (verb); **construction** (noun)   to build (usually by putting parts together)

Examples   One objective of science is to construct theories in order to explain natural phenomena.

A lot of American students take jobs as construction workers during the summer. You can earn good wages building houses and roads.

VOCABULARY STUDY: READING PASSAGE 3.5 ⎯⎯⎯⎯⎯⎯⎯⎯⎯⎯⎯⎯⎯

conflict (noun)   serious disagreement; fighting; **to conflict (with)** (verb)   to disagree
    Examples   Conflicting reports are coming in about the earthquake. One report says the damage is slight. Another claims that there is extensive damage and loss of life.
              One role for the United Nations is to prevent international disagreements from developing into armed conflicts.

fundamental (adjective)   basic (and therefore, very important)
    Examples   Most people believe that the freedom to think and speak as you want without fear of oppression is a fundamental human right.
              The views of the two governments are so fundamentally different that it is difficult to see a way to settle their dispute.

dispute (noun); **to dispute** (verb)   a serious disagreement or argument
    Examples   The workers at this factory have been on strike for a week now. The dispute between them and the company is mainly about health benefits, which the company wants to reduce.
              Some researchers claimed that learning a second language was just like learning a first. This claim, however, was hotly disputed by others who pointed out the obvious differences.

critical (adjective)   containing disapproval of someone of something; extremely important; serious and dangerous
    Examples   The report of the independent investigators was extremely critical of the government. They said the government had contributed to the disaster by not buying the best security equipment for its airports.
              The first few years of a child's development are critical to his or her future ability to learn and to form healthy relationships with other people.

proponent (noun)   a person who supports a particular idea; opposite: **opponent**
    Examples   Proponents of the plan to build a new mall in the center of town say that it will benefit everyone in the community.
              Proponents of the innateness theory of language argue that the human brain is biologically programmed to learn language.

vast (adjective)   very large; enormous; huge; immense
    Examples   It is difficult for humans to really imagine the vast distance that would be involved in traveling even to the nearest star.
              Today's computers are vastly superior to the computers of only fifteen years ago.

to accumulate (verb); **accumulation** (noun)   to gradually increase
    Examples   When I returned from vacation, I found that a lot of work had accumulated for me while I was away.
              The weather forecast is predicting a severe snow storm today. Accumulations of six to ten inches are expected.

flexible (adjective)   describes something or someone that can adapt to changed circumstances; or something that can bend; opposites: **inflexible, rigid, stiff**
    Examples   The government's economic policy needs to be more flexible because the economic conditions it was designed to deal with are changing rapidly.

The branches of some evergreen trees are very flexible so that they don't break under the weight of snow.

to gain (verb)   to gradually obtain something more of something (usually valuable); to profit or benefit from something; **to regain** (verb)   to get back something you lost; to recover

Examples   The doctors are happy with the premature baby's progress; she is now feeding and gaining weight.

After the accident, it took the patient a full year to regain complete use of the arm he had injured.

The car skidded on the ice, but the driver didn't panic and was able to regain control of it after a few seconds.

to halt (verb); **halt** (noun)   to stop

Examples   Drivers are expected to halt at red lights and stop signs.

The dispute between workers and management has caused a halt in production at the automobile plant.

counter- (prefix)   *counter-* placed at the beginning of another word changes its meaning to "opposite" or "against"

Examples   When a car moves forward, its wheels turn clockwise. When it reverses, the wheels move counterclockwise.

"Never have I been so surprised." This sentence is a counterexample to the rule that the subject precedes the verb in English statements.

valid (adjective); **validity** (noun)   usable and officially acceptable for a period of time; based on error-free reasoning

Examples   Your driver's license will no longer be valid at the end of this month. You need to renew it.

Some experts questioned the validity of the researcher's conclusions because her sample was very small.

VOCABULARY STUDY: READING PASSAGE 4.1 _____

ecology (noun); **ecosystem** (noun)   the complex relationships among all the plants, animals, humans, and the environment in which they live

Examples   In the 1980s, the public became aware of how acid rain could damage the ecology of the areas where it fell. It makes the water of rivers and lakes unlivable for many plants and fish.

A natural ecosystem consists of the interactions between its members—the many different kinds of plants, animals, and microbes that exist in a given area.

arid (adjective)   describes land that has little natural water to support plants

Examples   Most people think of a desert like the Sahara when they are asked to illustrate the word *arid*.

Many areas in the Southwestern states of the United States can be classified as arid; they receive less than fifteen inches of rain a year.

root (noun)   the part of a plant or tree that is under the ground; the original cause of something

Examples   If you want to get rid of a plant from your garden, you have to pull it up by the roots. If you don't do that, it will grow again.

The root cause of hostility to new immigrants in the United States is often economic hardship among poor Americans.

to irrigate (verb); **irrigation** (noun)   to supply water to land so that plants will grow there

Examples   For thousands of years, water from the River Nile has been used to irrigate farmland on both sides of the river.

Irrigation has enabled humans to turn arid land into productive agricultural land.

species (noun)   a class of animals or plants that have similar characteristics.

Examples   The diversity of natural species is one of the earth's most valuable resources.

Scientists have only studied a small percentage of the world's species.

climate (noun)   the weather patterns of a given region of the earth

Examples   The climate in England is well suited to growing flowers. It rarely gets very cold or very hot, and there is sufficient rainfall.

In the United States, many older people move to Florida, Arizona, New Mexico, and other southern states when they retire. Many are attracted by the warmer climates of those states.

crop (noun)   plants grown (usually in large quantities) for profit; the amount of plants that are successfully grown.

Examples   Wheat and corn are the two main food crops in the Midwestern region of the United States.

The unusually cold weather in Florida in January has reduced this season's crop of oranges and grapefruit.

fertile (adjective); **fertility** (noun)   describes land or soil when things grow well on it or in it; people are fertile when they are able to have children

Examples   For land to be fertile, it needs water and the nutrients that plants require for growth.

Married couples who are experiencing difficulty having children can go to fertility clinics, where they can receive expert medical help.

to evaporate (verb)   to become steam and disappear in the air; **vapor** (noun)   liquid in the form of a gas, e.g., steam or mist

Examples   Many methods of irrigation are very inefficient; they waste too much of the water they use by allowing it to evaporate in the sun.

Clouds are formed from water vapor in the atmosphere.

soil (noun)   the layer of earth or dirt in which plants grow on top of the ground

Examples   The soil in this area of my garden is very poor. I can't grow flowers or vegetables in it.

The soil on this hillside has been washed away by heavy rain. Now very little will grow here.

pesticide (noun)   a chemical substance that kills insects and animals that cause harm to crops or people (-*icide* is a word ending that means "killing." Other words with this ending are **suicide, homicide, herbicide.**)

Examples   For some time, pesticides like DDT were widely used. Then scientists discovered that their effects were not limited to the pests they were intended to eliminate.

Nowadays because of environmental awareness, people are becoming much more careful about using pesticides and herbicides.

to drain (verb)   (to allow liquid) to flow out of somewhere; **drain** (noun)   a pipe that carries water (or other liquids) away from where it is not wanted

Examples   When water drains into rivers and lakes from farmland, it carries with it some of the chemicals that have been used on the land.

This bathtub is not emptying. The drain must be blocked.

vulnerable (adjective)   not protected against attack; easy to hurt or damage; easy to influence; synonym: **susceptible**

Examples   A weak economy can affect almost everyone in a society, but in such times, the children of poor parents are often the most vulnerable.

A person whose immune system is damaged is much more susceptible to infection and disease than people with healthy immune systems.

measure (noun)   an official action (or step) taken by an organization to achieve some result
    Examples   The government is planning to take measures to control the use of pesticides in agri-
           culture.
           Because of the high number of people killed by guns annually, more people than ever
           believe that the U.S. government needs to take strong measures to limit the sale of
           guns here.

VOCABULARY STUDY: READING PASSAGE 4.2 _____

negligible (adjective)   small and unimportant; not worth considering; opposite: **substantial**
    Examples   Most experts are not impressed with the government's new tax plan. They say it will
           have a negligible effect on the country's economic problems.
           However, the new factory under construction here will have a substantial impact on
           the local economy. It is expected to provide two thousand new jobs.

to erode (verb); **erosion** (noun)   to be gradually weakened or destroyed (by weather, wind, or water)
    Examples   When humans clear trees from hillsides, the unprotected soil is often eroded by heavy
           rain.
           Experts claim that large areas of valuable farmland are lost through erosion each
           year.

to relieve (verb); **relief** (noun)   to lessen the bad effects of something
    Examples   You can relieve the pain of a headache by taking a couple of aspirin.
           I experienced a feeling of relief when I heard I passed the examination I thought I had
           failed.

cycle (noun)   a sequence of events that repeats itself again and again in the same order; **to recycle**
    (verb)   to process things so that they can be used again
    Examples   In the water cycle, water on the surface of the earth evaporates into the atmosphere,
           forms clouds, and then, in the form of rain, falls back to the earth, where the cycle
           begins again.
           If we recycle paper instead of throwing it away, we will be taking one step toward a
           sustainable economy.

to distribute (noun)   to share or deliver something to people; to spread
    Examples   People in some countries often go hungry. Sometimes there is just not enough food; at
           other times, however, the problem is that there is no reliable system of distributing
           the food.
           The population of the United States is not evenly distributed; some areas—for exam-
           ple, the Northeast—are densely populated; others have very few inhabitants.

contraceptive (noun and adjective); **contraception** (noun)   something used (e.g., a pill) to prevent a
    woman from becoming pregnant.
    Examples   Family-planning clinics give out contraceptive advice to people who have decided to
           limit the size of their families.
           The birth-control pill is one of the easiest and most reliable methods of contraception.

to collide (verb); **collision** (noun)   when two things collide, they hit each other or they come into
    conflict with each other
    Examples   The two trucks collided when their drivers lost control of them on the snowy road.
           Fortunately no one was injured in the collision although both vehicles were badly
           damaged.

to reproduce (verb); **reproductive** (adjective)   to produce young or seed (plants, animals, humans)
> *Examples*   If animals reproduce too rapidly, their numbers may increase to the point where the
> area they live in no longer has sufficient resources to support them.
>
> Some of the chemicals developed by modern industry can damage the human repro-
> ductive system. Infertility, unsuccessful pregnancies, and birth defects in children
> are found in cases where people have been exposed to the chemicals.

to exploit (verb)   to use something or someone for your own profit
> *Examples*   Humans have always exploited the world's resources; nowadays, however, they are
> more aware of the damage such exploitation can have on the environment.
>
> In nineteenth-century Britain, it was common for children to have to work twelve
> hours a day in factories or coal mines for extremely low wages. Legislation stopped
> this exploitation of children in Britain many years ago.

to cease (verb)   to stop
> *Examples*   The factory will cease production and close at the end of this month.
>
> After two months of fighting, the two countries accepted a United Nations plan for a
> cease-fire.

to exhaust (verb)   to use something until it is finished; to make someone very tired
> *Examples*   Some experts predict that the world's oil resources will be exhausted sometime in the
> mid-twenty-first century.
>
> After four soccer games in seven days, most of the players were exhausted and were
> looking forward to a week of rest before the next game.

to sustain (verb); **sustainable** (adjective)   to maintain X in existence for a (long) period of time
> *Examples*   The runner ran the first three miles of the race in under eighteen minutes, but he was
> unable to sustain his early speed and only finished in tenth place.
>
> Cutting down forests for profit without replanting trees is an example of an unsus-
> tainable economic activity. Sooner or later, the forests will disappear and the asso-
> ciated businesses will have to cease their activities.

VOCABULARY STUDY: READING PASSAGE 4.3 _____

perspective (noun)   a specific way of thinking about something
> *Examples*   People's perspectives on events in their lives often change as they become older.
> Things that seem so serious in the present will often seem less significant later
> when you look back at them.
>
> By showing us the damaging effects of industrial pollution on our environment, scien-
> tists are giving us a new perspective on the way we think about our world.

fossil (noun); **fossil fuel** (noun)   the hardened remains of a plant or animal from prehistoric times;
fuel (like coal and oil) that comes from the remains of plants
> *Examples*   Scientists have been able to discover a vast amount about life on prehistoric earth by
> examining fossils from that time.
>
> We now know that the burning of fossil fuels releases substances into the atmosphere
> that can damage the environment.

domestic (adjective)   describes things that are connected with your home or your country rather than
with the outside world; **to domesticate** (verb)   to control wild plants or animals for
human use

Examples Domestic car manufacturers in the United States have experienced a loss of sales in the past fifteen years because of foreign competition.

Cows, sheep, horses, and dogs are examples of domesticated animals.

to intervene (verb)   to take action in a dispute or conflict in which you were not originally involved

Examples In the case of a long strike in an important industry, sometimes the government will intervene and try to help settle the dispute.

The United Nations is not permitted to intervene in the affairs of a country unless it is invited to do so by that country.

strain (noun)   a situation where things or people are required to do more than they may be capable of

Examples Taking five courses in his first semester put too great a strain on the student. He finally had to drop two classes.

John is under a great deal of strain at the moment; his wife and children are ill and he is still unemployed.

flourish (verb)   to be healthy, successful; to develop well; to prosper

Examples This computer company has been flourishing since it moved its factory here.

The fishing industry is beginning to flourish again since the government's successful program to clean up pollution in the Great Lakes.

to flood (verb); **flood** (noun)   to cover a place that is usually dry with water

Examples While we were out of town, a water pipe burst and flooded our apartment to a depth of four inches.

Two weeks of heavy rain caused widespread floods in low-lying areas of the state. People had to leave their homes and move to higher ground by boat.

intense (adjective)   strong and powerful (e.g., feelings, heat, cold, pressure); **to intensify** (verb)   to increase in strength or degree

Examples The heat from the burning building was so intense that firefighters were not able to approach within one hundred feet of it.

As the economy worsens, pressure is intensifying on the government to take measures to halt its decline.

to collapse (verb)   to fall down; to fail completely

Examples During the earthquake, many badly constructed buildings collapsed and caused great loss of life.

The talks between the workers and management have collapsed. There now seems no possibility of avoiding a strike.

to harvest (verb)   to bring in crops from the fields when they are ripe or ready; **harvest** (noun)   the quality or size of the crops that are brought in

Examples Because of a warning that severe storms may be on the way, farmers have started to harvest their crops a week earlier than they planned to.

This year's weather was perfect for apples and similar fruit. The harvest was the biggest and best for twenty-five years.

to deteriorate (verb); **deterioration** (noun)   to become worse, to worsen

Examples The patient's condition deteriorated overnight, and he has been moved into intensive care.

The recent deterioration in the economy is of great concern to the government. Sales have been falling for four months, businesses are closing, and unemployment has reached its highest level in twenty years.

to abandon (verb)   to leave someone or something (usually in a difficult situation)

Examples When it became clear that the ship was sinking, the crew abandoned ship and took to the lifeboats.

It's very sad. Because of a severe injury, the athlete has had to abandon all hope of competing in the next Olympics.

VOCABULARY STUDY: READING PASSAGE 4.4 _____

to conserve (verb)   to keep something from being wasted, changed, or destroyed; to use something economically; **conservative** (adjective)   describes a person who is reluctant to accept change and new ideas; a *conservative estimate* is one that is cautious and intentionally not optimistic

   Examples   The 55 mile-per-hour speed limit in the United States was originally introduced in 1973 as an attempt to conserve fuel and decrease the country's dependence on foreign oil.

   In financial planning, it is advisable to plan conservatively. In other words, you should overestimate your possible expenses and underestimate your possible income.

to appreciate (verb); **appreciation** (noun)   to know the value or good qualities of something or someone; to be grateful for something

   Examples   After living in a tent in the wilderness for a month, I really appreciated the simple comforts of my apartment, especially hot showers!

   "Thank you. I really appreciate the help you've given me."

moist (adjective); **moisture** (noun)   containing water; slightly wet

   Examples   It is important to keep the soil around these new plants moist; otherwise they will die.

   The roots of this plant are very deep so that they can pick up whatever moisture is present in the soil.

to exceed (verb); **excess** (noun); **excessive** (adjective)   to be more than what is needed, or right, or legal

   Examples   In this state, drivers who exceed the speed limit by more than 20 miles per hour can lose their driver's licenses.

   During the storm, winds in excess of 100 miles per hour were recorded.

habitat (noun)   the natural environment in which a plant or animal lives

   Examples   Thoughtless development of the land by humans can destroy the habitat of natural species.

   Some zoos, instead of keeping their animals in cages, are spending a great deal of money to create surroundings that are similar to their natural habitats.

extinct (adjective); **extinction** (noun)   no longer existing (as a species) on the earth

   Examples   Dinosaurs, which used to be the dominant form of life on earth, have been extinct for about 60 million years.

   Because of illegal hunting and the destruction of their environment, a number of animals, fish, and birds are in danger of extinction.

precedent (noun)   an earlier event that establishes expectations or rules for the present; **unprecedented** (adjective)   describes something that has never happened before

   Examples   The Korean War established the precedent that the United Nations could intervene militarily to protect a country that was attacked by another country.

   The increase in the world's population in the late twentieth century is unprecedented in human history.

to utilize (verb)   to use something

   Examples   Some experts suggest that the United States should utilize more nuclear energy to generate electricity.

   It is estimated that about seventy-five thousand of the world's plant species have nutritional value for humans. However, we only utilize an extremely small proportion of these species.

prospect (noun); **prospective** (adjective)   the hope or possibility that something will happen

Examples   The prospects for an end to the dispute between the management and the workers are much better now. The two sides are finally talking to each other.

Students graduating from college in the early 1990s were worried about their prospects of finding good jobs. The country was going through some serious economic problems at that time.

to accelerate (verb)   to go faster; to make something go faster; synonym: **to speed up**

Examples   When driving, you can conserve gasoline if you accelerate slowly and smoothly.

This new car's acceleration is impressive—from 0 to 60 miles per hour in 6.2 seconds.

eventual (adjective); **eventually** (adverb)   occurring after delay or after a number of events or stages in a process.

Examples   After months of negotiations, the two countries eventually signed an agreement that was almost identical to the one suggested by the United Nations six months before.

The Mayas could not foresee the eventual consequences of their decision to cut down forests for agricultural land.

to retreat (verb)   to move back or away from someone or something; opposite: **to advance**

Examples   As human settlements advance, the tropical forests are retreating and becoming smaller every year.

The waters of the Aral Sea have retreated since 1950, and now the sea covers only a fraction of its original area.

VOCABULARY STUDY: READING PASSAGE 4.5 _____

to alter (verb); **alteration** (noun)   to change something

Examples   The bad weather forced us to alter our vacation plans. We decided to postpone our trip.

Extensive alterations will be necessary in order to convert this house into student apartments.

to deplete (verb)   to use up the supply of something without replacing that supply

Examples   CFCs, the chemicals used in air-conditioning, deplete the ozone (O_1) layer in the atmosphere, which protects us from ultraviolet radiation.

Extensive use of water for irrigation has significantly depleted the flow of water into the Aral Sea. As a result, the sea has shrunk to a fraction of its former size.

to interfere (verb); **interference** (noun)   to become involved in a situation where you are not wanted; to prevent the functioning of something

Examples   When the government introduces laws to protect the environment, some people think that it is interfering in the affairs of business. However, others feel that without such laws, businesses would continue to damage the environment.

Most people believe that a person's private life should only interest an employer when that person's private activities interfere with his or her ability to do the job.

to consume (verb)   to use something up; **consumption** (noun); **consumer** (noun)   any person who buys goods or services from someone who produces or offers them.

Examples   In the 1970s, the 55-mile-per-hour speed limit was introduced in the United States as an attempt to reduce the amount of expensive foreign oil the country was consuming. Around the same time, the government also introduced fuel consumption standards that new cars had to meet.

Most democratic countries have laws that protect the consumer from products that are clearly unsafe for human use.

to dispose of X (verb); **disposal** (noun)   to get rid of something you don't want; to throw away.

Examples Earlier this century, industries used to dispose of their wastes by dumping them in rivers or lakes.

Now we understand that such methods of waste disposal cause great damage to the environment.

legacy (noun) an inheritance; something that a person leaves for others when he or she dies or leaves a position

Examples Susan has received a considerable legacy from an unmarried aunt. She is going to use some of the money to establish her own business.

Often war causes more problems than it solves. Frequently it leaves a legacy of hate, starvation, and homelessness among the refugees it creates.

descendant (noun) a person who belongs to a later generation in a family; opposite: **ancestor** (noun) a person who belongs to an earlier generation

Examples In the eighteenth century, many French immigrants settled in the northeast of what is now Maine. Today many of the descendants of these settlers live in Louisiana.

Many Americans are interested in finding their "roots"; they do research to identify their ancestors and where they originally came from.

to oblige (verb); **obligation** (noun) to force someone to do something

Examples In some countries, every male above a certain age is obliged to do military service.

In stores you can just walk around and look at the goods. There is no obligation to buy.

to negotiate (verb); **negotiation** (noun) to talk with someone in order to reach an agreement or settle a dispute

Examples After ten years of war, the two countries decided to negotiate an end to the conflict between them.

In an attempt to prevent a strike, negotiations between the management and the workers continued through the night.

treaty (noun) a formal agreement between countries

Examples It took a number of years to negotiate a peace treaty between the two countries.

The Treaty of Versailles ended World War I. Inside Germany, however, it caused a great deal of hardship and resentment, which contributed to the rise of Hitler and the Nazi party in the 1930s.

to comply with (verb); **compliance** (noun) to obey (an order, law, rule, regulation)

Examples Negotiating an international treaty is difficult. However, an even more difficult task is to make sure that the countries who sign the treaty actually comply with it.

The government has introduced a new fuel efficiency standard of 30 miles per gallon for all passenger cars. Auto manufacturers will have five years to bring all their cars into compliance with this standard.

to compensate for (verb); **compensation** (noun) to give something valuable to someone in order to balance a loss of something.

Examples To compensate passengers for the inconvenience caused by the delayed flight, the airline paid for their meals and hotel rooms while they waited.

The people hurt in the train accident each received $100,000 to $200,000 in compensation from the government for their injuries.

VOCABULARY STUDY: READING PASSAGE 5.1 _____

structure (noun) the way in which the parts of something are organized to form the whole; something that consists of organized parts

Examples Subject-verb-object is the basic structure of an English sentence. However, each of these three elements also has its own structure.

The Statue of Liberty in New York Harbor is an impressive structure, especially when you consider that it was built in the nineteenth century.

to rear (verb) to take care of children (or domesticated animals) until they are mature; synonyms: **to raise, to bring up**

Examples In many traditional American families, the task of rearing the children still remains with the mother.

Child rearing is a job that requires lots of time, patience, and common sense.

to cooperate (verb); **cooperation** (noun) to work together towards a goal

Examples In 1992, many space scientists were hoping that the United States and Russia would cooperate in future space projects. Both countries had the expertise for such projects, but neither had the funds to do them alone.

The 1992 Rio de Janeiro treaty was the first real example of international cooperation to protect the earth's environment.

nucleus (noun); **nuclear** (adjective) the center of an atom, a cell, or some other organized group

Examples The police have arrested two important terrorists. With the arrest, the government believes that the nucleus of the terrorist group has been destroyed.

One of the main objections to nuclear, or atomic, energy is the questionable safety of nuclear power plants. The accident at Chernobyl in 1986 showed how dangerous they could be.

companion (noun); **companionship** (noun) a person who spends time and shares experiences with another person; Same word family: **company, to accompany**

Examples In 1912, the British explorer Scott and his companions died in Antarctica during the return part of their journey to the South Pole.

People who travel overseas to study often miss the companionship of the friends and family they've left at home.

affection (noun); **affectionate** (adjective) kind, gentle feelings of liking or love for a person

Examples Children who don't get enough affection from their parents or from other caring adults often grow up to have problems in their relationships with other adults.

Mary held her daughter in her arms and looked at her affectionately.

to compel (verb) to force or oblige someone to do something; **compulsory** (adjective) obligatory; not something that you can choose to do or not to do

Examples A serious illness compelled the politician to retire from politics.

Compulsory education for children only began in England in 1870. Before then parents could send even young children to work in factories and mines.

to consult (verb) to go to a source of information (e.g., a person, a book, etc.) for advice, help, information

Examples If you want to start an exercise program after years of being inactive, you should first consult your doctor. The doctor may recommend that you get a complete physical examination.

For information on the meaning of a new English word, students should consult a good ESL English-English dictionary.

to dominate (verb) to have the most important position; to have power; **dominant** (adjective) more or most important, powerful, or influential

Examples The teacher was concerned about her class. One student dominated most of the discussions; the other students were reluctant to speak.

Among animals that live in groups, large mature males tend to be the dominant members of the group.

to isolate *X* (verb); **isolation** (noun) to separate *X* from other members of the group

Examples Often international students are rather isolated from the rest of the student community by language difficulties. This can be a factor in culture shock.

Patients with dangerous infectious diseases often have to be kept in isolation. This helps prevent the disease from spreading to the general population.

criterion (noun) the standard(s) that you use as a basis for a decision or judgment; plural: **criteria**

Examples Safety is becoming an important criterion in people's choice of automobile. People are no longer basing their choice exclusively on price and comfort.

Before you buy a house, you should list your criteria, in other words, the features you want in your house, for example, privacy, space, nearness to good schools, etc.

to desire X (verb); **desire** (noun); **desirable** (adjective) to want X; a strong wish for X

Examples Most immigrants to the United States had one thing in common—the desire to live in a land where there was more freedom and economic opportunity.

Sometimes job advertisements will say "Experience desirable." This means that an applicant with experience will generally be preferred; but it does not mean that experience is essential.

compatible (adjective); opposite: **incompatible** (adjective); **compatibility** (noun) able to exist together without fundamental disagreement

Examples People who get divorced often say that they cannot live together because they have very different interests, opinions, and values; in other words, they are incompatible.

Compatibility is an important criterion for any organization buying new computer equipment. They have to be sure that the new equipment will be able to function with the equipment they already have.

VOCABULARY STUDY: READING PASSAGE 5.2 _____

to constitute X (verb) to be (the components of) X; to make up X

Examples What constitutes happiness? Different people have different ideas on what makes them happy.

The number of marriages where husband and wife both work constitutes about 66 percent of all marriages.

to grant X (verb) to give or allow officially (request, permission, admission); **grant** (noun) money given by an authority for a certain purpose

Examples After a long delay, the reporter was granted permission to look at secret government documents from forty years ago.

The scientist received a large grant to continue her research into genetic factors in heart disease.

era (noun) a period of years that begins with an important development; synonym: **epoch, age**

Examples The era of space exploration began in 1957 with the launching of the U.S.S.R.'s first satellite, Sputnik 1.

The development of the jet engine in the 1940s brought in a new era in airplane design.

to decay (verb); **decay** (noun) to lose health and strength; to go bad; to disintegrate; synonym: **to rot;**

Examples The soil in tropical forests gets its fertility from decaying leaves and other material.
When sugar comes into contact with your teeth, it can cause rapid tooth decay.

to inhibit (verb); **inhibition** (noun) to discourage something (usually natural) from occurring

Examples People's upbringing can often inhibit them in certain ways. For example, if our parents could not talk freely to us about sex, we may feel certain inhibitions about talking to our children on the same subject.
People often lose some of their inhibitions after they consume some alcohol.

to sue (verb); **lawsuit** (noun) to start a legal action (= a suit) against someone who you believe has harmed you in some way

Examples The workers are suing their employer for damages of $50 million. They claim they were exposed to extremely hazardous chemicals at work.
However, the company is expected to settle the lawsuit out of court because it wants to avoid the negative publicity that a trial would bring.

to dissolve (verb); **dissolution** (noun) to break up, to end; to disappear in liquid

Examples Sugar dissolves quite quickly in hot coffee.
After the dissolution of his fifth marriage, the movie star said he would never get married again.

stable (adjective); unlikely to move or shift or collapse; opposite: **unstable, shaky; stability** (noun); opposite: **instability**

Examples Tests have shown that certain automobiles are very unstable. They tend to roll over very easily.
The early 1990s was a period of great political and social instability in Eastern Europe and Central Asia. The instability followed the disintegration of the former Soviet Union.

to prevail (verb); **prevalent** (adjective) to be widespread, common.

Examples If you compare life in modern Germany to the terrible economic conditions that prevailed immediately after World War II, you can appreciate how far the country has come in the last forty years.
Statistics show that divorce is becoming more prevalent in Western societies. It used to be a much rarer occurrence than it is today.

for the sake of X (phrase) for the welfare or benefit of X

Examples The doctor told John to stop smoking for his own sake as well as for the sake of his family.
A generation ago, parents who were having problems in their marriage often thought they should avoid divorce for the sake of the children. Nowadays many people feel that a bad marriage can harm children more than a divorce.

to fulfill (verb); **fulfillment** (noun) to satisfy (a requirement, condition, need or demand); to carry out (a promise, task, function, duty, responsibility)

Examples The workers claimed that the company had failed to fulfill its side of the agreement; they are planning to go on strike tomorrow.
Teaching and nursing are often not well-paid jobs. However, teachers and nurses often get a great feeling of fulfillment from their work.

to opt (verb); **option** (noun) to choose to do something or not to do it

Examples In the late 1980s and early 1990s, a growing number of parents opted to send their children to private schools. They were concerned that the U.S. public schools were not doing a good job of educating young people.
The average high-school graduate in the United States has a broader range of options than the average young person in Europe. For example, he or she will probably be able to attend a university. In Europe, on the other hand, only a small minority of young people are able to find a place in a university.

VOCABULARY STUDY: READING PASSAGE 5.3

blank (noun and adjective)   empty; without writing or expression (describes pages, faces, minds, screens)

Examples   After the accident, the survivors wandered around, their faces blank from the shock.
In some vocabulary tests, students only need to fill in the blanks in sentences with an appropriate word.

wise (adjective)   showing knowledge and good judgment (usually based on experience); **wisdom** (noun)   the quality or the thoughts of wise people

Examples   In certain parts of the city, it's not wise to leave your car unlocked. It's likely not to be there when you return.
Conventional wisdom says that politicians who support raising taxes cannot win in an election.

to devastate (verb); **devastation** (noun)   to cause immense damage or harm to X

Examples   German cities were devastated by U.S. and British bombing during World War II.
Environmentalists are trying to halt the devastation that occurs when people cut down the tropical rain forests for quick profits.

grief (noun)   great feelings of sorrow or suffering after a sad event

Examples   The community was filled with grief by the report that many of its members had lost their lives in the factory fire.
Divorce can cause a great deal of grief for children who feel they are losing their home and one of their parents.

incidence (noun)   the rate at which some phenomenon occurs

Examples   Medical experts are extremely concerned; the incidence of AIDS among teenagers has almost doubled in two years.
The high incidence of divorce is changing American family life. Fewer children now live with both biological parents than used to be the case.

adolescence (noun); **adolescent** (noun and adjective)   the period in life when a person is between twelve and sixteen or seventeen years old (approximately)

Examples   Adolescence is often a difficult period in a person's life. He or she often wants to be treated like a mature adult but does not have the experience and wisdom to behave like one.
Many Americans are extremely concerned about the growing number of inner-city children and adolescents who become involved in illegal drugs.

miracle (noun); **miraculous** (adjective)   an unexpected event that has good results but cannot be explained scientifically.

Examples   In the middle of the devastation caused by the earthquake, a church remained undamaged. People called it a miracle.
The doctors are describing the patient's recovery as almost miraculous. They had believed that she would not survive her injuries.

to reconcile (verb); **reconciliation** (noun)   to bring about agreement between two hostile sides or between apparently contradictory ideas

Examples   The dispute between the two sides was so long and bitter that it will be difficult for them to become reconciled.
The process of reconciliation after World War II was made easier by the Marshall Plan. Under this plan, the United States provided funds to rebuild the devastated economies of Western Europe.

despondent (adjective); **despondency** (noun)   unhappy, without hope, depressed about problems you can't overcome

Examples After he lost his job and had been unemployed for six months, John became very despondent.

The despondency among the workers was lifted when the company announced it was not going to close the factory.

to resign (verb); **resignation** (noun) 1. to give up a job; 2. to accept something unpleasant that you cannot change

Examples The government's housing minister had to resign because of a newspaper report that he had given government contracts to a company owned by his wife.

When our flight to London was canceled, we were disappointed, but there was nothing we could do about it. We resigned ourselves to it and took a later flight.

to abuse (verb); **abuse** (noun); **abusive** (adjective) to treat someone badly; to use something for the wrong purpose

Examples In many countries, there are cases when police are charged with physically abusing people they arrest. This naturally weakens the public's confidence and trust in the police.

Drug and alcohol abuse are two major problems in the United States.

When parents become abusive toward their children, the children are often removed from their care and placed with other relatives who will take better care of them.

subsequent (adjective); **subsequently** (adverb) later; happening afterward

Examples Winston Churchill was giving warnings about Hitler as early as 1933, but few people paid any attention. Subsequently, events showed how right Churchill had been.

The first large waves of immigrants to America came from the British Isles and north-western Europe. Subsequent waves in the 1890s came from central, eastern, and southern Europe.

VOCABULARY STUDY: READING PASSAGE 5.4 _____

to witness (verb) to see something because you are present at the time when it occurs; **witness** (noun) a person who gives evidence in a court of law; a person who was present when an event occurred

Examples Through live television, the world is now able to witness historical events as they happen, for example, the April 1992 riots in Los Angeles.

The police have not been able to find any witnesses to the accident. All they have are the two contradictory stories of the two people involved.

prominent (adjective); **prominence** (noun) very well known; easily noticed

Examples A number of prominent scientists have urged the government to reduce the emission of CO_2 by industry. The scientists, all leading authorities in their fields, are extremely concerned about global warming.

Ronald Reagan, president of the United States 1981–1988, first came to prominence as a movie actor in the 1940s and early 1950s.

to shortchange to give back less change to customers than what they are entitled to; to treat people unfairly by not giving them what they are entitled to; synonym: **to cheat**

Examples Inexperienced tourists are sometimes shortchanged on vacation by dishonest store-keepers or taxi drivers.

People in a number of states in the United States feel they are being shortchanged by the federal government. They feel they are not receiving enough federal support in return for the federal taxes they pay.

dimension (noun)   one measurement of size (length, height, or width); size, extent, or importance; aspect

Examples   To calculate the area of a room, you need its floor dimensions—its length and width.

Some scientists are accusing the government of failing to appreciate the dimensions of the problem of global warming. They warn that it is a much more serious problem than the government claims.

eminent (adjective); **eminence** (noun)   Highly respected (usually because of your expertise)

Examples   Some of the most eminent scientists in the United States have criticized the government for its lack of leadership on environmental issues.

Salk won eminence as the scientist who developed the world's first effective vaccine against polio.

routine (noun and adjective)   a regular, normal, and frequently used way of doing something

Examples   John's routine every morning is to get up, shower, dress, read the newspaper during breakfast, and leave for work at 7:30. He is not happy if anything interferes with this routine.

Many types of surgery, for example, to remove cataracts in elderly patients' eyes, used to be complex and difficult. Now, with new surgical techniques and technology, they are almost routine.

rank (noun); **to rank** (verb)   the position (relative to the position of others) in a list or an organization.

Examples   In the military, the rank of captain is higher than the rank of sergeant.

If we rank developed countries on the basis of their infant mortality rates, the United States surprisingly ranks fairly low.

profound (adjective)   deep; to a great degree

Examples   I have profound respect for that politician. He will tell the truth even though doing so might cost him popularity and support.

The anxious patient experienced a profound sense of relief when the doctors told him that his illness was not serious.

counterpart of X (noun)   the person or thing equivalent to X in another place or system

Examples   The U.S. president is meeting with his European counterparts next week. The leaders are expected to discuss economic issues.

The U.S. secretary of defense and his German counterpart are meeting in Washington, D.C., today. They are expected to sign an agreement on troop withdrawal from Germany.

eager (adjective); **eagerness** (noun)   full of desire and enthusiasm (to do something)

Examples   At the end of the long semester, most students were eager to get away for a complete break from classrooms and books.

In my eagerness to get rid of my old car, I sold it for a lot less than I could have got if I had been more patient and had taken my time.

elite (noun and adjective)   a small group of people who are considered superior to the others in a community by some criteria (e.g., the richest and most powerful, the most intelligent, the best trained people)

Examples   Most countries have a small number of elite universities. Oxford and Cambridge in Britain, and Harvard, Yale, Stanford, and MIT in the United States are examples.

In the former Soviet Union, high government and Communist party officials and their families constituted an elite. They enjoyed many privileges as a result of their positions.

to neglect X (verb); **neglect** (noun)   not to give X the attention and care it needs; not to do something you should

Examples This house has been neglected for the last fifteen years. It is now in need of extensive repairs.

Unfortunately, I neglected to lock my car when I parked it on the street. When I returned, it had disappeared.

to disregard X (verb)   to feel that *X* is unimportant and can be ignored

Examples During the conflict, a number of television reporters disregarded warnings to stay away from the fighting. Many brought back memorable pictures of the war, but some lost their lives.

In the 1930s, the majority of politicians disregarded Churchill's warnings that Hitler and his Nazi party were an immense danger to world peace. Britain and France did not act until 1939, when it was almost too late.

VOCABULARY STUDY: READING PASSAGE 5.5 _____

to endure X (verb); **endurance** (noun)   to continue to exist (in spite of difficulties); to suffer *X* without giving in

Examples The friendship between us has endured although we live on opposite sides of the Atlantic and see each other infrequently.

Immigrants to the United States often have to endure great hardship and loneliness when they first arrive here.

You need great endurance to be a 5,000-meter runner. You need much less to compete in 100- and 200-meter races.

ideal (noun and adjective)   a perfect example of something; an idea or standard that you try to achieve because it seems perfect; **to idealize** (verb)   to imagine or describe things or people as much better than they are in reality

Examples Ideally, these flowers should be planted in a shady place. However, they will also grow quite well in a place where they get the early morning sun.

U.S. television shows tend to idealize American family life. They do not give an accurate picture of what family life is really like.

to merit X (verb)   to be good enough to deserve *X;* **merit** (noun)   value; good qualities of something

Examples Leading scientists argue that the problem of global warming merits the government's immediate attention.

His proposal has some merit. I think we should consider it carefully.

affluent (adjective); **affluence** (noun)   wealthy; enjoying a high standard of living

Examples When you are asked to think of an affluent country, you think of countries like Switzerland, Germany, and the United States.

However, you need to remember that the affluence in these societies does not extend to all sections of the population. In some of these countries, in fact, the differences between rich and poor are vast.

drama (noun)   an exciting situation (which people can watch on television, in the theater, or in real life); **dramatic** (adjective)   impressive; noticeable and exciting

Examples In 1968, the world watched the drama of the first landing by humans on the moon.

August 1991 was a time of dramatic events in the former Soviet Union. A group of politicians tried to take over the government by force; the population resisted, and the attempt failed.

radical (adjective)   complete; far-reaching; extreme

Examples Some people believe that the health-care problems of the United States cannot be solved without radical changes in the system. They feel, for example, that the entire system of private health insurance needs to be replaced by a publicly funded system.

The professor told the student that his report was in need of radical revision in order to merit a passing grade.

stigma (noun)   a sense that something is bad or shameful (usually because society disapproves of it)
>*Examples*   In some societies, being an unmarried mother carries little or no stigma. In other societies, however, it is considered a disgrace.
>
>Fifty years ago in Western countries, it was practically impossible for an unmarried woman and man to live together. However, the stigma attached to such living arrangements seems to have weakened considerably.

to seek (irregular verb)   to try to find or obtain something; to try to do something; past: **sought**
>*Examples*   Immigrants came to America to seek freedom and economic opportunity for themselves and their children.
>
>To solve the worst social problems of the country, the government must seek ways to relieve poverty and create more jobs.

steep (adjective)   rising or falling quickly
>*Examples*   There is an extremely steep hill on this road. It's therefore best to take a different way into the city in icy and snowy weather.
>
>Bad harvests in many coffee-producing countries has caused a steep increase in the price of coffee here. It has gone up 40 percent in the last three months.

to strike (irregular verb)   to hit; to attack suddenly; to stop work because of a dispute (to go on strike); past: **struck; strike** (noun); **striking** (adjective)   so unusual or noticeable that it cannot be ignored
>*Examples*   An electricity transformer was struck by lightning in the thunderstorm last night. Part of the city lost power for three hours.
>
>It was a very pleasant house, but the most striking thing about it was the enormous living room with its 12-foot-high windows.

to transform X (verb); **transformation** (noun)   to change X completely or radically
>*Examples*   In the last ten years, the appearance of this city has been transformed. Many old buildings that had been neglected for decades have been torn down and replaced by impressive new buildings.
>
>The development of agriculture transformed human life on earth. With agriculture, for example, people could settle permanently in one place.

VOCABULARY INDEX

The words printed in capital letters are introduced in the Vocabulary Study pages. Most of the words printed in small letters are introduced in the reading passages and listed in the Vocabulary in Context sections of each unit. Some occur in the Text Study sections.

ABANDON, 353
ABNORMAL, 330
ABORTION, 331
absorb, 249
ABUSE, 361
ABUSIVE, 361
ACCELERATE, 355
access, 58
accessible to, 61
accompany, 82
ACCOMPLISH, 346
ACCOMPLISHMENT, 346
accountable, 257
account for, 154
ACCUMULATE, 348
ACCUMULATION, 348
ACCURACY, 345
ACCURATE, 345
achievement, 5
acknowledge, 121
acquire, 82
actually, 96
ADAPT, 340
ADAPTATION, 340
address, 96
ADEQUATE, 327
adjacent, 249
ADJUST, 336
ADJUSTMENT, 336
admit, 96
ADOLESCENCE, 360
ADOLESCENT, 360
adopt, 93
ADVANCE, 329
ADVANTAGE, 329
advocate, 253
AFFECTION, 357
AFFECTIONATE, 357
AFFLUENCE, 363
AFFLUENT, 363
afford, 54
agenda, 323
aid, 62

ALARM, 328
ALARMING, 328
allegation, 118
aloof, 288
ALTER, 355
ALTERATION, 355
ALTERNATIVE, 334
amused, 294
ANALYSIS, 338
ANALYZE, 338
ANCESTOR, 356
ANNUAL, 332
apparatus, 281
apparently, 179
appliances, 253
applicable, 182
APPLY, 346
APPRECIATE, 354
APPRECIATION, 354
approach, 180
appropriate, 136
APPROVAL, 340
APPROVE, 340
approximately, 93
ARID, 349
arouse, 119
artificial, 197
aside from, 323
ASSESS, 346
ASSESSMENT, 346
ASSIMILATE, 340
ASSIMILATION, 340
assistance, 7
ASSOCIATE (X with Y), 326
ASSOCIATION, 326
ASSUME, 342
ASSUMPTION, 342
at will, 320
attain, 159
attainable, 159
attempt, 7
attitude, 5
attribute, 19

autonomy, 300
avoid, 154
AWARE, 327

BACKGROUND, 338
bargain, 255
basin, 197
BENEFIT, 328
beyond, 183
biased, 96
bilingual, 118
blame, 19
BLANK, 360
bond, 320
breakdown, 150
brief, 121
BRING UP, 357
brings about, 19
burden, 190
by no means, 154

CAPABLE, 333
CAPACITY, 347
CASE, 332
case, to be the ___, 116
CATASTROPHE, 333
CATASTROPHIC, 333
categorize, 130
category, 130
CAUTION, 331
CAUTIOUS, 331
CEASE, 352
CHALLENGE, 338
characteristic, 82
characterize, 257
charge, 118
CIRCUMSTANCES, 334
CITATION, 341
CITE, 341
class, 130
classification, 129
classify, 130
CLEAR, 347

8205